D1739372

# SCHOLARLY COMMUNICATION AND BIBLIOMETRICS

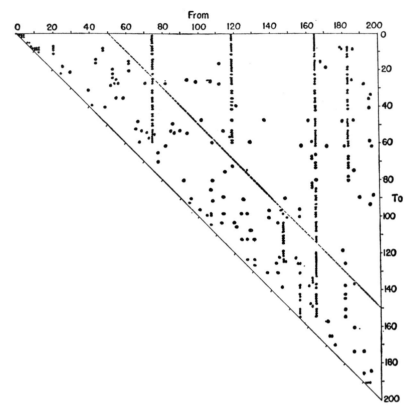

Matrix showing the bibliographical references to each other in 200 papers that constitute the entire field from beginning to end of a peculiarly isolated subject group. The subject investigated was the spurious phenomenon of N-rays, about 1904. The papers are arranged chronologically, and each column of dots represents the references given in the paper of the indicated number rank in the series, these references being necessarily to previous papers in the series. The strong vertical lines therefore correspond to review papers. The dashed line indicates the boundary of a "research front" extending backward in the series about 50 papers behind the citing paper. With the exception of this research front and the review papers, little background noise is indicated in the figure. The tight linkage indicated by the high density of dots for the first dozen papers is typical of the beginning of a new field.

Price, Derek J. deSolla. Figure 6 from: (1965) Networks of scientific papers. Science 149: 514.

# SCHOLARLY COMMUNICATION AND BIBLIOMETRICS

edited by
## Christine L. Borgman
*University of California, Los Angeles*

## EDITORIAL BOARD

**Belver C. Griffith**
*Drexel University*

**Donald Case**
*University of California, Los Angeles*

**William Paisley**
*Knowlege Access*

**Everett M. Rogers**
*University of Southern California*

**Henry G. Small**
*Institute for Scientific Information*

**Linda C. Smith**
*University of Illinois*

**SAGE PUBLICATIONS**
*The International Professional Publishers*
Newbury Park   London   New Delhi

*For information address*:

 SAGE Publications, Inc.
2455 Teller Road
Newbury Park, California 91320

SAGE Publications Ltd.
6 Bonhill Street
London EC2A 4PU
United Kingdom

SAGE Publications India Pvt. Ltd.
M-32 Market
Greater Kailash I
New Delhi 110 048 India

Printed in the United States of America

Library of Congress Cataloging-in-Publication Data


Borgman, Christine L., 1951-
    Scholarly communication and bibliometrics / edited by Christine L. Borgman.
        p.    cm.
    Includes bibliographical references and index.
    "A revision and extension of the special issue of Communication research (16(5), October, 1989)"—
    ISBN 0-8039-3879-9 (C)
        1. Communication—Research—Methodology. 2. Bibliometrics. 3. Learning and scholarship.  I. Title.
    P91.3.B67   1990
    302.2′244′01—dc20                                    90-8745
                                                             CIP


**FIRST PRINTING, 1990**

Sage Production Editor: Astrid Virding

# Contents

**Part III: Empirical Studies**

**Part IV: Conclusions**

# Preface

This volume is a revision and extension of the special issue of *Communication Research* (Volume 16, number 5, October 1989) on "bibliometric methods for the study of scholarly communication" edited by me and William Paisley. Four of the nine articles from that issue appear here in the same form (Brooks; Griffith; Miyamoto, Midorikawa, and Nakayama; and Zsindely and Schubert). Four other articles have been revised and extended (Borgman; Lievrouw; McCain; and Small and Greenlee). Paisley's closing synthesis from the special issue has been replaced by a new chapter that is broader in scope.

Eight new chapters appear in this volume that were chosen to complement the *Communication Research* articles. These chapters provide additional theoretical perspectives, research methods, and disciplinary traditions. In addition, they extend the geographic representation from three regions—North America, Eastern Europe, and Asia—to an additional two regions—Western Europe and Scandinavia.

The resulting volume of 16 chapters is intended to provide a comprehensive overview of current research and theory at the intersection of scholarly communication and bibliometrics. Our hope is that it will serve as both an introduction to the topic and help to set an agenda for scholars interested in this burgeoning area of research.

The volume has been closely edited to resolve redundancies among chapters and to avoid omissions of important topics. Drafts of complementary chapters were shared among authors, allowing them to reference others in this volume. The reference lists of the individual chapters were merged to provide a comprehensive bibliography, and the text has been professionally indexed by Dee Michel of UCLA. The resulting volume should be far more useful as a textbook than is usually the case with an edited book.

The *Communication Research* special issue and this volume are an outgrowth of William Paisley's and my continuing interest in the intersection of the fields of communication and information science. In our other writings we each have noted signs of the convergence of these two fields such as the appearance of information science concepts in communication journals and vice versa, the hiring of faculty across these disciplinary boundaries, and even the merging of academic programs. An increasing number of scholars have allegiances to both fields, in no small part due to the emergence of important shared research topics. Both fields long have had an interest in one or more aspects of scholarly communication, from the information needs and uses of scholars to the study of the formal and informal channels through which they communicate.

Also in common between communication and information science is an interest in communication technologies, from electronic mail to information retrieval systems. These technologies have changed the way scholars communicate with each other.

The two fields share essentially the same repertoire of methods: surveys, experiments, case studies, content analyses, and historical analyses. However, these methods have been applied and defined differently in each field because of the public focus of the majority of communication studies and the business, professional, or specific focus of the majority of information science studies. Communication research has developed standard batteries of items for use in surveys and experiments, while information science has developed standard content measures that tap its richest source of data, the written record in books and journals.

The production of this volume and the special issue became experiments in the use of communication technologies to conduct a dialogue among far-flung scholars. We received papers from 11 countries and inquiries from several more. Most parts of the northern hemisphere, all levels of economic development, and a variety of political systems were represented. Our communication channels included electronic mail, telex, international telepost, postal special delivery, private express mail, telefacsimile, domestic postal mail, author hand delivery, telephone, and face-to-face contact. We relied heavily on the international Bitnet, CREN, and Internet networks to communicate among the editors, reviewers, and authors. Not only did we handle administrative matters this way, we shipped entire papers and reviews over the network. After this experience we cannot imagine how international scholarship could otherwise be conducted!

As is the case with all large projects, many people made important contributions who are not fully acknowledged in the text. We owe a great deal to our editorial board members, who shared the reviewing of many submitted papers and who read multiple drafts of the accepted papers. We thank the authors of all of the contributed papers for providing us with such a rich pool from which to select, and we especially thank the authors of the accepted papers for producing the requested revisions to bring them together into a cohesive whole and for their patience with the many demands of the editorial process.

We enjoyed the nearby support of the editor of *Communication Research*, Peter Monge; his assistant, Linnea Berg, who drew all of the figures; and the cover artist, Carmen Corona, who ably sketched many representations of these abstract concepts.

Several people provided forums for public presentations of papers originating in the special issue or this volume: Everett Rogers (the 1988 conference on scientific communication at the University of Southern California and the 1990 Social Networks Conference); James Danowski (a 1989 ICA panel); and Leah Lievrouw (a panel at the 1989 meeting of the Society for Social Studies of Science).

Very special gratitude is due to William Paisley, who would not accept title-page credit for his contributions to this volume but who provided extensive intellectual and editorial assistance throughout. Both the special issue and this volume bear the unmistakable marks of his intellect, representative of his 25 years of contributions to the fields of communication and information science.

The experience of producing the special issue and this volume was both intellectually demanding and professionally rewarding. We hope you will find that our many efforts were worthwhile.

—*Christine L. Borgman*

CHRISTINE L. BORGMAN

# Editor's Introduction

In recent years there has been a resurgence of interest both in scholarly communication as a research area and in the application of bibliometrics as a research method. This volume is a compilation of current theory, method, and empirical studies at the intersection of scholarly communication and bibliometrics. We consider scholarly communication to be the study of how scholars in any field use and disseminate information through formal and informal channels and bibliometrics to be the application of mathematics and statistical methods to books and other media of communication. We propose a matrix for the intersection of these two topics of variables studied (producers, artifacts, and concepts of communication) by research questions asked (characterizing scholarly communities, evolution of scholarly communities, evaluation of scholarly contributions, and the diffusion of ideas). Research in these areas is reviewed, and chapters in this volume are set in the context of the matrix. Reliability and validity issues in the application of bibliometrics are discussed briefly.

Several years after Thomas Kuhn's classic work on the nature of science (Kuhn, 1962) was published, he wrote a postscript to a later edition as a "chance to sketch needed revisions, to comment on some reiterated criticisms, and to suggest directions in which my own thought is presently developing" (Kuhn, 1970, p. 174). In this postscript he reiterates the central importance of the community structure of science and calls for empirical research, noting that "preliminary results, many of them still unpublished, suggest that the empirical techniques required for its exploration are non-trivial, but some are in hand and others are sure to be developed" (Kuhn, 1970, p. 176).

AUTHOR'S NOTE: This introduction and the corresponding article in the *Communication Research* special issue benefited substantially from long discussions with William Paisley, Henry Small, and Leah Lievrouw. I am also thankful for the extensive comments on earlier drafts by Marcia J. Bates, Belver C. Griffith, William Paisley, Sydney J. Pierce, Henry Small, and Linda C. Smith. I retain responsibility for all opinions and errors of fact, of course.

Kuhn cites several studies in support of the latter point (Crane, 1969; Garfield, 1964; Hagstrom, 1965; Kessler, 1965; Mullins, 1966; Price, 1965; Price & Beaver, 1966). Each of these studies relied wholly or in large part on *bibliometrics*, or the application of mathematics and statistical methods to books and other media of communication (Pritchard, 1969), as a research method.

In the 20 years since Kuhn called for empirical research on the processes of communication in science, the research methods have matured, the amount and accessibility of the data have increased, and the research questions to be addressed have become richer and more central to the communication sciences. For all of these reasons, we found it timely to assemble this volume on scholarly communication and bibliometrics.

## Bibliometrics

Bibliometric methods have been applied in various forms for a century or more (Pritchard & Wittig, 1981) but, until recently, the data collection was an extremely tedious process and the methods often were lacking in rigor. The last two decades have seen the provision of vast portions of the scholarly record, about both bibliographic and full-text data, in computer-readable form. More than 3,000 publicly available databases already exist on commercial (e.g., Dialog, BRS, Lexis/Nexis) and government (e.g., Medlars) systems. Of particular interest for bibliometrics are the citation databases produced by the Institute for Scientific Information: the *Science Citation Index*, the *Social Sciences Citation Index*, and the *Arts & Humanities Citation Index*. The use of these large datasets makes possible analyses at a scale that cannot be achieved by traditional methods such as surveys and case studies.

As we have gained experience in bibliometrics, the methods have matured significantly, moving from mere counting of citations to an understanding of the content and purposes of citations and the relationships among different methods (Chubin, 1985; Narin & Moll, 1977; White & McCain, 1989). Bibliometrics encompasses a number of empirical indicators that can be found in the formal record of scholarly communication, including authors, citations, and textual content.

## Scholarly Communication

Interest in scholarly communication has increased for reasons both external and internal to the communication and information sciences, both of which (as well as others) lay claim to this research area. Among the external reasons are the increasing competition in science for scarce research funds and pressures to show contributions to international competitiveness. Scholars and policymakers alike are concerned about understanding the flow of research findings and improving technology transfer.

Interest internal to these fields is exemplified by their continued introspection about their constituency and viability as disciplines, considering works such as "Ferment in the Field" (1983), Paisley (1984), Delia (1987), and Wiemann, Hawkins, and Pingree (1988) in communication research and Nakayama, Ueda, and Miyamoto (1979), Borgman and Schement (1990), and Prentice (1990) in information science. A field's interest in its own scholarly communication is a sign of its maturity. Fields such as physics, chemistry, and medicine have standing committees and/or publications concerned exclusively with the "fullness of communication" (Kuhn, 1970, p. 177; 1977, p. 461) within the field and with other fields.

Social science researchers have analyzed their own fields as well. Early notable work includes the multiyear "Project on Scientific Information Exchange in Psychology" conducted by the American Psychological Association (Garvey & Griffith, 1964) and the studies of sociology by Crane (1967) and of communication research by Parker and Paisley (1966).

Relatively young fields like communication research and information science need to be aware of the strategies by which older fields manage their growth and assert their self-interest vis-à-vis institutional status, access to research support, recognition for their contributions to the whole of science, and so on. These strategies may not be entirely appropriate for all fields at all times but they are a part of the "disciplinary self-awareness" that marks any maturing field.

# Bibliometrics and Scholarly Communication: Definitions

## Bibliometrics

The most widely accepted definition of *Bibliometrics* is that of Pritchard (1969), which is quite broad in scope:

(1) "to shed light on the processes of written communication and of the nature and course of development of a discipline (in so far as this is displayed through written communication), by means of counting and analyzing the various facets of written communication." (Pritchard, 1968)

(2) "the assembling and interpretation of statistics relating to books and periodicals . . . to demonstrate historical movements, to determine the national or universal research use of books and journals, and to ascertain in many local situations the general use of books and journals." (Raisig, 1962)

Citation analysis is the best-known bibliometric technique, although other analyses of written materials also fall within the scope of bibliometrics. We note that bibliometrics consists of empirical research methods and does not necessarily have any inherent social science content.

Bibliometric methods have been applied not only to the study of scholarly communication but for various other purposes including the evaluation of library collections and as a basis for information retrieval algorithms (Belkin & Croft, 1987; Smith, 1981; White & McCain, 1989). Although these are important applications, they are outside the scope of our current interest.

## Scholarly Communication

By *scholarly communication* we mean the study of how scholars in any field (e.g., physical, biological, social, and behavioral sciences, humanities, technology) use and disseminate information through formal and informal channels. The study of scholarly communication includes the growth of scholarly information, the relationships among research areas and disciplines, the information needs and uses of individual user groups, and the relationships among formal and informal methods of communication (Compton, 1973; Crane, 1971, 1972; Garvey, 1979; Garvey & Griffith, 1964; Meadows, 1974; Paisley, 1968).

Bibliometric methods are applicable only to the study of the *formal* channels of scholarly communication, that is, the written record of scholarship. In combination with data gleaned from other methods, they can provide a large, rich characterization of communication processes not otherwise possible.

# A Model for the Intersection of Scholarly Communication and Bibliometrics

The single greatest difficulty in developing this volume, and the *Communication Research* special issue that preceded it, has been reaching a common understanding of the scope of the intersection of scholarly communication and bibliometrics among its editors, advisers, and contributors. Some view the intersection narrowly, constituted only by the use of clustering methods to map relationships among disciplines or to identify scholarly communities. Others view the intersection broadly, considering any bibliometric study necessarily to concern scholarly communication and almost any quantitative analysis of scholarly communication to be bibliometric.

The editors of both the book and the special issue have sought a middle ground. The chapters we considered in scope incorporate quantitative analyses of the written record of communication, either the bibliographic description or the content of the communication artifact, *and* a behavioral interpretation of the communication process under study. We have included theory, method, and empirical studies within these boundaries. Specifically excluded were studies that examine communication *structure* without examining the communication *process*.

We are encouraged to find that a core bibliometrics journal compiled a similar special issue concurrently with our preceding *Communication Research* special issue, suggesting a convergence of interests. The *Scientometrics* issue is titled "The Relationship Between Qualitative Theory and Scientometric Methods in Science and Technology Studies" (Leydesdorff, 1989). The editor's introduction illustrates the common interest in this intersection, although his terminology varies slightly from ours:

> There is growing recognition of the need to integrate qualitative theorizing in the philosophy, sociology and history of science with the quantitative perspectives provided by scientometric studies. . . . Questions are raised such as: can scientometric indicators be used to measure institutional performance, reputational structure or knowledge growth? How do various bibliographic representations ("maps") of science relate to the actual structure of research fields? How do indicators and constructs based on aggregates of citations relate to authors and the "quality" of their publications? Is it possible to bridge the gap between the policy relevance of indicators and the theoretical perspectives of more qualitative S&T [science and technology] studies? (Leydesdorff, 1989, p. 333)

We propose that research applying bibliometrics to scholarly communication can be organized into a two-dimensional matrix with axes of "variables studied" and "research questions asked." The variables chosen largely define the bibliometric techniques applied, while the research questions are driven by the theoretical framework of the studies. Such a matrix is useful for organizing prior bibliometric studies of scholarly communication and for placing the articles in this volume in context.

## Variables Studied

Bibliometric studies of scholarly communication use one or more of three theoretical variables: *Producers* of the communication, *artifacts* of communication, and communication *concepts*. Leydesdorff (1989) independently arrived at a similar taxonomy of *scientists*, *texts*, and *cognitions*. Each of these variables may result in multiple operational definitions, resulting in different levels and types of analyses.

### PRODUCERS

*Producers* of written communication may be operationalized as individual authors or as aggregates such as research teams, institutions, fields, or countries. In a communication context, producers are studied both as senders and as receivers of scholarly communications.

Bibliometric analyses typically represent producers by the embodiment of their ideas in one or more of their published documents. When precision is required in tracing the influence of a communicator's idea, one or a few documents will be used and citation patterns will be obtained. When the study is focused on a producer's overall influence, the unit of analysis will usually be the author's *oeuvre*, or body of work (White & Griffith, 1981a).

## ARTIFACTS

*Communication artifacts* are the formal product, or output, of a sequence of informal communication activities—reading other documents, translating their ideas into their own terms, talking with others (Bazerman, 1988; Callon, Law, & Rip, 1986; Latour & Woolgar, 1979; Small, 1988)—as well as the input to the scholarly communication of others. Artifacts may be studied at the level of the individual article, conference paper, or book. They may also be studied at aggregate levels such as journals or conferences.

Most studies that use the individual article or book as a unit of analysis are considering the artifacts as the message, or the embodiment of an idea. Studies that use the journal as a unit of analysis are likely to view the artifact as the channel through which producers communicate with one another.

## CONCEPTS

We combine two somewhat disparate types of research under the label of *communication concepts*: (a) studies that use the authors' own terms (i.e., words in the title or text) or assigned terminology or classification added through the publication process and (b) studies that focus on the purpose or motivation of a citation. Both ascribe meaning to the content of the artifact—one to the substantive content, the other to the links made to other artifacts.

Research on authors' terminology or assigned terminology is most often used to trace the flow of ideas within and across disciplines and is closely related to content analysis (Paisley, this volume). Research on the context of citations includes that on citer motivation (e.g., Kochen, 1989; Moravcsik & Murugesan, 1975) and that which studies the actual content of citations as symbols (Small, 1978).

## Research Questions Asked

The range of research questions asked in bibliometric studies of scholarly communication does not fall into categories as neatly as do the variables studied; nor can the list be fully enumerated (as elaborated by Paisley, this volume). Many of the research questions can be addressed at different levels of analysis, using different variables. Other questions are closely linked to a unit of analysis, thus leaving some cells in the matrix empty. Here we discuss four of the major research questions that have been addressed, providing examples from past work. These questions are similar to those stated by Leydesdorff (1989), quoted earlier. A subsequent section places the articles in this volume within the same matrix.

### CHARACTERIZING SCHOLARLY COMMUNITIES

The most commonly asked research questions are of the form: "What is the scholarly community of X?" and "Of what types of scholars is the community composed?" Studies asking these questions attempt to characterize a scholarly community as it exists at some moment in time. Longitudinal studies of a scientific community usually ask questions about the growth or evolution of an area and are corollaries of these questions. We treat these separately below.

We are combining studies of invisible colleges and studies of research specialties, which, although theoretically distinct, have much in common methodologically. Invisible colleges comprise social and other links among scholars, although the concept of "invisible college" has never been well explicated (Lievrouw, this volume). Reference specialties, in the sense used by Kuhn (1970), are formed by the focus on a common problem. The cluster of scholars focusing on that problem may or may not have a full complement of social links.

Scholarly communities have been studied through producers, artifacts, and concepts. Most common are artifact studies, counting either individual links among journal articles, as was done by Price (1965; shown as the frontispiece to this volume), or overall counts of links among journals, as was done by Reeves and Borgman (1983) for journals in the field of communication, later replicated by Rice, Borgman, and Reeves (1988) and So (1988). These journal citation maps reveal distinct clusters of mass and interpersonal communication research with a citation "bridge" between the two communities; the maps are further explicated by Reardon and Rogers (1988) and Wiemann, Hawkins, and Pingree (1988).

Much of the mapping of communication artifacts relies on clustering of documents. Bibliographic coupling (Kessler, 1965) and document co-citation analysis (Griffith & Mullins, 1972; Small, 1973; Small & Griffith, 1974) both involve the distance between authors in an intellectual space on the basis of citations they give to or receive from other authors.

Authors may be studied directly to characterize scholarly communities. These studies usually begin with a list of authors that was generated from one or more sources. The authors are then mapped directly, as in sociometric maps, or clustered using author co-citation analysis (White, this volume; White & Griffith, 1981a).

Concepts, in either of the senses used above, may be applied to define scholarly communities. Lievrouw, Rogers, Lowe, and Nadel (1987) identified invisible colleges among lipid metabolism researchers through the use of co-word analysis of document texts combined with co-citation, sociometric, and qualitative analyses and interviews. Small and Greenlee (1980) mapped the community of researchers studying recombinant DNA by combining context analysis of citations with document co-citation analysis.

## EVOLUTION OF SCHOLARLY COMMUNITIES

Most of the work that has followed scientific communities over time has relied on citation analysis of artifacts, especially document co-citation analysis. By comparing the rate at which clusters of co-cited documents change in composition, it is possible to identify both the rate and the direction of change in research topics. Garfield, Malin, and Small (1978) report on four years of data (1970-1973) for 31 specialties, finding an average 55% change in the constituency of the clusters over that period, with about one-third experiencing major shifts in research direction, with an almost entirely new set of documents appearing. The quantitative record of such shifts may be compared with results of interviews with scholars about trends in their research areas, as was done by Small (1973). Changes over time in the composition and relationships among entire disciplines can be mapped also, as demonstrated visually in a videotape produced by Small (1988).

## EVALUATING SCHOLARLY CONTRIBUTIONS

Bibliometric techniques have been used widely to evaluate the contributions of producers and of artifacts. Most studies of producers' influence appear to rely on citations received by particular pieces they have written, although direct studies of an author's body of work are possible (White, this volume). An example is Garfield (1985), who analyzed Derek J. deSolla Price's influence through a citation analysis of *Little Science, Big Science* (1963).

The "importance" of an idea is measured by the number of citations received by the document(s) in which it is embodied. In this way a reference to an artifact is viewed as a sociometric choice (Garfield, Malin, & Small, 1978). Garfield systematically reports on highly cited documents, or "citation classics," in his regular column in *Current Contents*. The reports are complemented by comments from their authors about the origin of the article and their views of its subsequent impact (e.g., Crane, 1989, commenting on her 1972 book, *Invisible Colleges*).

Bibliometric analyses are particularly useful when compared with influence measures obtained from other methods, as was done by Latour and Woolgar (1979) in conducting an anthropological study of scientists in a laboratory. Among the bibliometric dimensions they used to measure the scientists' productivity were the proportion of literature in the specialty being produced by the laboratory, the channels through which papers were disseminated, the audience to which they were directed, and computations of the production cost per article as a portion of the total laboratory budget.

Other research evaluates artifacts, principally scholarly journals, as channels of communication. Rather than producing maps most of these measures are applied to journals individually, assessing their influence relative to other journals. Todorov and Glanzel (1988) review the many measures of journal impact that have been applied, such as "impact factors," "immediacy index," and "half-life."

DIFFUSION STUDIES

Bibliometrics may be used to trace the evolution of an idea within and across disciplines. At the earliest stages of diffusion, the idea is linked with the document in which it was first presented, thus allowing tracing through citations. As an idea diffuses further, it may become dissociated from its bibliographic origins, thus requiring tracing through terminology.

Among the ideas traced through citations are the "double helix" (Winstanley, 1976), Shannon's information theory (Dahling, 1962), and topics relevant to psychiatry originating in related fields (Davis, 1970).

Several studies of the diffusion of ideas have been done within the field of communication. Paisley (1984) traced the concepts "information society," "uses and gratifications," and "knowledge gap" from their origins in communication research through their appearance in the publications of other disciplines. Beniger (1988) recently traced the concept of "information" across a wide range of disciplines using citation indexes and then analyzed the context in which the terminology was applied.

## Chapters in This Volume

The goal for the composition of this volume was to compile a complementary set of theoretical essays, methodological discussions, and empirical studies distributed across this matrix of variables and research questions.

The 15 chapters forming the body of this volume are organized into the three parts noted below, bracketed by this editorial introduction and a closing synthesis by the coeditor of the special issue, William Paisley. The chapters are fairly evenly distributed across the matrix shown in Table I.1 and are discussed in sequence below.

### Part I: Theory and Perspective

We first present three essays, by Griffith, Pierce, and Lievrouw, that provide historical perspective, explicate concepts, and lay the theoretical framework for the later chapters addressing methods and results.

TABLE I.1
Scholarly Communication and Bibliometrics: Matrix of Variables Studied and Research
Questions Asked by Chapters in this Volume

|  | Variables | | |
|---|---|---|---|
| *Research Questions* | *Producers: Authors, Institutions, Nations, and so on* | *Artifacts: Articles, Journals, Books, and so on* | *Concepts: Words, Meanings, and so on* |
| *Scholarly communities and networks* | Griffith Lievrouw White Rogers & Cottrill Moed & de Bruin | Pierce Swanson Rice | Beniger |
| *Growth and evolution* | Griffith White Rosengren McCain Moed & de Bruin | Swanson Small & Greenlee Brooks | Brooks Beniger |
| *Influence and importance* | Griffith Rosengren Zsindely & Schubert |  | Beniger |
| *Diffusion and gatekeeping* | Griffith |  | Beniger |

NOTE: Miyamoto, Midorikawa, and Nakayama and Paisley chapters omitted from
matrix, as they are reviews that cover topics in most of these cells.

We open the volume with the essay by Belver Griffith, who sets
bibliometrics in the context of the sociology of science by tracing the
influence of three central figures: Robert K. Merton, Thomas S.
Kuhn and Derek J. deSolla Price. Griffith's chapter is placed in all
cells of the "Producers" column, as he addresses all of these research
questions (and more) in the context of the communication behavior
of individual scholars (Table I.1).

Next is Sydney Pierce's chapter. A sociologist by training, she
asks what a contemporary sociology of science might contribute to
bibliometrics. Among her proposals are that bibliometrics can benefit from the sociological research that characterizes the nature of
scholarly disciplines and particularly from the renewed interest in
the scientific paper as the embodiment of the scientific process. She
suggests that the "new seriousness" afforded the scientific paper will
lead to a new seriousness for bibliometrics in the sociology of science.

The chapter by Leah Lievrouw focuses on the intersection of four fields concerned with the sociology of science by examining their treatment of the concept of "invisible college." She attempts to reconcile research on the structure of the invisible college (using bibliometrics) and research on the informal communication process underlying that structure.

## Part II: Bibliometric Research Methods

All five of the chapters in this section provide both methodological discussions and empirical results and are placed in this section because each is more heavily weighted toward explaining the method than toward explaining the results.

We open Part II with a chapter by Sadaaki Miyamoto, Nobuyuki Midorikawa, and Kazuhiko Nakayama covering bibliometric research in Japan published both in Japanese and in English. Theirs is a comprehensive review of several dozen papers, organized by application and by research method. They close with data of their own, mapping the field of library and information science within the behavioral sciences. Because they touch on almost every cell in the matrix, we have not placed them explicitly in Table I.1.

Howard White, among the developers of the author co-citation method, discusses the method and reviews the research in which it has been applied. In doing so he presents a rich discussion of the validity issues in citation analysis, responding to those who have attempted to discredit the method. We place his chapter at the intersections of the "Producers" column in both of the "Scholarly Communities" and "Growth and Evolution" rows, as most of the research applying the author co-citation method attempts to characterize a community of scholars in some way, either statically or over time.

White, among others, acknowledges Karl Erik Rosengren, a Swedish sociologist, as the first to invent the author co-citation method, which he calls "co-mentions" (Rosengren, 1968). Rosengren's chapter, which reviews his work on the co-mentions technique, follows the chapter by White. His chapter appears in the second and third cells of the "Producers" column, as he is more interested in identifying changes in scholarly communities over time than in characterizing existing communities and is perhaps most interested in identifying the influence of earlier scholars on current writing.

Don Swanson's brief chapter discusses the extensive research he has done in identifying literatures that are logically but not yet bibliometrically related, thus predicting future document co-citation. His work is among the rare predictive research in bibliometrics.

Ronald Rice discusses the use of network analysis on journal-to-journal citation maps to elicit the deep structure of journal relationships, a method not otherwise covered in this volume. The method is illustrated with data from the intersection of the fields of communication research and information science.

## Part III: Empirical Studies

As with the above section, all seven of these chapters provide both methodological discussions and empirical results. These are more heavily weighted toward explaining the results of the research than toward providing examples of the method. Each quantitative analysis is complemented by one or more analyses of the underlying communication processes.

We open this section with a brief chapter by Everett Rogers and Charlotte Cottrill that compares the scholarly communities of "diffusion of innovation" and "technology transfer," which were found to be almost unrelated bibliometrically. Rogers, a central figure in diffusion of innovations research, and his coauthor provide an insightful explanation of this result. This is the only one of the empirical chapters that falls in the "Scholarly Communities and Networks" row.

In the "Growth and Evolution" row is the chapter by Henry Small and Edwin Greenlee, who have performed a comprehensive study of AIDS research using the document co-citation technique first developed by Small (1973) and others (Griffith & Mullins, 1972; Small & Griffith, 1974). They document the evolution of AIDS research from its first identification as a clinical disease in 1981 through its state as a full-blown research area in 1987. This is a massive study, providing maps of the emergence of this important new research area at multiple levels of detail. The structural analyses are complemented by contextual analyses of the references, thus showing the intellectual content of each shift in research direction. The Small and Greenlee article in the *Communication Research* special issue is the first publication (to our knowledge) of a bibliometric analysis of AIDS research; this is a revision and extension of that article.

Complementing Small and Greenlee's document co-citation study, we have Katherine McCain's author co-citation study of population genetics researchers. She attempts both to validate research trends identified by other means and to validate a developmental model of the growth of science, comparing the structural maps produced by bibliometrics with prior sources and with results of interviews with authors studied.

Henk Moed and Renger de Bruin of the Netherlands provide their first report on a large study of scholarly communication in the field of agriculture, done for the Commission of European Communities. They focused on the awareness of European Community (EC) scholars of work done in other EC countries and collaborations across international boundaries, both within EC nations and in links outside the EC. These are analyses over time, assessing the impact of EC funding to encourage cooperative research.

Terrence Brooks bounds an active research area, superconductivity, by articles indexed under that terminology in a major indexing and abstracting source. He then analyzes the distribution of journals in which they appeared, comparing the results with an established empirical law of bibliometrics (Bradford's law), thus assessing the influence of these journals as communication channels. Because he used both concepts in the journals and the journals themselves in his analyses, we place his chapter in two cells in the "Growth and Evolution" row.

We close the empirical results section with two chapters looking at the influence of individual scholars. The chapter by Sándor Zsindely and András Schubert, two Hungarian bibliometricians, assesses the role of editors of medical journals or gatekeepers. They are clearly authorities, by nature of their positions, but are they also experts? Are they now or were they ever highly cited scholars in their fields?

The last empirical chapter is one by a communication scholar, James Beniger, that analyzes the roles of individual scholars and the influences of multiple disciplines on the field of communication. He does so via a content analysis of the new and comprehensive *International Encyclopedia of Communications*. His use of content analysis and his multiple research questions place him in all cells of the "Concepts" column. Beniger's is the only chapter in the volume that relies on a content analysis of a single text, providing a suitable bridge to Paisley's proposals for the direction of future research.

William Paisley, who has studied scholarly communication and bibliometrics for 25 years (Paisley, 1965), reflects on the history of each of these areas. He finds that the rapidly increasing availability of electronic texts and analytical tools will lead to burgeoning interest in the use of bibliometric techniques to study scholarly communication. He compares bibliometrics with complementary research methods, including content analysis, indicators research, sociometrics, and unobtrusive measures, showing what might be learned from each. Paisley closes with his reflections on the model presented in this chapter, suggesting how the model might evolve in the future.

## Reliability and Validity Issues

Bibliometrics has been heralded as providing invaluable insights into the scholarly communication process that could not be obtained by any other method. At the same time the methods have been criticized as being overly rationalized and promoting a positivist, realist view of science (Edge, 1979) and as being both unreliable and invalid (e.g., MacRoberts & MacRoberts, 1987b, 1989).

Reliability, or the amount of error in measurement, and validity, or the degree to which we are measuring what we think we are measuring, are an inseparable pair of issues in assessing the value of bibliometrics or any other research method.

### Reliability

One of the major strengths of bibliometrics is its high reliability. Bibliometric methods rely on unobtrusive measurement of readily accessible data, and results can be replicated easily. Although reliability problems do exist in individual data sources (e.g., Moed & Vriens, 1989; Rice, Borgman, Bednarski, & Hart, 1989), they generally can be identified and corrected by the careful researcher.

### Validity

Critiques of the validity of bibliometrics have focused on the assumptions underlying citation analysis. Although citation analysis assumes *some relation* between a citing and a cited document, it does not assume that all citations are made for the same purpose or that all citations are thus equal (Cole, 1970; Smith, 1981; White, this volume). Although critiques of citation analysis have attributed such assumptions to citation researchers (notably Edge, 1979; MacRoberts & MacRoberts, 1989), a close analysis of citation studies rarely reveals such assumptions, as White discusses at length.

Citation analysis is most useful for achieving a macro perspective on scholarly communication processes through the use of voluminous datasets. In doing so we are seeking the aggregate of links among authors, or their writings, that emerges. Citation analysis assumes that authors or documents that are frequently cited have some importance, even if the reasons for the citations vary. Study of the individual links between authors or documents is better pursued by methods that provide more behavioral insights.

On one central point both citation researchers and their detractors agree: Citation data are most useful when they are supported by other evidence (Edge, 1979; White, this volume). As reviewed earlier, the results of bibliometric analyses have been compared with sociometric data, survey data, case studies, usage statistics, and various other indicators, often with very strong results.

Reviews of correlations among bibliometric and other measures include Narin and Moll (1977), Todorov and Glanzel (1988), O'Connor and Voos (1981), Chubin (1987), Garfield, Malin, and Small (1978), Porter, Chubin, and Jin (1988), and Pritchard (1980). As most of these authors note, any comparison between citation measures and subjective measures must also compare the objectives of study. Differing results can often be explained by differing research motives. Pritchard (1980) uses the example of comparisons between bibliometric and journal usage studies on factors such as ranking of journals and obsolescence rates. Although the variables appear similar, the citation studies are measuring formal communication (documents publicly cited as a source of information) while the journal usage studies are measuring informal communication (browsing documents for various purposes). The existence of lack of correlation between these measures is meaningful in and of itself and may be used to address such questions as the degree to which scanned journals are actually cited later.

Because bibliometrics captures data on a scale larger than that of other social science methods, full validation of bibliometric results by other methods is virtually impossible. Conversely, however, we can use bibliometric data to validate other measures, such as sociometrics, because they use a subset of the respondents provided by bibliometrics.

In selecting chapters for this volume, we have carefully chosen work that reflects a sensitivity to reliability and validity issues and that provides support from other data sources and interprets the communication processes studied. Each chapter addresses the validity of its method in some way; White provides the most extensive discussion. Other useful reviews of these issues can be found in Smith (1981) and a recent issue of *Scientometrics* (1987, Volume 12, numbers 5-6) that contains a critique of one aspect of citation analysis (MacRoberts & MacRoberts, 1987b) and 16 responses to the critique.

## Conclusions

This introduction has attempted to provide an overview of the substance of bibliometrics and of the ways in which it may be applied to the study of scholarly communication. The large volume of work published in this area has given us many insights into the nature of the scholarly communication process and of the community structure of science. At the same time past research has generated an ever-larger number of research questions of increasing urgency. The rapidly increasing data sources, improved tools, and increased understanding of the research questions involved offer exciting and challenging directions for the communication and information sciences.

# PART I

# Theory and Perspective

BELVER C. GRIFFITH

# 1. Understanding Science:
## Studies of Communication and Information

A diverse group of researchers and scholars have achieved a better under-standing of social and cognitive processes that are general throughout science. The key elements proved to be communication and information. Communication is the only general scientific behavior; other behaviors are mostly specific and technical. Information and its representations are its principal and general artifacts. This chapter explores the development of theory and the discovery of some strong empirical relationships among measured communication and information that, in turn, capture important features of social process and cognitive change in science.

The goal of studying science is to seek an understanding of it as human behavior, not as technical subject content. For most investi-gators, the goal does not lie in using science to understand behavior as behavior or communication as communication. Modern science is too laden with complexity to serve well as a laboratory; the goal, instead, is to seek understandings of social and cognitive processes general to science.

Figure 1.1 illustrates one schema for approaching science. I argue that we are trying to understand the bottom six boxes through studying the top three. Communication is the only general scientific behavior; other behaviors are mostly specific and technical. Infor-mation and its representations are its principal and general arti-facts. Scholarly syntheses are its final integrations and mechanisms for conservation of scientific achievement. These three are the prin-cipal data for understanding general social and cognitive processes in science. This chapter explores the discovery of some strong rela-tionships among measured communication and information and social and cognitive events. (The lines in Figure 1.1 are discussed in the Summary, below.)

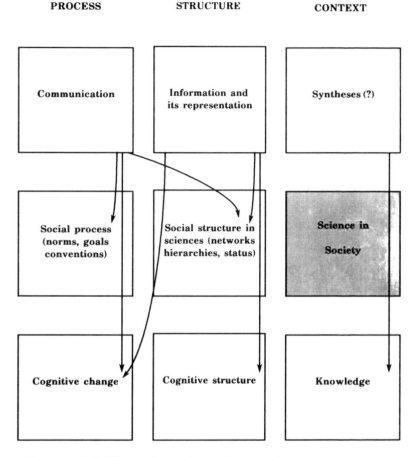

**Figure 1.1.** A Schema for studying Social and Cognitive Processes in Science

NOTE: The top three boxes indicate behaviors and artifacts used to analyze social and cognitive events in the bottom six boxes.

A diverse group of scholarly works on science appeared within a half decade around 1960 (see Figure 1.2). The abscissa is years; the contributions are roughly divided between sociology and the history and philosophy of science. These were amplified by a number of researchers, listed under "empirical findings and models for information" within the dashed lines that are discussed later. When all

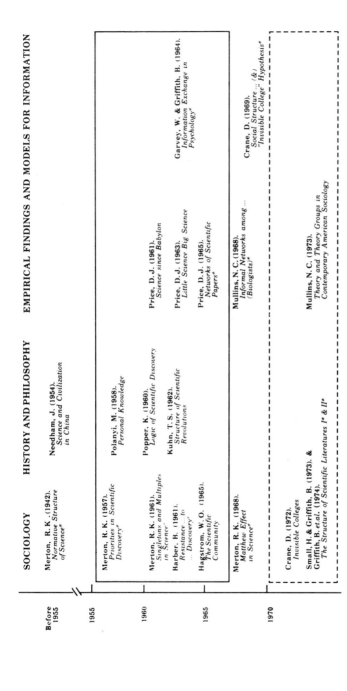

**Figure 1.2.** Scholarly Research and Quantitative Research on the Nature of Science Displayed Against a Time Line

NOTE: Citations within the solid line were written in the major period of new theory and results. Those within the dashed line were written within the speciality analysis period. Articles are noted by asterisks; the other entries are books.

these writings are considered as a group, they afford a major change in understanding science. The result is a "powerful," not "immature and ineffective" (Ravetz, 1971), social science of science that has developed several technologies for objective science policy.

## Social Process and Structure: Merton as Theorist

The major ideas that related communication to social processes were Merton's. They make up, in essence, the "Laws of Rugby" for science. Merton stated how a scientist scores in the game of science and the social rules that make this highly competitive, intricate activity possible. There is also another aspect to his writings that places these efforts and motivations in a deeper context. He explores the response of science as a social system subject to various historical stresses and thus suggests the ways in which the game evolves. Most important are those social processes and structures designed to protect awards for a most fragile prize, cognitive achievement and originality.

The ideas were presented in a series of major papers, highly distinctive in form. A hypothesis is developed and commented upon at length; then Merton, ranging broadly over the history of science, attempts to isolate instances that amount to naturally occurring critical experiments testing the hypothesis. The paper often has several iterations of this process, each extending or amplifying the hypothesis. These contributions appear independent of context and seem to stride across the decades in Figure 1.2. The "normative structure" paper was far too early—appearing in 1942. Several fall within the time slot of particular interest in this chapter but they do not link clearly with other events.

The most outstanding contributions were the paper on the normative structure of science (Merton, 1942) and the paper on priority in scientific discovery (Merton, 1957). The first paper, apparently stimulated by the extreme nationalism of the beginnings of World War II (and the historical record of similar more extreme events during World War I), was critically important and stated the basic rules for science as a social activity controlled by four norms:

"universalism," "communism," "disinterestedness," and "organized skepticism."

Many critics, for example, Mitroff (1974), have focused with unerring insensitivity on the failure of scientists to observe norms strictly as disproof of the theory. To understand Merton on this point, one must recognize norms as standards that are not rigidly defined or precisely restricted to a single specific behavior. They are far too deeply embedded to be easily legislated into a code of ethics for science or to be taken out for daily discussion and assessment. Private and consensual discomfort are the usual response to violations of norms and are also the important indicators of their presence.

The "priorities" paper (Merton, 1957) began by developing an impressionistic but scholarly calendar of priority disputes in science. The paper ends up as a great articulation of the importance of originality, judged by peers, as the governing force of scientific ambition.

Some of Merton's handling of evidence is illustrative:

> "The peerless Newton fought several battles with Robert Hooke over priority in optics and celestial mechanics and entered into a long and painful controversy with Leibniz over the invention of the calculus. Hooke, who has been described as the universal claimant" because "there was scarcely a discovery in his time which he did not conceive himself to claim" (and it might be added, often justly so, for he was one of the most inventive men in his century of genius), Hooke, in turn, contested priority not only with Newton but with Huygens over the important invention of the spiral-spring balance regulating watches to eliminate the effect of gravity [sic]. . . . The incomparable Euler withheld his long-sought solution to the calculus of variations until the twenty-three-year-old Lagrange, who had developed a new method needed to reach the solution, could put it into print, " 'So as not to deprive you,' Euler informed the young man, 'of any part of the glory which is your due.' " (Merton, 1973, pp. 287-290)

Note that this worked for a communication database to social process and structure. Nearly always Merton is concerned with communication as the basis for analyzing social structure and process.

## Cognitive Change and Structure:
## Kuhn as Theorist

Kuhn's remarkable essay on scientific revolutions (Kuhn, 1962) is best understood in terms of the intellectual positions he was against. Understanding his specific complaints requires an appreciation that goes well beyond his own writing. His reader must already have some frustration with the sources of Kuhn's frustrations. Thus the book is seemingly easy to read but has a capacity to mislead even the wary. Never have so many not-quite-correct ideas been generated or so many revolutions been claimed as in the several years immediately following the publication of Kuhn's book.

Kuhn has rejected the cumulation of knowledge view as the basis of scientific advancement; there were periods of time when very little seemed to happen, while great science represented quantum jumps, not gradual change. He had also rejected the validation of science as a hierarchical system that could be properly tested for internal logical coherence and for unvarying definitions rooted in empirical operations and measures.

Other historians of this period had begun to conclude that many of the classical early scientific experiments could not have been done at the reported time and place. Therefore, many of the proofs in scientific arguments were actually *Gedankenexperiments* performed only in the mind of the writer. Since then they have reversed themselves in some specific examples as having underestimated the skills of medieval and renaissance craftsmen. Apparently, therefore, not even empirical proof was essential. Kuhn also rejected the criterion of accuracy in prediction as a measure of the quality of scientific theory because, for example, Copernican astronomy was not, at first, as accurate as Ptolemaic. He recognized that a single disconfirmation, or even many, rarely led automatically to the rejection of a theory, hence the persistence of astrology.

Kuhn, in brief, systematically examined the conventional beliefs regarding science and destroyed them; he pointed constantly to underdeterminations of theory. He showed that the historians and philosophers of science, including the logical positivists and Popper, had not gotten it right. In these arguments lies Kuhn's great negative message.

His most general positive statement is that science involves cognitive states and cognitive changes that would necessarily resist the earlier formalisms. The detailed statement, the part about revolutions that everyone knows, is more problematic. It may be consistently wrong in the future because a revolution requires an established order to overthrow. Modern science's eclectic treatment of theories and evidences may preclude neat revolutions.

The remaining works between 1957 and 1962 in Figure 1.2 are extremely important. A fine model is developed for the exemplar historical scientist, shown in these writings as a knowing human being filled with hypotheses, ambitions, and restraints.

## Modeling Science:
## Communication and Information as Data

The works listed under "empirical findings and models for information," shown to the right in Figure 1.2, present a series of new contributions, each concerned with data, and quantitative models have been added and related to the time scale on the left. This literature is not humanistic, feeding on history, but is a series of concepts, definitions, and models usually derived from and tested by data. The concepts discussed here are those that deal directly with the social and intellectual operation of science, and selection may have been a bit arbitrary.

Price was, in contrast to the others discussed in this section, a remarkable humanist and one of the finest writers anywhere. He was especially a first-rate historian of scientific instruments and artifacts. These feats often represented skills in linguistics, detection, general science, and tinkering. His work on instruments poses enduring questions in those fields, and, in the field I am discussing, he is the most important researcher.

Some parts of Price's contribution to the understanding of the behavior of scientists were in the humanistic tradition. Drawing on his diverse experiences, he identified and defined "new invisible colleges," groupings of elites, as the site of productive work. Later, the concept would lose the "new" (and the implied, but accurate, historical reference) and become overused and problematic.

Among other essays on widely assorted topics, his first book, *Science Since Babylon* (Price, 1961), included one on "diseases of science," in which he discussed exponential growth. His second book, *Little Science, Big Science* (1963), and the paper on networks of scientific papers (1965) present an extensive menu of models and their application. The short and elegant "networks" paper was orders of magnitude better than any previous study of citations and launched serious research.

Figure 1.3 presents an instructive example of Price's method—although, in part, he was later proved incorrect. It shows growth of the number of journals over several centuries. It was probably less than completely accurate, but not to the degree that would invalidate the approach. The number of journals founded grew exponentially from a date circa 1700 after some perturbation at the end of the seventeenth century. When there were several hundred journals, the first abstracts journal was founded. They reached several hundreds in the 1950s, and I quote Price as to the issues he saw in the data:

> Thus, by about 1950 abstract journals had attained the critical magnitude of about three hundred. . . . It is interesting to reflect that, on the basis of this historical evidence, one can show that any new process would bear the same relation to abstracts as the abstracts have to original papers. This relation involves a compression by a factor of about three hundred—the number of journals that seem to have necessitated the coming into being of the abstract journal.

> Now it seems that the advantage at present provided by the electronic sorting may be of a considerably smaller order of magnitude—perhaps a factor of the order of ten. If this is so, it follows that the new method must be no more than a palliative and . . . can only delay the fateful crisis by a few decades. (Price, 1975, pp. 167-168)

The achievement, over the next several decades after 1950, was to be speed and ease of access, and not compression. Price had misread the major dimensions in the computerization of bibliographic information. Obviously there is a compression technology in process and the likely advantage will be in the range of six orders of magnitude.

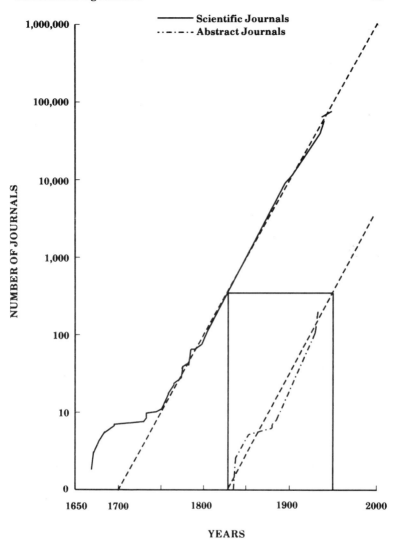

**Figure 1.3.** The Growth in the Numbers of Journal and Abstract
Services Displayed Against Time in Years

SOURCE: From *Science Since Babylon* (p.166) by D. J. deS. Price, 1975, New Haven,
CT: Yale University Press. Reprinted by permission.

Such a lapse is rare, and Price's approach to modeling lives on in many active researchers and publications, including this volume. Price established the measurability of communication and information and the feasibility of developing and testing theories on the operation of science through the counting of communicators and communications.

It is probably impossible to identify the first behavioral studies of the use of information. Bernal's (1948) must be noted as an early and professional effort. In a short period of time, there were many able and well-supported researchers working on scientific communication and information issues. For example, the following had all done research before 1960: J. D. Bernal, S. Herner, M. Herner, H. Menzel, R. H. Orr, R. Ackoff, H. Fussler, A. Kent, R. R. Shaw, and D. J. Urquhart. Their results showed the scientist to be active and aggressive in seeking information; identified and examined a surprising range of sources, including informal ones; and showed information seeking and processing to be a major activity of scientists. If one examines an early, formally published grouping of such studies in the *Proceedings of the International Conference on Scientific Information* (Washington, DC, November 16-21, 1958 [1959]), one is surprised by the high quality. There were excellent tools to study the user and to obtain input to the design of information products and services. There was a good understanding of the context set by the user's immediate environment. Quickly, parallel studies were carried out in industry, especially by Pelz and Andrews (1966) and Allen (1966 to present).

The studies of psychology by Garvey and Griffith (1971) were different. These studies made three general contributions, namely (a) the development of a model for disciplinary processing of information, (b) the important distinctions in function and structure between the formal and informal realms of information dissemination, and (c) the identification of the role of the productive scientist as driving and controlling scientific information exchange. No amount of studying the user and, especially, studying the "use" of published information, could have discovered that the system was designed mostly about the needs and activities of the productive scientist.

Figure 1.4 illustrates these ideas. The shaded areas marked "informal" are the means of communicating among productive researchers and involve those persons in the free and unrestricted

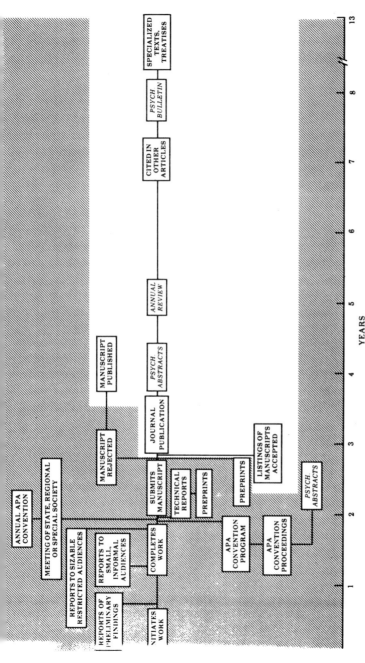

**Figure 1.4.** Informal and Formal Realms of Scientific Information

SOURCE: From "Scientific Communication: Its Role in the Conduct of Research and the Creation of Knowledge," by W. D. Garvey and B. C. Griffith, 1971, *American Psychologist*, 26. Reprinted by permission.
NOTE: The shaded portions of the figure contain informal media of communication.

dialogue that is essential for their development as scholars. The formal-informal distinction is an extremely useful one. Informal exchanges atrophy under conditions of high competition; researchers speak only to "trusted assessors" (Mullins, 1973), and, in the extreme case, they may eliminate vital communicative activities. For example, AIDS researchers apparently are not exchanging biological material freely. Informal domains may expand or become nearly invisible when there is low competition—one reason Merton and Kuhn have not traveled as well abroad as here, where "big science" with many competitive individuals and institutions first arrived.

Normally, the immediate research community should at least know of the work prior to journal publication, which marks the entry of information into the formal domain. Students of science were at first surprised by Garvey and Griffith's (1971) findings that few people cared to read the published article when it finally appeared. Price saw these findings at an early stage in their own informal dissemination and steered the discussion at that time by stating something like the following: You people are treating the scientific journal as though it were a newspaper. You should think of it as a registry of births.

The critical features, following that metaphor, are the claim of legitimacy and the official presentation to the world, not just the reading of the report by other researchers. What occurs after publication is essential to the impact of the research and furnishes strong tests of the degree of institutionalization of the discipline.

Once published, the article is cited, reviewed, and evaluated. Eventually, some portion of its content is—or is not, the most likely outcome—integrated into the discipline as basic knowledge. Garvey and Griffith (1971) saw the evaluative steps in citing and reviewing published research and the syntheses that appear as major reviews and technical texts, as establishing the basic knowledge base of the discipline. This knowledge base is the discipline's understanding of its subject matter: It improves professional practice; it is popularized and incorporated into educational and professional training programs. The extent to which this process occurs and is controlled by the discipline seems to be the measure of the importance and stability of the discipline.

Before examining the study of specialties, there is a major point that deserves detailed elaboration impossible here: The system must afford some measure of fairness and large amounts of skeptical testing of ideas and findings—hence the importance of processing information from raw journal articles into reviews and texts, the importance of maintaining distinctions between informal and formal channels, and the importance of scientists controlling the system. The influential scientists who run the system seem to adhere slavishly to Mertonian norms in the formal domain. The most protested perturbations, and there are many over the years in these systems, are those that defeat or suspend rules of fairness.

## Specialties: Clusters of Ideas, People and Documents

Figure 1.2 includes only the Crane and Mullins contribution that led to very interesting and very different books, Crane focusing on communication and Mullins on historical processes of institutionalizing "schools" within sociology. These books and the many researches performed in this period became models for the study of specialties. From this point, the typical study had several interrelated foci: first, the sociometry and constitutional affiliations of the group; second, scientific achievements and patterns of publication and dissemination; and, finally, in highly coherent groups, social actions in recruitment, in the acquiring and allocation of resources, and in managing the presentation of the group's work to the world. There are usually a variety of communication and leadership roles. Griffith and Mullins (1972) contain primitive analyses of these themes.

It became clear as this evaluation grew that there are very strong social organizations underlying scientific work, possibly some of the strongest voluntary organizations ever studied. They focus on and support the more productive scientist and are a principal mechanism for recruiting persons into research areas. On a continuing basis, they are the means of disseminating research results and the "craft knowledge" underlying research work.

In a prescient article, Crane (1969) speculated whether it would be possible to discern "cores" of scientists that correspond to the "cores" of scientific literature revealed by Bradford's law. The most useful "cores" would prove small and quite analogous to the groups studied sociometrically. Almost immediately thereafter, Small (1973) realized that one could group documents on the basis of their being cited together by new documents and involved me, who (a) recognized that co-citation was a link with an equal interval metric and who (b) knew lots of things that could be done with that type of measure (Griffith, Small, Stonehill, & Dey, 1974; Small & Griffith, 1974). The co-citation methodology created a realistic picture of differentiation in science and the speed and extensiveness of change. Small's analysis of changes within the specialty built about the connective material, collagen, was a particularly strong, and easily understood, demonstration of the power of the technique (Small, 1977). After that paper, it would have been difficult for anyone to have missed the point and not recognize the potential power of the methods.

The discovery of a bibliographic, information structure that parallels social and intellectual structure was of major importance. As I have observed elsewhere, the discovery of rapid changes in that structure instantly integrated Kuhn's revolutionary groupings and changes with Price's modeling of the overall community (Griffith, 1979). Further, by furnishing an automatic method of grouping documents and persons, co-citation completed an armamentarium for the analysis of scientific behavior and for the development of policy analysis.

## Summary

Turning back to Figure 1.1, it is possible to recognize that the lines and arrows represent the patterns in theory and data discussed in this chapter. The theories of Merton principally created ties between behavior and the analysis of social process and structure. Implicit in this work was the recognition that cognitive achievement required complex mechanisms of promotion and protection. Kuhn analyzed the relation of behavior and cognition and firmly established the fundamental character of science as cognitive. Price established the boundaries of the realms, in science, of information and social structure and created a new approach in modeling these areas. A host of researchers have developed these theories into a useful corpus of work through

(1) the study of communication and information use and the role of the scientist in seeking and disseminating information;

(2) the analysis of social processes that have developed about information;

(3) the continued mathematical modeling of information and social mechanisms; and

(4) the analysis of interrelationships among the structures of the literature, cognition, and social micro structures in science and the analysis of changes in those structures.

The chapter has not examined ties among these behaviors and the role of science in society, as considered by scholars like Ben-David and Nelkin—hence the shading of that block in Figure 1.1. Apparently only Garvey and Griffith (1971) have examined the relation between various levels of synthesis and a hypothetical process for the creation of knowledge and for the growth and support of disciplines (as discussed above). Their approach has not attracted other investigators, although it would seem to offer a natural measure of the strength and integrity of the disciplines, a seemingly interminable issue in the social sciences.

SYDNEY J. PIERCE

# 2. Disciplinary Work and Interdisciplinary Areas:
## Sociology and Bibliometrics

The development of a unified body of explanatory theory in bibliometrics is made difficult by the need to reconcile different disciplinary perspectives. Work done in citation analysis, for example, may not interest sociologists of science because its basic assumptions conflict with assumptions made in sociological studies. Disciplinary communities rely on universities for institutional support and for the recruitment and training of new members. Universities encourage disciplines to function as closed communities, promoting their own research traditions and discouraging work across disciplinary boundaries. Resistance to interdisciplinary communication may prevent dissemination of some work (for example, recent sociological studies of research literatures) to bibliometric researchers with relevant interests. Disciplines that are self-contained may build stronger research traditions, but interdisciplinary work is needed to disseminate findings more widely and integrate work done by different disciplines on similar topics.

Many disciplines have an interest in constructing theories of scientific information use. Researchers in such disciplines face a common problem: the identification of what Merton (1987) terms "strategic research materials," sources of data that will provide insight into the phenomena under investigation. Bibliometrics—and especially citation analysis—appears to offer a solution. One of the more attractive features of citation data is that they provide researchers trained to do empirical work with large bodies of data needing only the elaboration of explanatory theory. Better yet, citation data are relatively easy to collect, and they display the sort of regular and predictable patterns often believed to contribute to the construction of fruitful theory in the natural sciences.

AUTHOR'S NOTE: I am grateful to Marcia J. Bates, Donald O. Case, and John E. Clemons for comments made on an earlier draft.

Developing explanatory theory, however, is not as simple as it may seem. Bibliometrics is a research area that derives much of its unity from the use of similar datasets and methodologies. The success that its researchers have so far achieved in the study of scientific communication has been in the identification of characteristic statistical distributions of data. What bibliometrics lacks, as Edge (1979) and Cronin (1981) have pointed out, is a unified body of explanatory theory. The interdisciplinary nature of bibliometric research may be part of the problem: focal points for theories vary by discipline. For a sociologist, theories should logically focus on the social significance of actions (e.g., the act of citing) and should relate this behavior to other sociological theories of human social behavior.

This chapter deals with the question of what sociology (specifically contemporary sociology of science) might contribute to bibliometric theory. In addressing this topic, it also deals with the general question of what disciplinary bodies of research contribute to the study of interdisciplinary areas. Because, normally, contributions are needed only in areas where something is lacking, the first section of the chapter deals with what a sociologist might find lacking in one area of bibliometric research (citation analysis). The second section discusses ways in which interdisciplinary research may be affected by barriers to communication across disciplinary boundaries. The final section briefly describes some recent sociological work dealing with the place of research literatures in scientific communication that might contribute to new theoretical perspectives in bibliometric research.

## Sociological Theory and Citation Analysis

To a sociologist, much of the citation analysis literature is lacking in appreciation of citation as a social act. Where a contemporary sociologist may be interested in the part played by citation practices in social relations in scientific communities, a bibliometric researcher seems likely to treat them as part of scientific research itself. Citations are taken at face value in much bibliometric research: They are treated as identifications of sources from which researchers acquire the theoretical perspectives and previous research findings on which their own work is then based. The difference in perspectives is not hard to explain: Sociologists and bibliometric researchers focus on different aspects of researchers' behavior. The result, however, is that there are serious discrepancies between the assumptions made in the bibliometric analysis of citations and the assumptions made by sociologists studying the conduct of the researchers producing the citations.

## Assumptions Made in Citation Analysis

The assumptions made in citation analysis have been summarized by Smith (1981; and Garfield, 1979a) as (a) citation implies use; (b) citation is based on merit; and (c) citation reflects similarity of content. A fourth assumption, that all citations are equal, is more easily criticized but is less problematic to a sociologist: It is in the nature of empirical research to deal in variables that reduce complex behaviors to simple indicators. Less attention has been given to problems that a sociologist might have accepting the first three assumptions, given sociological studies of the actual practices of authors of scientific papers.

That citation implies use—indeed, that cited works have been consulted at all—one must take on faith (perhaps not without an uneasy awareness of the ease with which citations can be lifted from one work and incorporated into another, without the author having gone to the trouble of actually consulting the original source). That the use may not occur until after the completion of the research project is more widely acknowledged. Wilson and Farid (1979), for example, present the search for relevant citations as a process quite separate from the performance of the research project itself, often done at a later date and/or by a junior member of the research team. The citations collected at this point are not materials actually used in research but materials from which supporting argumentation can be constructed (in a process described at length by Latour, 1987, pp. 21-62).

Assumptions that citation is based on merit or on similarity of content might also be questioned. Since Medawar's (1964) discussion of the "fraudulent" nature of research reports, it has been widely recognized that a paper's content is not intended to be a full and accurate description of the work of the researcher, and there is no good reason to believe that citations are any less governed by convention than are other portions of a research paper. It has long been known that much material found useful by researchers is not cited—for example, older publications (see Line & Sandison, 1974) and reference materials (see Brittain, 1979). Moravcsik and Murugesan (1975) demonstrate that the use of much of what is cited in research literatures is perfunctory, having little to do with a paper's content. Certainly a knowledgeable selection based on either merit or similarity of content would require a wider acquaintance with the potentially relevant literature than one normally attributes to researchers. Explanations for bibliometric distributions based upon cumulative advantage processes (see Bensman, 1982) suggest that the visibility and prestige of an author attract citation much more effectively than the nature or merit of the cited research.

## Other Problems with Citation Analysis

Several recent studies of scientific communication give added reason to doubt the validity of citation as a measure of either the merit or the importance of research. Hurt (1983), for example, finds that citation patterns in quantum mechanics do not identify the same body of important early work as do disciplinary histories and that bibliometric data may correlate poorly with other objective measures. Gilbert and Mulkay (1984) find that authors frequently do not hold the opinions attributed to them based on analyses of their citation patterns and that their actual evaluations of each other's research may be so complex as to defy analysis. MacRoberts and MacRoberts (1986, 1987a) demonstrate that many researchers neglect to cite sources fully or equally and that citation often goes to secondary rather than to primary sources (thereby denying the original authors citation as recognition for their work).

The situation is further complicated by variations in bibliometric distributions when merit and similarity of content give no reason to expect variation. Evidently, citation patterns are affected by more factors than are normally taken into account in bibliometric studies. Chubin and Moitra (1985) find citation patterns in physics dependent on the type of paper being presented: formal research papers differ from briefer reports and theoretical papers from experimental ones. Others (e.g., Line, 1979) find that citation patterns in monographs differ from those in journals. Patterns also vary by country and by research specialty (see, for example, Chubin & Moitra, 1975; Garfield, 1979a; Moravcsik & Murugesan, 1975, 1979).

On the other hand, differences long held to exist between disciplines in such factors as the rate of obsolescence of their literatures are now being explained in terms of resources available to the group. Differences in the age of publications cited seem to disappear when the relative ages of the available disciplinary literatures are taken into account (Cole, 1983; Hargens & Felmlee, 1984; Marton, 1983). Cole (1983) goes so far as to suggest that differences in citation patterns between the natural sciences, social sciences, and humanities may not reflect differences in research in these fields. These differences may instead be due simply to differences in the ages and growth rates of their literatures.

Whatever citation patterns do reflect, they appear to be strongly influenced by such social factors as the communities to which researchers belong and the publication formats in which researchers choose to present given findings. Citation analysis is of interest to sociologists; indeed, much work in the area has been done by sociologists. But to many contemporary sociologists of science, a failure to deal with the nature of the groups contributing to research literatures and with the social meaning of their contributions leaves citation analysis unable to address the complexities necessary to a well-articulated body of social theory. Instead citation analysis gives us statistical distributions of bibliometric data. To understand how and why citation patterns may vary, both within and between disciplinary groups, bibliometric researchers might seek greater understanding both of the nature of disciplinary literatures and of the social significance of citation practices.

## Disciplinary Boundaries and Interdisciplinary Areas

To approach bibliometrics from a disciplinary perspective is a complicated matter. Disciplines are large and complex groups, the common bond being the body of knowledge in reference to which members do their work. Members of a discipline have an education and a research literature in common, and both the education and the literature provide more common points of reference than are identifiable in citation studies of their published research. These common points of reference are central to the definition of what is meant by a *discipline*. We tend to speak of disciplines as if they were subject areas, and yet all publications on a subject of interest do not automatically become part of a discipline's literature. Disciplines recognize only such work as their members are willing to use; they do not function as abstract categories in a taxonomy of knowledge.

To work in bibliometrics from a disciplinary perspective means one's work is in some way (through the problems addressed, the previous work acknowledged, the publication channels used) connected to that of others in the relevant discipline. There is no better way to define what *discipline* means, because any more abstract mapping of disciplinary boundaries leads to inconsistency and conflict. As Gieryn (1983) demonstrates, interested parties can always redraw the boundaries of a subject matter more narrowly when they wish to shut others out, and others may broaden them in order to draw in unaffiliated others (see Debons, King, Mansfield, & Shirey, 1981, for an example of this). Perhaps for this reason true membership in a "discipline" traditionally has been taken to mean involvement not on the level of interest in its content but in what one does for work (see, for instance, the *Oxford English Dictionary*'s explanation that *discipline* always implies "practice or exercise"). The boundaries of a discipline reflect the knowledge, interests, and practices of researchers actively working in the field. Without some generally recognized body of work on which researchers build, a research tradition will not survive long (as Oberschall, 1972, demonstrates).

## Self-Contained Nature of Disciplinary Research

Working within their disciplinary boundaries, researchers in different disciplines tend to simplify approaches to their special subjects, focusing only on factors of disciplinary interest (see Cambrosio & Keating, 1983; Storer & Parsons, 1968; Whitley, 1982). Where disciplines have overlapping areas of interest, each develops its own approach to the subject, ignoring the complex interrelationships of factors of interest to other disciplines. Sociological approaches to the study of information use need no more resemble those of other disciplines than sociological approaches to the study of contemporary society need resemble those of such disciplines as political science or economics. Sociologists, political scientists, and economists may do work on the same problems and may even at times refer to each other's work. However, they use and generate different bodies of knowledge and do not normally view themselves as participating in the same field.

Working from the perspective of a specific discipline is an exclusionary process, and this causes special problems in interdisciplinary areas like bibliometrics. Researchers may not use, or even attend to, the same literatures. As Cambrosio and Keating (1983) demonstrate, one of the most important attributes of a discipline is its power to set its own rules for participation. Disciplines establish academic departments and, through them, define the specific knowledge and skills that all new members of the discipline must possess. The knowledge and skills, therefore, become identified with competence in the discipline (see Whitley, 1984). The skills, concepts, and theoretical orientations that are taught come to be expected of all members, promoting cohesion and ease in reaching consensus on matters of disciplinary importance. Bourdieu (1975), Hagstrom (1976), and Cambrosio and Keating (1983) all suggest that one distinguishing feature of disciplines as social institutions is that they reserve all roles (researcher, referee, audience) for members possessing this special knowledge. Disciplines do not formally limit those allowed to participate, but they create an exclusive society of their own and refuse to attend to the work of outsiders.

## Barriers to Interdisciplinary Work

Though members of most disciplines may be aware of work done in other disciplines on research problems relevant to their own interests, and may even make use of material from other disciplines in their work, participation in the most important disciplinary activities is difficult for those who do not participate in this common culture. Attaining competence in a discipline, as Collins (1975) and Wilson & Farid (1979) illustrate, involves mastery not only of relevant intellectual content but also of what is not written down but is imparted through the experience of interacting with others in the field. The competent have special knowledge, needed to perform successfully in disciplinary contexts, that is never explicitly taught or discussed in the literature.

When researchers do work in interdisciplinary areas, they thus have three choices. The simplest is to continue to orient their work on the content of their own disciplines (though this may make it poorly understood by those approaching similar problems from other disciplinary perspectives). It is also possible to attempt a shift to other disciplinary perspectives, though this risks having the research defined as irrelevant by researchers in one's own discipline and in the new discipline as well (because the full content of a disciplinary perspective is not easily mastered). It is also possible for a group of researchers to try to find a common meeting point, a body of research representing input from several fields on which to base a new research tradition. This may well be what most interdisciplinary researchers hope to do. Sociological studies of the disciplinary formation process (e.g., Clark, 1973; Farber, 1982; Graham, Lepenies, & Weingart, 1983; Oberschall, 1972; Oleson & Voss, 1979) provide interesting views of the necessary resources.

## Contemporary Sociology of Science and Bibliometric Research

Considering what the common body of research might be on which bibliometrics may be founding its own traditions lies outside the scope of this chapter. It is, however, well within its scope to ask what sociology might have to contribute to such a body of research. An understanding of the need for a commonly recognized knowledge base on which research traditions may be built might be part of this contribution. Building a commonly recognized body of knowledge is seen as the ultimate goal of scientific research by most theorists interested in the social study of science, whether sociologists or not (e.g., Hagstrom, 1965; Merton, 1973; Polanyi, 1958; Price, 1963; Ziman, 1968). There are many theorists currently working in the sociology of science whose research seems relevant to citation analysis, or at least to the study of research literatures, and whose work seems worthy of inclusion in any interdisciplinary review of contributions to bibliometric research.

### Mertonian Influences on Bibliometric Research

Any consideration of the relevance of contemporary sociology to bibliometric research must begin with Robert Merton. His influence has been so pervasive in the sociology of science, particularly in the United States, that discussion of research in the field is impossible without at least implicit reference to his work. He is of particular interest in bibliometrics because so much of his work deals directly with published literatures. Papers on the scientific publication system, on the experience of publication, and on priority disputes (see Merton, 1973) are an important part of his work as a sociologist of science.

Merton's broader influence lies in theoretical perspectives not always apparent to those approaching sociological work in bibliometrics from other fields. His contribution to bibliometrics does not lie solely in his own use of bibliometric data or in his analyses of the scientific publication system. It also includes a view of how scientific research works, an acceptance of Merton's description of the "normative structure of science" (so described in a well-known paper originally published in 1942—see Merton, 1973, pp. 267-278). The norms of science described in this paper are familiar to any researcher in the sociology of science: communism, universalism, disinterestedness, and organized skepticism.

Merton's normative view of science describes scientists as freely disseminating (communism), testing (organized skepticism) and using research results, evaluating them on the basis of their intrinsic merit (disinterestedness) rather than their origin (universalism). Such an approach to science makes it possible to measure scientific productivity through numbers of publications and to measure the influence of published work through numbers of citations. Merton's work has influenced a long series of studies using such bibliometric data to study science and scientific careers, from Hagstrom's *The Scientific Community* (1965) to Jonathan and Stephen Cole's study of social stratification in science (1973) and Mullins's network analysis of theory groups in sociology (1973) to Zuckerman's study of Noble prize winners (1977). It is a view of science entirely compatible with the assumptions of citation analysis as summarized by Smith (1981): Selection of scientific findings for use is based on merit and acknowledged through citation.

## Contemporary Departures from Mertonian Approaches

But change is inevitable in disciplinary bodies of research. Research done in sociology by one generation of researchers is questioned by the next, and recent sociological studies of research literatures tend to be critical of Mertonian norms. Researchers in bibliometrics may still accept such idealistic views of science, but contemporary sociologists of science tend to be much more relativistic in their approach. Some newer work includes direct attacks on conventional uses of bibliometric data. One such study recently attracting attention is Gilbert and Mulkay's *Opening Pandora's Box* (1984, pp. 112-160), in which researchers are asked about their reception of a specific discovery, to test the conclusions derived from a citation study of their published work. Their responses often conflict, both with the bibliometric data and with each other. The authors conclude that the reception given to scientific work is too complicated and too unstable to be subject to bibliometric measurement. They suggest that the best approach to understanding it is to study the presentational strategies controlling the interpretation and use of scientific content, instead of seeking to gather evidence on the reception of specific papers.

To anyone with an interest in bibliometrics, Gilbert and Mulkay's work is representative of one of the more interesting trends in contemporary sociology of science. The more sociologists seem to depart from traditional Mertonian perspectives and from conventional bibliometric data analysis, the more they seem to turn to direct study of published research in search of data. This in itself is very Mertonian. As Zuckerman and Merton point out (see Merton, 1973, pp. 460-496), what is scientific about scientific research lies not in its execution but in its publication. Scientific research is recognizable as such not because of the conditions under which it is performed but because of the way it is presented and published. As researchers begin to question conventional wisdom regarding the workings of science, they turn to research papers as one directly observable scientific output available for analysis.

## New Approaches to Scientific Literatures

Contemporary sociology of science may be of greatest interest to bibliometric researchers because of this renewed interest in the research paper. Bazerman (1983) provides a useful review of much of the relevant sociological literature. Published research is the most popular source of data in bibliometrics. Any new understanding of what a scientific literature is and how it relates to the research activities on which it reports, therefore, should be of potential interest.

Much of this renewed interest in the research paper began with Latour and Woolgar's *Laboratory Life* (1979). In this anthropological study of researchers at the Salk Institute, the authors represent the writing desk, not the laboratory bench, as the "hub of the productive unit" in the creation of science. The raw material from which science is made is paper: laboratory records, readings from equipment, other research papers. And more research papers, not scientific discoveries in the abstract, are the product. The authors use bibliometric data to analyze researchers' activities that contribute to the "construction" of discoveries and to the accumulation of personal "credibility." However, their view of authors as engaging in strategies to promote their own careers departs both from Mertonian norms of science and from the conventional bibliometric approach.

Latour's more recent work even more strongly rejects universalism and disinterestedness as norms of science. In *Science in Action* (1987), he considers the question of how scientists manage to perform experiments on small samples in highly localized settings and then present the results of their work as universal truth. Though the book concerns science as a social institution as a whole, much discussion centers on the presentational strategies used in scientific literatures to make arguments convincing (without reference to the evidence on which they are based).

Latour's *The Pasteurization of France* (1988) deals with a new problem, the complex process through which the work of a particular researcher (Louis Pasteur) comes to be recognized as a major scientific achievement. Much of the evidence is drawn from examination of contemporary scientific writing, and the book is methodologically interesting for this reason. It also represents a much stronger rejection of the objective content of science. Rather than treating papers as descriptions of actions performed in research, the construction of convincing research papers, to Latour, *is* the action. Scientific knowledge rests on foundations no more secure than those of knowledge in any other field.

Not all studies of research papers go so far in their rejection of a special status for scientific knowledge. Charles Bazerman's work might be more compatible with the views of many bibliometric researchers studying scientific work. He too focuses on the research article as the product of science most worthy of study but is somewhat more optimistic about the epistemological status of the research paper. He is particularly interested in the development of the research paper as a genre and does not present reliance on written communication as incompatible with communication of content. An earlier study of the evolution of research papers in physics (Bazerman, 1984) suggested that the definition of a disciplinary form for the presentation of research results is a fundamental step in the evolution of a discipline. His recent book, *Shaping Written Knowledge* (1988), describes the evolution of scientific papers, in general and in specific disciplines. Like Latour, Bazerman recognizes that papers are not transparent media through which "science" itself is observed directly, but he does suggest that they are intended to convey content to properly educated readers. For Bazerman, shared disciplinary perspectives make it possible for research papers to communicate some content in a reasonably objective fashion.

This sociological trend toward treating research literatures with new seriousness means bibliometric data may itself be viewed with new seriousness. Instead of treating the research papers from which data are taken as description after the fact, many researchers now see them as essential parts of scientific research efforts. Sociologists, however, are still focusing on the sociological, on the writing of research papers as a social act. Their research is oriented to their own discipline and may or may not be relevant to understanding what other disciplines find of interest in scientific communication systems. What bibliometric researchers may make of their work depends on the different contexts in which they encounter and use it.

## Conclusions

The orientation of researchers from different disciplines to different bodies of research and different sets of problems limits the relevance of work done across disciplinary lines. Researchers in interdisciplinary areas may have the most severe problems, because the body of knowledge in reference to which they work is less clear. A sociologist may find that bibliometric research in scientific communication omits social factors of interest in sociology, but the same sociologist may fail to deal with other factors of more interest to researchers approaching bibliometrics from other fields. The problem is not unique to bibliometrics or to studies of scientific communication. Interdisciplinary researchers in other areas (e.g., those in women's or African American studies) whose work is evaluated by researchers in related disciplines become accustomed to hearing that it deals with the wrong problems, cites the wrong research, and is disseminated through the wrong publication channels.

It is the function of a discipline to provide its researchers with its own problems, its own body of accepted knowledge, and its own publication channels for disseminating research. This is the strength of disciplinary research. It is fundamental to scientific research that the process be cumulative, that disciplines give their members a commonly accepted body of knowledge on which to construct new work. Researchers in an interdisciplinary area, lacking a clearly defined disciplinary mainstream, enjoy more freedom to define their own interests but also receive less understanding and support.

The interdisciplinary research they produce, however, is a necessary counterbalance to work done in the disciplines on which they draw. If the separate bodies of knowledge of different disciplines provide strength, they are also a weakness. Disciplines build their exclusive communities by stressing social participation over subject matter. At some point, work on the same subject done in different disciplines must be recognized and dealt with as a whole, or the insights originating in a discipline are lost to those outside its circles. This is what researchers in bibliometrics and in scientific communication seek to do. Sociology's contribution to such research may lie in two different areas. The most obvious are the studies of scientific communication done in sociology of science that stress an aspect of scientific research, its social significance, not frequently addressed by researchers from other disciplines. The other contribution may lie in research on disciplinary formation processes and disciplinary functions, important both because of the role disciplines play in scientific communications and because greater theoretical understanding of disciplines may ultimately give us better understanding of the role and function of the interdisciplinary area.

LEAH A. LIEVROUW

# 3. Reconciling Structure and Process in the Study of Scholarly Communication

In this chapter the relationship of bibliometric techniques (especially citation analysis) to scholarly research is examined, using the invisible college
as the principal example. The invisible college is used because it is the
best-known model of scientific communication and because it is based in
bibliometric studies of science. As such, the *invisible college* is typical of
constructs that describe processes yet are founded on the study of structures;
the ambiguity surrounding the use of the term is symptomatic of the
confounding of structure and process in the study of scholarly communication. A revised definition of the invisible college is proposed that reempha-
sizes its fundamentally communicative nature, and issues for future theory
building in scholarly communication are suggested.

Social studies of research and scholarship, including studies of
scholarly communication, tend to be characterized by two major
research problems: the study of the social *structures* of scholarship
and the study of its social *processes*. Each problem poses different
methodological and theoretical challenges, yet their boundaries
have sometimes been blurred as investigators have tried to understand just how new knowledge is created, communicated, and used
in the research context. Paradoxically, researchers have often attempted to understand scholarly communication processes by studying the structures and products of research.

In this chapter, the relation between scholarly communication
structures and processes is examined, using the construct of the

AUTHOR'S NOTE: I would like to acknowledge the careful reading and
helpful comments of Pam Snelson and Chris Borgman, but especially of
Belver Griffith, who pointed out a number of difficult issues and supplied
several useful and important references that I had overlooked in the preparation of early drafts. His forbearance and attention to detail were extraordinarily useful and greatly appreciated.

invisible college as the focal example. The invisible college is of particular interest in the context of this book because it is widely accepted as a model of scholarly communication, and yet it is based on structural (bibliometric and sociometric) analyses of the literature and analyses of social links among scientific researchers. Therefore, it reflects a recurrent problem in studies of scholarly communication, which tend to examine the products of scholarship (e.g., published documents, professional organizations, research institutions) in an effort to reveal the communication processes of the people who do scholarly work. It is argued that, although past studies of scholarly communication have benefited from structural analyses, future studies should focus on the development of more direct methods for the observation of communication processes in scholarly and research settings.

## Studying Scholarly Communication Structures: Bibliometric Analysis

In social science research, statistical clustering techniques are used to organize many types of data, such as family ties, bureaucratic structures, professional relationships, or economic dependencies. In studies of scholarly communication, clustering techniques have been used to organize the relationships among communication artifacts (typically research articles published in scholarly journals) and to represent that organization in a meaningful way (Chubin, 1983; Lievrouw, 1988; Paisley, 1965). The family of techniques used to discern relationships in the published literature are collectively referred to as *bibliometrics*.

*Bibliometrics* is defined by Pritchard (1969, p. 349) as "the application of mathematics and statistical methods to books and other media of communication" and, more recently, by Broadus (1987, p. 376) as "the quantitative study of physical published units, or of bibliographic units, or of the surrogates for either." Bibliometric techniques have been used primarily by information scientists to study the growth and distribution of the scientific literature, Pritchard's somewhat disingenuous reference to "media of communication" notwithstanding. However, occasionally, certain of these techniques (especially citation analysis: see Garfield, Malin, &

Small, 1978; Rice, Borgman, Bednarski, & Hart, 1989; Snelson, 1989) have been used by communication researchers studying scientific or other scholarly communication.[1] Indeed, communication research is a relative latecomer to the use of citation analysis (Griffith, 1987; Thackery, 1978); communication researchers became interested in citation analysis only in the 1980s (Parker, Paisley, & Garrett, 1967).

It can be argued that the fundamental process of research is communication. Several investigators have pointed out that, without communication, science as a social activity cannot exist (Paisley in communication, 1984; Garvey in information science, 1979; and Whitley in sociology, 1989). Bibliometric studies are of interest to communication researchers because scholarly communication *artifacts* result directly from a process that involves, first, the authors' expression of their own and others' expert ideas. Scholarly research publications are written according to a strict set of conventions regarding the presentation of original concepts. To attribute credit to other researchers, the authors make specific bibliographic references to their works, and these references (citations) are usually construed to stand for interaction among the authors and those they cite.[2] Second, the authors' expressions are reviewed and evaluated by others with similar expertise, with publication contingent upon the evaluation. Scholarly works are published on the basis of this peer review, and the appearance of a manuscript in print is usually taken to indicate that communication has also occurred among the author and the evaluators.

In scholarly communication research, the patterns of references among publications are often used as operationalizations of the authors' interpersonal interactions. Such maps can be very suggestive conceptually (for example, see those in Small & Garfield, 1985) and have in fact inspired a number of structural analogies for the shape, or "geography," of scholarship, including the research front, the social circle, the leading edge, frontiers, fields, scientific communities, and, of course, the invisible college. Furthermore, clusters, or maps, of research articles resulting from bibliometric analysis can be *interpreted* as networks of interpersonal contacts, that is, *communicative* interaction can be inferred from clusters of documents. This assumption has been referred to variously as the "implicit theory of citing" (Mulkay, 1974, p. 111) and the "normative theory of citing" (MacRoberts & MacRoberts, 1987a).

By the same token, citation analysis is often criticized on the grounds that the citation links from one academic paper to another may not actually represent communication among the papers' authors (for a more thorough discussion of this ongoing debate, see Williams, this volume). However, it would be a mistake to conclude, on the grounds of such criticism, that citing behavior has *no* communicative meaning and, therefore, that bibliometric citation analysis yields interesting but invalid snapshots of the literature. Citing behavior as it is understood by the researchers themselves might be reexamined instead or the way their referrals to one another may be a simple indicator of more complex behaviors or social relationships.

# The Invisible College:
# At the Intersection of Structure and Process

The term *invisible college* has been used since the founding of the Royal Society of London in the seventeenth century (Lingwood, 1969; Paisley, 1972; Price, 1961), but in a modern context it was revived by Derek Price in his book *Little Science, Big Science* (1963). The members of the early Royal Society adopted the term to emphasize the fact that they were geographically close together, and shared common scientific interests, yet had no institution of their own (Lingwood, 1969). In contrast, Price (1961, 1963) used "invisible college" to denote the *informal* affiliation of scientists with common interests who were already strongly embedded in other institutions—indeed had risen to the upper ranks of those institutions—and who might live some distance from one another.

Following Price's lead and the work of sociologist Warren Hagstrom (1968), Diana Crane published her watershed work *Invisible Colleges* in 1972. In this book, Crane documented the growth of communication networks among rural sociologists and mathematicians specializing in finite group theory, using both survey and citation data to support her conclusions.

Despite the emphasis on informal social relationships in her work, Price's definition of the invisible college seems to be a strong influence on Crane's understanding of the concept. In an article that preceded the publication of *Invisible Colleges*, she says that

Price uses the term "'invisible college' which refers to an *élite* of mutually interacting and productive scientists within a research area" (Crane, 1970, p. 34, emphasis added). In her book, Crane's citation data are striking. Dramatic curves illustrate the growth of the two specialties' literatures (confirming Price's earlier findings). By the same token, her survey data suggest that *informal* communication relationships may explain the bibliometric results. She visualizes these communication relations as networks and dubs them "invisible colleges" because of the geographic scatter of their members. Though she borrowed the term from Price, Crane integrates it with the idea of informal communication in science as articulated by Menzel (1968) and the construct of the social circle (Kadushin, 1966).

The first apparent difficulty with Crane's treatment of "informal" communication is that she uses the self-reports of scientists about their communication behavior (survey data) in lieu of direct observation of scientists as they communicate. Crane does not explicitly define the invisible college, although she describes the activities of invisible college members (such as the exchange of preprints, coauthorship, and so on), which paradoxically center on the formal communication channels among the scientists she studied. Such channels are admittedly attractive because they facilitate the production of documents, which are then construed by Crane as representations of other informal behaviors. The lack of "real" information about informal communication in Crane's book prompted one critic to note: "Crane presents almost nothing about the intellectual content or the personalities working in diffusion theory or finite groups" (Hagstrom, 1973; quoted in Chubin, 1983, p. 6).

Subsequent invisible college studies (such as those reviewed by Chubin, 1983, 1985) continued to focus on network structures among individuals, institutions, or documents of scholarship rather than on communication processes or the content of those structures. Griffith (1987, p. 9) points out that the invisible college concept eventually lost Price's "implied, but accurate, historical reference and became overused and problematic." Of course, structural data *can* indicate the presence of communication relationships; however, they do not in themselves reveal the *nature* of those relations or how specific types of communicative acts might lead to corresponding social structures.

Crane's analysis, then, may be confounded. She proposes that invisible colleges are informal structures that serve as conduits for both formal and informal communication; yet she implies that such informal structures can grow only from preexisting formal structures. Significantly, Crane (1973, p. 3) frames her argument in terms of "institutions that produce scientific ideas" rather the reverse, that is, ideas that produce institutions via communicative behavior. She adopts Price's general definition of the invisible college, that is, informal links across *existing* formal social structures rather than the original definition of informal links established in the *absence* of formal social structures. Therefore, Crane's findings tend to obscure the central role of communication behavior and interpersonal processes and emphasize the mapping of institutional structures. She uses citation data as evidence of the informal communication relations among her subjects; yet, by using structural data, she reinforces the primacy of structure over process.

Other researchers have attempted to define the invisible college or other "informal" social structures, only to discover similar difficulties. Susan Crawford contrasts informal communication—"a person-to-person relation in which a scientist selects out of the population other scientists to communicate with on aspects of his work" (Crawford, 1971, p. 301)—with "formal or *organized* methods of communication" including publishing and the presentation of papers at meetings (emphasis added). Essentially, this distinguishes communication in terms of the channels used (and social organizations that support them), not in terms of the behavior involved. Her operational measure of informal communication is sociometric: Subjects were asked to name "all persons they contacted at least three times during the past year concerning their work" (Crawford, 1971, p. 302). From the point of view of communication behavior, the issue of "contact" is problematic because it does not describe what scientists actually do in the course of communicating but instead measures the frequency or strength of the relation. As a result, Crawford's findings are similarly sociometric. Her sociograms of sleep researchers illustrate structures of relationships, but the processes of communication that might constitute or result in those structures are much less clear.

Lingwood (1969, p. 172) uses a more open-ended definition: "An invisible college may be defined as a system of scientist-units interacting frequently about some shared topic of research interest."

However, he also relies on a sociometric criterion (the frequency of interaction) to determine the existence of an invisible college among "scientist-units," leaving the *nature* of the interaction as an open question.

Similarly, in his discussion of the conceptualization of "scientist specialties" in the wake of Crane's book, Chubin (1976, p. 449) outlines what he believes to be the critical questions for social studies of science or other research. His use of the term *specialty* implies the technical nature of the work being done, while *invisible college* has a more social, informal connotation. Nonetheless, Chubin sees them as closely related concepts. The prominence of structural issues in his list, and the corresponding secondary role of communication, are clear:

1. What are the social and intellectual properties of a specialty?
2. How do specialties grow, stabilize and decline?
3. What are the temporal and spatial dimensions of a specialty?
4. How do specialties vary in size, scope and life expectancy?
5. Who are the institutional arrangements that support specialties?
6. What impact does funding have on the kind and volume of research produced in a specialty?
7. What kinds of communication relations sustain research activities in a specialty?

Chubin's list reiterates some of Crane's assumptions, for example, that institutions precede communication relations, that specialties have specific boundaries apart from human actions, and that communication "sustains" social structures instead of being the fundamental activity that *constitutes* those structures.

Mullins (1968) found that every researcher in his sample of the *American Men of Science* defined his or her own group of social contacts differently, leading him to conclude that invisible colleges do not exist as Price defines them. Instead, he suggests that a single large network may exist for all of science and that the part of the network that the individual researcher "sees" is what he or she considers to be his or her invisible college. However, Mullins does not find any grouping or structure that corresponds to the invisible college, at least as seen from outside the perceptions of individual researchers.

Mullins's findings, in fact, raise a critical question about invisible colleges: Are they *structures* (discernible and measurable from outside) or are they *processes* (in which only the scholars involved might participate, therefore, perceivable only by them)? The dilemma illustrates again how difficult it is to look for informal communication processes by identifying and measuring social structures. It may be that, if invisible colleges are seen as the constructions of the scholars involved, they can only be known, as it were, from inside the college itself. The large "network" of research, as measured via its publications or other structural indicators, is an indicator of underlying communication processes, but ultimately the individual researchers' views of the college may say more about the "reality" of the processes in which they engage.

Crane's principal legacy for communication research then is a theoretical construct that is highly suggestive but difficult to operationalize. Paradoxically, the term *invisible college* denotes an informal communication *process*, yet researchers look for it in formal social structures and documents. The resulting ambiguity, built into the construct in the absence of a clear definition, has led researchers to use the term very differently from study to study. Why has a construct as popular and apparently rich as the invisible college yielded such as scattered and unfocused body of studies of scholarly communication? Would a more coherent definition help to reestablish communication as the central concern in invisible college studies as well as other social studies of scholarship?

## Studying Scholarly Communication Processes: Future Directions for Research

If the invisible college is considered to be an informal social phenomenon, then a revised definition can be proposed: *An invisible college is a set of informal communication relations among scholars or researchers who share a specific common interest or goal.*

Essentially, this definition removes a number of assumptions that have grown up around the invisible college concept, such as prerequisite formal institutional structures or the importance of geographic distance. The definition refocuses the concept on communication processes and suggests a new set of research issues for the study of scholarly communication:

- What kinds of communication behavior produce an invisible college? Is the presence of certain kinds of communication acts (e.g., the exchange of article preprints or face-to-face meetings) sufficient for a group of acquaintances to be considered an invisible college?
- How do individuals perceive their interactions with others within, versus outside of, the invisible college? Do outsiders perceive the invisible college the same way that insiders do? How do insiders' perceptions vary from person to person?
- What is the effect of time on the communication processes in an invisible college? What measures might be developed for observing this effect?
- What does "closeness" mean within an invisible college? What amount of cohesion must members experience in order to define themselves as a group? Is cohesion within an invisible college based on the sharing of information, on interpersonal/ emotional affinity, or both?
- How do individual scholars use invisible colleges as resources to help fulfill their information needs? How does the invisible college relate to other types of scholarly information systems?

## Methodological Implications for Studying Scholarly Communication

Where, then, does this leave bibliometrics as a methodological tool for studying communication behavior among researchers? Obviously, few of the questions listed above can be answered using only the measurement techniques that have dominated invisible college studies in the past. The bibliometric links among publications, or, analogously, the sociometric links among the members of professional societies or the faculties of certain institutions, may provide clues about the existence of an invisible college, but by definition an informal relationship would not appear fully formed in its formal products or structures.

Certainly, bibliometric techniques are important because they give analysts the ability to crystallize abstract ideas into apparently concrete forms. They can inspire theoretical thinking—and in this respect the durability of the invisible college construct testifies to the fundamental value of bibliometric analysis for communication research. By allowing us to construct "maps" of documents, bibliometrics gives us a systematic glimpse of the communication acts that produced the documents in the first place.

However, scholarship is a multilayered world composed of and driven along by the communication behavior of individuals. Scholarly communication might be explored in more depth using the fieldwork techniques typical of ethnographic studies of communication in neighborhoods or families, for example. Participant observation and interviewing have seldom been used to understand the unique nature of research processes like mentoring, coauthorship, or collegiality. Discourse analysis of face-to-face conversations, phone calls, or even presentations at professional meetings might reveal communication patterns that distinguish one specialty from another (e.g., the work in progress by Knorr-Cetina, 1988). These methods offer the communication researcher a great deal of interpretive and heuristic power when combined with the results of strictly structural analysis.

Moreover, the use of ethnographic approaches is a separate issue from the dichotomy between formal and informal scholarly communication that has been emphasized in social studies of scholarship in the past. Griffith (1987, p. 9) notes that, like bibliometric studies, studies of informal communication have been "infected with Price's ideas about counting people and acts of communication and bits of information." The typical informal communication study might be characterized as a quintessential "artifact" or "user" study (Lievrouw, 1988), where the assumption is that information (and communication) are material commodities that can be operationalized and counted.

Alternatively, communication researchers might take the example of constructivist sociologists like Knorr-Cetina (1981, 1988), Restivo (1983), or Latour and Woolgar (1979), who, in their "lab studies" of science, assume instead that knowledge is phenomenological and ephemeral, a social construction of the researchers involved. From this perspective, documents are "data" without intrinsic meaning of their own. They remain data until individual scholars make sense of them—until scholars engage in the act of "informing" themselves and their colleagues via communication.

The main advantage, then, of ethnographic methodology in studies of scholarly communication is that it would allow researchers to make more powerful interpretations of the quantitative analysis of

communication artifacts. In a famous essay on the use of ethnographic methods in organizational communication research, John
Van Maanen (1983) points out that "the territory is not the map."
Nor, we might add, is the "territory" of scholarly communication to
be found intact in the maps of bibliometrics. However, we also know
that the territory cannot easily be navigated without a map and that
the map is meaningless unless the traveler can interpret it. Both
the bibliographic map and its ethnographic interpretation are necessary to move through the territory of scholarly communication.

## Notes

1. With few exceptions, in the past there has been an overwhelming
emphasis on the study of science as opposed to other scholarly specialties.
However, the study of scholarly communication includes the humanities,
arts, and social science as well as the natural sciences as subjects for study.
For examples of studies that examine communication patterns in specialties outside the physical, mathematical, and biological sciences, see Crane
(1987), Paisley (1984), and Burt (1978).

2. For example, co-citation analysis relies on the patterns of documents
in which the same two papers are cited together (Griffith, Small, Stonehill,
& Dey, 1974; Mullins, Hargens, Hecht, & Kick, 1977; Small, 1973). This
consistent relationship of two papers together in other papers is usually
interpreted to mean that the two papers have something to do with each
other and, therefore, that there may be a social link between the authors of
the two papers (see also Lievrouw, Rogers, Lowe, & Nadel, 1987).

# PART II

# Bibliometric Research Methods

SADAAKI MIYAMOTO
NOBUYUKI MIDORIKAWA
KAZUHIKO NAKAYAMA

# 4. A View of Studies on Bibliometrics and Related Subjects in Japan

This chapter surveys studies on bibliometrics and related subjects in Japan. Reviewed articles are classified according to the following categories: (a) studies on bibliometrics, including bibliometric laws, citation studies, scientific communication, and software tools for bibliometrics, and (b) application of bibliometrics, including policies for scientific reference, bibliometrics and information retrieval, and databases in oriental languages. An interesting characteristic in the Japanese studies is that databases of texts in oriental languages such as Japanese and Chinese have been developed. Applications of fuzzy set theory to document retrieval using bibliometric techniques are also observed. We emphasize the models and methods used in common between bibliometrics and other fields of sciences.

The purpose of this chapter is to review studies on bibliometrics and related subjects in Japan. First, we observe the following characteristics:

(1) Development of large-scale databases has stimulated research on statistical analysis of documents in the databases.

(2) Researchers in different scientific disciplines in Japan are interested in bibliometrics. Accordingly, their works can be divided into two categories: (a) Researchers in library and information science are interested in citation behavior, communication studies, and the use of information in libraries, and (b) researchers in other fields, such as chemistry, management science, and system science, are interested in bibliometric laws, mathematical models, information retrieval databases in oriental languages, and the social use of statistics for bibliographic databases.

In this chapter, we review works on these subjects in two sections. The first section contains studies concerning library and information science: bibliometric laws, citation studies, and communication research. The second section deals with the application of bibliometrics such as evaluation of research, information retrieval, and development of text databases. We emphasize interaction between bibliometrics and studies in other fields.

We do not attempt to include all important studies on bibliometrics in Japan. We focus more on articles written in English than on those in Japanese. Therefore, many significant studies written in Japanese are omitted.

## Bibliometrics and Scientometrics

### Bibliometric Laws

It is little known that a Japanese botanist (Tamiya, 1931) published a paper on the increase of bibliography for a particular subject far earlier than Price; the latter is known to have demonstrated that the number of publications grows according to the logistic curve (Price, 1963). In his 1931 paper, Tamiya showed the same type of logistic curve as the one Price discussed later, using a nonlinear differential equation and data of bibliography concerning *Aspergillus*.

More recent studies on fundamental laws in bibliometrics include papers by Fujiwara, Yokoyama, and Ueda (1981), Eto (1984a, 1984b, 1988), Eto and Makino (1983), Onodera (1988), and Asai (1981a). Asai (1981a) proposed a general model that describes the Bradford curve. He used a weighted error sum of squares criterion for determining parameters to fit the model to bibliographic data. Different models formerly proposed were considered as special cases of his general model. Results of the curve fitting according to these models were compared using 11 different databases. Eto (1984a, 1984b, 1988) and Eto and Makino (1983) discussed the Bradford distribution according to a stochastic model of difference equations and differential equations. Although they were more interested in the distribution of technological innovation in firms than the distribution of bibliography, their works are still interesting as studies of bibliometric laws. Taking the same stochastic modeling approach, Onodera (1988) considered an extension of Simon's (1955) model of a skew distribution that describes Zipf's law, Bradford's law, and Lotka's law.[1] He compared his model with distributions of classification items of actual databases. Fujiwara, Yokoyama, and Ueda (1981) and Fujiwara (1984) investigated the distribution of key words in *Chemical Abstracts*. They measured the cross-correlation between a pair of sections in *Chemical Abstracts* using the number of common key words. Fujiwara (1984) found a linear relationship between the logarithm of the frequencies of key words and the order of appearances for the key words based on the same data.

On bibliometric laws, a good review in Japanese by Harada (1974) is well known to researchers in this field in Japan.

## Citation Studies

Works by Garfield (1979b) and his colleagues on citations have had a major influence on bibliometric studies. New techniques of analysis such as clustering and multidimensional scaling have been used, and citation measures have been investigated.

Asai (1981b) proposed a way of modifying the impact factor and immediacy index introduced by Garfield (1979b). He used a probability distribution of citations over 12 months for calculating citation measures more precisely. In this method, the ages of citations are adjusted according to the distribution, and the adjusted ages are applied to the impact factor and immediacy index. Midorikawa, Ogawa, Saito, Kaneko, and Itsumura (1984) investigated several measures of citations of journals including impact factor, immediacy index, number of citations, number of source articles, and a cited-citing ratio, the last of which they proposed. They calculated cross-correlations of these measures using the *Journal Citation Reports* from the *Science Citation Index*. They found that the cited-citing ratio correlates less strongly than the impact factor and immediacy index with the number of articles and the number of citations.

The contexts of citations were investigated by Mayumi (1984). She studied meanings of citations of articles on Shakespeare and categorized the citations using a modification of the categories proposed by Moravcsik and Murugesan (1975).

Miyamoto and Nakayama (1980) proposed a method of graphic representation of citation relationships among journals using both digraphs and hierarchical clustering. The method was later modified to include statistical hypothesis testing for generating edges of a digraph of citations (Miyamoto & Nakayama, 1984). These researchers also proposed a technique of hierarchic clustering of source articles using a similarity measure based on a citation space: They compared clusters of documents with clusters of journals (Miyamoto & Nakayama, 1983).

## Scientific Communication

Many works on scientific communication using bibliometric techniques have been done by Japanese library scientists; most of these works are written in Japanese. These works are summarized in two textbooks also written in Japanese (Midorikawa, Kurata, Mayumi, Oka, & Sugimoto, 1986; Ueda et al., 1987). Ueda et al. (1987) used statistics on bibliography to exhibit characteristics of scientific and technological literature. Midorikawa, Kurata, Mayumi, Oka, and Sugimoto (1986) reviewed various bibliometric techniques and their use in library studies.

Studies on scientific communication can be divided into three groups. The first group contains studies on features of the production of scholarly information. The second group is concerned with the ways that the information is transferred. The third group deals with how the information is used.

Kurata (1984, 1985) investigated factors that influence productivity of publication of 828 Japanese political scientists and 100 Japanese physical scientists. She found that a considerable percentage of the total information has been produced by scholars graduated from a small number of universities in Japan.

Kaneko, Itsumura, Saito, Ogawa, and Midorikawa (1983) studied time lags in information transfer. They investigated times between submission and publication for letter journals and other journals and compared the time lags between these two types of journals. Kaneiwa et al. (1988) investigated time lags for publication of papers written by Japanese that were submitted to *Science* and *Nature*. They found that time lags were longer for papers with Japanese first authors than for those with foreign first authors in the case of *Science*. On the other hand, they found no remarkable difference in the case of *Nature*. Ogawa et al. (1989) investigated the effectiveness of the two major bibliographic tools: abstracting and indexing services. They found that general bibliographic tools that cover all types of publications, such as *Physical Abstracts* and *Chemical Abstracts*, had lower ratios of coverage of conference materials, while special tools, such as *InterDoc*, covered an average of 80% of available conference materials.

Citations are a main tool for measuring information use. Miwa, Ueda, and Nakayama (1980) analyzed citations in the *Social Sciences Citation Index* using the six academic disciplines of law, economics, politics, psychology, sociology, and education. They investigated the number of citations per source article, distribution of ages of citations, distribution of titles, and other measures for these six disciplines. Features of the citations were summarized. For example, publications in political science cite more books than journal publications, whereas articles in psychology cite more journal publications than books. Using *Chemical Abstracts*, Tamura, Midorikawa, and Inoue (1985) examined patterns of citation in papers by Japanese and Soviet authors. One of their results showed that Soviet chemists cite Soviet publications more frequently than those in English, whereas Japanese chemists cite Japanese publications less than those written in English. Midorikawa (1983) investigated half-lives of citations of journals on physics.[2] His results reveal two groups of journals: The group with shorter half-lives contains subfields of physics that use large experimental devices; the group with longer half-lives includes subfields that use smaller experimental devices.

## Software Tools for Bibliometrics

Given that bibliographic databases are well developed, efforts should be directed to the development of software tools for analyzing bibliographic data. Asai (1987) described his software developed on a microcomputer that includes models for Bradford curves. He also implemented a document database with citations on the microcomputer.

## Application of Bibliometrics

### Policies for Scientific Research

Hayashi and Yamada (1975) discussed the use of statistics in scientific literature from the viewpoint of policy and decision making for scientific research and education. They investigated life cycles of research activities, such as chronological changes in numbers of publications on specific subjects and the growth and decline of a number of new technological products. They suggest that their analysis is useful for improving systems for education and for research.

Arima and Kanada (1984) investigated the numbers of publications and citations of various research organizations in Japan, with the purpose of using the statistics for evaluation of research activities and groups of researchers. They used *Chemical Abstracts*, *INSPEC*, and *The Science Citation Index*. Their results include tables of the total numbers of publications of universities, research institutes, and several large companies in Japan for 13 years. Ichikawa, Kanada, Oe, and Momota (1979) investigated research activities on plasma physics using *INSPEC* and showed that the cumulative number of publications and the temperature of plasma are highly correlated.

### Bibliometrics and Information Retrieval

As discussed by Garfield (1979b), bibliometric techniques such as clustering are useful for developing advanced techniques of information retrieval. Miyamoto, Miyake, and Nakayama (1983b) proposed the use of citations that are compiled as a thesauruslike structure. Their basic tool is fuzzy set theory[3] (see also Miyamoto, Miyake, & Nakayama, 1983a). Nomoto, Wakayama, Kirimoto, and Kondo (1987) also used fuzzy sets for realizing information retrieval with a citation index. They implemented a system of fuzzy information retrieval on a database with a citation index. They considered citation networks of documents: Their system enables retrieval of all documents associated on the network. In another work, Miyamoto (1989) showed that, using a composition rule of fuzzy relations, the clustering of documents can be represented theoretically as feedback from the information retrieval process.

## Databases in Oriental Languages

One notable characteristic of Japanese research on document databases is that databases in oriental languages have been studied. The databases include not only Japanese but also Chinese and other languages. Hoshino (1988) reported development of such databases as Ancient Japanese documents, texts of Japanese classics, Chinese texts, and various historical records. Some of these databases include the whole texts of the documents. Indices such as KWIC, KWOC, and concordances were constructed on the databases, and statistics on frequencies of occurrences of words were calculated.

Sometimes advanced methods of analysis are applied to these databases of texts. Matsumoto, Miyamoto, and Nakayama (1982, 1984) used cluster analysis, factor analysis, and multidimensional scaling on a set of important key words in a Chinese classic and found the structure of ideas in the text. Their result is useful as a guideline for understanding the text.

# Discussion

As shown above, researchers in different scientific fields are studying bibliometrics and related problems in Japan. Accordingly, some of the works have the characteristics of interdisciplinary studies. We recognize common mathematical models between bibliometrics and other fields, the application of bibliometric methods to other disciplines, and the use of techniques developed for other fields in bibliometrics.

In general, information exchange between library and information science and other areas of science that include bibliometrics is not remarkable. In a previous study (Nakayama, Ueda, & Miyamoto, 1979), we investigated information exchange among 11 disciplines of behavioral science. Table 4.1 shows frequencies of citations among the 11 disciplines. The disciplines are economics and business, law, education, library and information science, political science and history, psychiatry, psychology, sociology/ anthropology/linguistics, social issues and philosophy, health and rehabilitation, and management and planning. This table is based on data from the *Social Sciences Citation Index* (*SSCI*) in 1976: Source articles were randomly sampled from the *SSCI* database, and citations to journal articles were examined. Most of the scientific journals are classified into different disciplines by the Institute for Scientific Information (ISI). The source articles and the cited articles were classified into the 11 disciplines following the ISI classification. Table 4.1, showing calculated frequencies, indicates that library and information science is an isolated discipline. As we look at that column, we find that it takes 89% of its journal citations from itself. As we look at the row, we see that the other 10 disciplines rarely cite library and information science. If this field of library and information science continues to give and receive so little information to and from other disciplines, it may lapse into irrelevancy. It seems that an effort should be made to exchange more information with other disciplines.

Nevertheless, methods and results of investigations in bibliometrics and related areas of study in library and information science can be interesting and useful for other disciplines. As Eto and Makino (Eto, 1984a, 1984b, 1988; Eto & Makino, 1983) showed, a stochastic model for the Bradford distribution is applicable to management science. Methods of management science can also be applied to problems in bibliometrics. Using mathematical programming, Miyamoto and Nakayama (1981) reformulated a problem of discarding periodicals in a library that had formerly been considered by Brookes (1971).

Many scientists in different fields consider that bibliographic databases provide interesting material for analysis, aside from their usefulness as a tool for information retrieval. Works by Hayashi and Yamada (1975) and Arima and Kanada (1984) emphasized the practical usefulness of analyses of document databases. These works have been done from the viewpoints of researchers outside bibliometrics. As document databases provide interesting material for such analyses, bibliometrics should provide more methods and software tools for data analysis (see Asai, 1987).

The clustering of documents can be considered to be a standard technique of bibliometrics. Different methods of cluster analysis for large numbers of documents have been proposed (e.g., Garfield, 1979b). They are more or less ad hoc techniques based on experience or heuristics. It should also be noted that the clustering of

**TABLE 4.1**
Citation Frequencies Among 11 Disciplines in the Behavioral Sciences

| Citations | Source Articles | | | | | | | | | | |
|---|---|---|---|---|---|---|---|---|---|---|---|
| | Economics and Business | Law | Education | Library and Information Sciences | Political Science and History | Psychiatry | Psychology | Sociology/ Anthropology/ Linguistics | Social Issues and Philosophy | Health and Rehabilitation | Management and Planning |
| Economics and business | 652 | 108 | 6 | 2 | 47 | 0 | 2 | 112 | 36 | 3 | 83 |
| Law | 287 | 3031 | 35 | 5 | 12 | 18 | 0 | 26 | 3 | 3 | 40 |
| Education | 0 | 2 | 541 | 15 | 4 | 23 | 81 | 8 | 13 | 9 | 0 |
| Library and information science | 0 | 0 | 0 | 591 | 0 | 0 | 1 | 0 | 1 | 0 | 3 |
| Political science and history | 8 | 63 | 37 | 3 | 164 | 1 | 1 | 124 | 47 | 1 | 71 |
| Psychiatry | 0 | 0 | 24 | 1 | 0 | 1337 | 101 | 52 | 32 | 110 | 16 |
| Psychology | 7 | 3 | 312 | 5 | 9 | 253 | 2492 | 123 | 67 | 102 | 71 |
| Sociology/ anthropology/ linguistics | 19 | 7 | 73 | 3 | 64 | 54 | 64 | 1450 | 112 | 36 | 41 |
| Social issues and philosophy | 9 | 42 | 30 | 5 | 14 | 44 | 37 | 107 | 225 | 16 | 32 |
| Health and rehabilitation | 0 | 15 | 68 | 0 | 1 | 82 | 44 | 10 | 12 | 342 | 4 |
| Management and planning | 39 | 46 | 13 | 13 | 8 | 2 | 2 | 50 | 12 | 2 | 180 |
| Other | 88 | 39 | 67 | 18 | 17 | 744 | 219 | 225 | 32 | 309 | 28 |

documents is a typical and interesting example of a real cluster analysis problem, due to the following characteristics:

(1) A very large number of data should be analyzed.
(2) Mathematical models based on Euclidian space are useless.
(3) An expected number of clusters is not given beforehand.

Observing these characteristics, we can deduce that (a) the method should be a hierarchic cluster, considering the third point, above; (b) a minimal spanning tree algorithm for the single linkage method should be applied, because this is the most efficient technique to deal with a large number of data by hierarchic clustering; and (c) an effective way to summarize information in the obtained clusters should be developed. A good example of this is the graphic representation of biomedical clusters by Garfield (1979b).

Points a and b above mean that advanced methods in statistics and computer science can be applied to document clustering; c implies that techniques in document clustering may be useful for problems outside bibliometrics.

Miyamoto and Nakayama (1984) applied the method of digraph representation, which was developed for information exchange among journals, to the measurement of cognitive structure. Later, they used the same method for analyzing data obtained by questionnaire (Oi, Miyamoto, Abe, Katsuya, & Nakayama, 1986).

Bibliometric techniques may also be useful for analysis of texts or content analysis. As noted above, various types of text databases have been developed, and analysis of them will be an interesting subject for further research. This means, at the same time, that good software tools are necessary for database analysis.

Fifteen years ago, few works on bibliometrics by Japanese authors had been published in English. The situation has improved, and a number of studies have now been published in the United States and Europe; but the majority of these studies are still written in Japanese. As we emphasized in the previous section, more information exchange is necessary for progress in bibliometrics. In this sense, the fact that researchers in different disciplines are interested in bibliometrics in Japan will greatly activate studies of this field, because document databases and methods of bibliometrics should reveal themselves to be more useful in many areas of scientific research.

## Notes

1. Zipf's law of rank-productivity relation, Bradford's law of rank-cumulated productivity relation, and Lotka's law of productivity-frequency relation are clearly described in Onodera's paper (1988), with their mathematical formulas. A Bradford curve is the plot of the mathematical formula of Bradford's law.

2. In statistical terms, a half-life of citations is the median age distribution of citations.

3. *Fuzzy sets* refers to a mathematical theory of dealing with vagueness. The use of fuzzy sets in information retrieval means introducing a degree of relevance in retrieved sets of documents. Fuzzy information retrieval may be considered to be a mathematically elaborated version of a weighted retrieval.

# 5. Author Co-Citation Analysis:
## Overview and Defense

Author co-citation analysis reveals the changing linkages of writings as they are used jointly over time. It is a highly specialized form of quantitative history that offers relatively objective insights into the intellectual structure of science and scholarship by clustering and mapping their constituent works. It shades, moreover, into techniques for retrieving the documents in which the co-citations occur. Although the retrieval techniques will be touched on here, this chapter focuses on co-cited author analysis as a way of studying the intellectual structure of scholarly fields. It gives some conceptual and historical background, argues against critics, and sums up some major findings of author co-citation studies to date.

## Authors as a Unit of Analysis

As practiced by its chief exponent, Henry Small, *document* co-citation analysis maps linkages among individual articles or books on the basis of their joint citation by later writers. *Author* co-citation analysis, on the other hand, uses computational and graphic display techniques to produce maps of prominent authors in selected areas of scholarship. This innovation was made by White and Griffith (1981a), who used *oeuvres*—sets of documents by authors, as opposed to single articles or books—as the unit of analysis, and the co-citation of pairs of oeuvres as the variable that indicates authors' distance from each other in maps. An "author" can be construed as both an oeuvre, or body of writings, and a person. (Thus "Pauling" = a body of works including *The Nature of the Chemical Bond*; "Pauling" = a chemist who twice won the Nobel Prize.) Just as with co-citation of papers, this method assumes that two authors are somehow related to each other if they are often jointly cited and that, the more frequently they are co-cited, the more closely they are related.

The maps are the two- or three-dimensional solutions when author data are submitted to multidimensional scaling by computer. Within a given map, each point represents an author, and the proximity of points reflects relationships as perceived by multiple citers. Closely placed authors are seen as similar, generally in content and approach; distant authors, as dissimilar. *Clusters* of authors, also computer derived, can be identified with subject areas, research specialties, or schools of thought. Cluster boundaries, with identifying labels, are often drawn around authors to enhance the map. Axes on the map are sometimes interpreted and labeled as well—for example, the poles of one axis might reflect qualitative versus quantitative tendencies. The power of maps to synthesize large amounts of information is thus applicable to intellectual fields as well as to actual terrain.

If author data are submitted for factor analysis, the factors, too, usually correspond to specialties or schools of thought. In this they resemble clusters. But with commonly used clustering techniques, each author appears in only one cluster, whereas an author may load on more than one factor. Thus factor analysis can reveal authors whom citers perceive to be useful in more than one specialty, along with a rough indication of the degree of usefulness (the factor loadings).[1]

Analysis using oeuvres results in groupings similar to those at the level of individual articles. But there are advantages to analysis at the author level. First, the co-citation counts can be obtained through publicly available databases—Scisearch, Social Scisearch, and Arts & Humanities Citation Index, all published by the Institute for Scientific Information (ISI) and offered widely through vendors such as DIALOG and BRS. Thus the methodology is open to the international online/community. In contrast, to do large-scale article analysis, one needs insider's access to ISI files.

Second, one needs only the names of prominent authors, which requires relatively little foreknowledge of a field and no detailed bibliographic information. Moreover, the author co-citation technique allows one to characterize an entire field with relatively few authors' names—far fewer than the number of papers one would need to conduct an article-level analysis.

Third, the use of authors as the unit of analysis opens the possibility of exploring questions concerning both perceived cognitive structure and perceived social structure of science. If co-citation analysis shows close relationships between oeuvres, is it the case that the *persons* who wrote them are socially connected? Anecdotal evidence points to a qualified "yes," but the matter has received less systematic attention than it deserves.

## Information Scientists

White and Griffith (1981a) mapped and clustered 39 authors in information science, a demonstration also reproduced in Griffith (1980), Garfield (1986), and, with additional names, Vickery and Vickery (1987). Comparable maps using information scientists' articles rather than oeuvres have been produced by Small (1981) and by Saito (1984); these yielded results congruent with White and Griffith's.

It may be possible to evoke the power of co-cited author mapping in the present context without recapitulating much of the earlier paper. From a multidimensional scaling of the original White and Griffith data, three-dimensional coordinates were obtained. These were submitted to a graphics program called Three-D for labeled plotting in two-dimensional space. The result is the starburst pattern of Figure 5.1, which represents the field as of about 1980.

As an intellectual construct, the map seems to capture information science reasonably well, according to knowledgeable persons. It also captures a certain amount of social structure. Upon seeing it, Derek Price, one of the mapped authors, said he knew "everyone about halfway across and then no one." Several retrievalists would doubtless say the same for their half of the map.

Many readers will find the groupings interpretable.[2] The horizontal axis of Figure 5.1 conveys an obvious subject gradation, but there is a subtler division as well. The authors on the right side tend to deal ahistorically with relatively permanent features of human language and psychology. Those on the left side are more oriented toward dynamic social and historical data. Although many of the authors in the map use mathematics or statistics in their work, those in the upper half of the map are possibly somewhat more mathematical in style, and less wide-ranging in subject matter, than those in the lower half.

It is pleasant to imagine entering any comparable list of authors at a terminal and, through algorithmic processing of their ISI co-citation data, having such a display flash onto the screen. I can

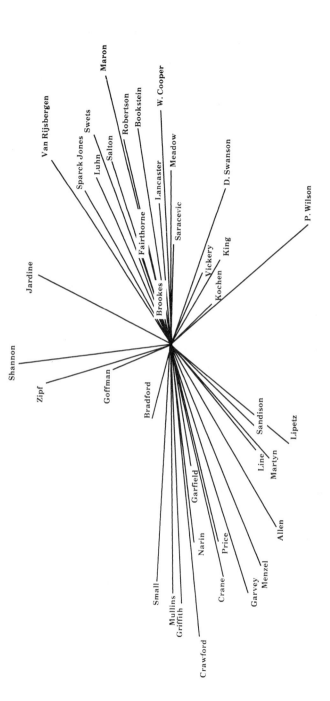

**Figure 5.1.** Information Scientists, circa 1980

87

think of nothing better for reconnoitering "macro-level" intellectual structure as it evolves in fields of science and scholarship, in particular because co-occurring authors' names have greater human interest than co-occurring subject headings.

This orientation to "macro-level" structure is not, of course, a replacement for *reading* the authors involved. However, the groupings in Figure 5.1 aid reading in two ways. First, they suggest *co-cited* authors to read together—for example, William D. Garvey, Herbert Menzel, and Thomas J. Allen. Second, they yield names for retrieving additional, *co-citing* authors who do not appear in the map—for example, those who, by citing Garvey, Menzel, and Allen jointly, reveal an interest in the topic *communication in research settings*. The latter retrieval technique, explained in several papers (Chapman & Subramanyam, 1981; Knapp, 1984; McCain, 1988; White, 1981a, 1981b, 1986), usefully complements searches with subject terms. By drawing on what authors' names imply jointly, it helps the searcher express aspects of content not expressed by available subject indexing.

## Earlier Lines of Research

Author co-citation studies can be linked to three lines of research:
(1) *Analysis of the citation (or other bibliographic) records of major authors in specialties or schools of thought.* These are generally done by academics studying their own fields or by sociologists of science and scholarship using manual, ad hoc data gathering techniques. ISI citation data are not used.[3]
(2) *Mapping of specialties, schools, and disciplines by citation or (since the mid-1970s) co-citation analysis of members' highly cited publications.* The main practitioners of this sort of analysis are Garfield, Small, and their colleagues at the ISI who have privileged access to the ISI citation databases. They use single articles or books, rather than oeuvres of authors, as their unit of analysis.[4]
(3) *Online gathering of bibliometric data, as described by several writers.* (See, for example, Hawkins, 1977; McGhee, Skinner, Roberts, Ridenour, & Larson, 1987; Oppenheim, 1985; Persson, 1986.)

These precedents are conjoined in the stream of author co-citation studies, which take authors as their unit of analysis like the studies in the first group; use co-citation measurement like many of

the studies in the second; use mapping, clustering, and factor-ana-
lytic techniques eclectically like both groups (see McCain's chapter
in this book); and draw data from online sources. More specifically,
they use author co-citation counts gathered from ISI databases in
settings external to ISI.[5]

Credit for the earliest co-cited author mapping that I have seen
must go to Rosengren (1968), with a book in English based on a
dissertation at the University of Lund. Rosengren was studying not
scientists or social scientists but Scandinavian and world literary
figures (mostly European). His raw data are counts of what he
calls "co-mentions" of figures such as Ibsen, Strindberg, Zola, and
Flaubert (along with lesser lights) in the texts of critical reviews.
His technique is fully bibliometric. In fact, five years before Small
introduced co-citation in 1973, Rosengren anticipated the work of
the next two decades. (Nevertheless, Small's, 1973, paper is generally taken as the founding paper of the co-citation literature.)

One can sense Rosengren's groping for precedents on which to
build: In his bibliography, he includes works on content analysis, quantitative linguistics, numerical taxonomy, the sociology of
knowledge, and the statistical sociology of literature as well as
Price's "Networks of Scientific Papers" (1965). But co-citation analysis as we know it had not been invented, and Rosengren succeeded
in inventing it to an astonishing degree. Unfortunately, despite its
methodological interest, a Swedish contribution to the sociology of
literature was not likely to be discovered soon in other fields and
countries. So, although Rosengren has cited some of the bibliometricians in more recent articles—and has contributed to this
volume—his own pioneering work is only now entering mainstream
bibliometrics.

## Citing and Voting

There is another body of citation research that bears on the line
represented here. Several investigators have attempted to characterize citers' possible motives in citing. Others have attempted,
from reading the documentary contexts in which citations occur, to
characterize them by their different functions. (See Cozzens, 1989;
McCain & Turner, 1989; Small, 1982, for reviews of this literature.)
Although these efforts at creating a "psychology of citation" are

perfectly proper, they are sometimes used to cast doubt on the whole enterprise of citation counting, the message being that aggregated citations are questionable as indicators until we know better what citers' norms are and what citers mean when they cite.

In co-cited author studies, however—as in bibliometrics generally—the psychological approach is usually bracketed as irrelevant. These studies involve a file of authors as units of analysis, and the variables are how often each has been co-cited with every other author in the file. The data are the overall magnitudes of citation and co-citation, regardless of citers' reasons for contributing to these counts or the differing functions of the citations in citers' papers. Exactly the same is true in other citation research when the unit of analysis changes from cited authors to cited papers, journals, universities, or countries.

An analogy with certain studies in political science may help make the point. Citing an author is in some ways like voting for a candidate. It is well known that there are various reasons for voting and various accompanying states of mind. In one kind of political study, it is perfectly proper to examine voter psychology and to categorize why votes were given. These correspond, of course, to the psychologies of citing mentioned above. But whole other classes of studies ignore the motivations underlying the votes and focus instead on the magnitudes and distributions of the vote counts. The fact that many votes were ill informed, perfunctory, and the like does not invalidate an election or render the study of election data meaningless. In other words, it does not matter to some scholars *why* the votes were given; what matters are the tallies and patterns that emerge over the whole electorate and perhaps over more than one election. Analyses of American "critical elections" and of Congressional roll calls are of this latter kind, and bibliometric analyses are comparable.

Thus it does not matter in bibliometrics that some of the citations to, say, Thomas S. Kuhn's works are perfunctory, ritualistic, negational, and so on. What matters is that his overall count is very high relative to most other authors in the sociology of science and that he is highly co-cited with many, but not all, of them. Even if all of the citations to Kuhn were critical or negational of his work (which they are not), he would still emerge, by bibliometric evidence, as a very important figure. (Analogously, so would Ronald Reagan even if all the votes he received in 1980 and 1984 were actually votes against Jimmy Carter or Fritz Mondale.)

Those who want to "psychologize" citing as a way of undermining trust in the counts seem to overrely on individual experience in a way typical of humanists, who tend to see universals in anecdotal particulars (for example, MacRoberts & MacRoberts, 1988, 1989). Anyone who has ever cited can, simply by introspection, arrive at ways in which citations might mislead or fail to tell the whole story. Anyone who has ever pored over the citations of others can furnish further evidence of the same things—for example, omission of items that should be included. The critiques of citation analysis by those working with their own small samples are almost uniformly of this kind. Cronin (1984) has a sympathetic review of their arguments.

What the anticitationists generally miss is the liberating effect of using data from very large files, such as those available from ISI. When one sees that scores, hundreds, and even thousands of citations have accrued to a work, an author, a set of authors, it is difficult to believe that all of them are suspect. It is also difficult *not* to believe that individual vagaries of citing behavior cancel each other out, corrected by the sheer numbers of persons citing. At a deeper level, one may ask why we should even think in terms of "vagaries"— individual peculiarities and deviations from the norm—in citing behavior. Why not believe that there *is* a norm in citing—straightforward acknowledgment of related documents—and that the great majority of citations conform to it?

Since the question is not likely to be settled empirically any time soon (see Small, 1982), one's answer reveals, ultimately, one's side in a permanent division of taste or style. On the one hand are persons willing to think only biographically, in terms of particular instances and individual peculiarities. On the other are persons willing to trust, and look for patterns in, highly aggregated data, which exist at a high degree of abstraction. The anticitationists, who might be characterized as humanist historians, are, of course, in the first camp; the citationists, who are cliometricians of sorts, belong to the second. Because the two groups work at such different levels of reality, the rift between them cannot really be closed. It is as if each were studying a town but could do so in only one way: either by living among its people or by flying over it. The "ground-level" and the "aerial" views lead to descriptions of reality that at some point become incommensurable.

Unquestionably, the anticitationists can give richer accounts of science and scholarship from the "ground-level" view, and such "aerial" techniques as co-cited author analysis should be considered as secondary to their accounts. I would also hold, however, that co-cited author studies (and bibliometrics generally) represent contributions to history that humanist historians using traditional methods cannot make.

For example, insofar as a field can be represented by its literature, a co-cited author map actually shows a kind of consensus. It shows how citers, often numbering in the hundreds, *jointly* perceive the relationships (or lack of them) among key writers in their field. The map cannot be obtained by interviewing any one citer or by reading and judging on one's own. But it can be created from unobtrusively gathered citation data—objective markers linking texts. The map based on these links neatly operationalizes the elusive notion of "consensus," so that the field, in effect, reveals itself. (As one completes a co-cited author map, there is a sense of "bringing out" what would otherwise be hidden, as if one were developing a photograph from a satellite.) Furthermore, the same technique by which the articles or authors of a single field are mapped can be used at higher levels of aggregation to display the relationships of multiple fields within a discipline or even of whole disciplines within science (Small & Garfield, 1985). At whatever level, the maps are informed by large amounts of data, often reflecting a multiyear period, from the very people who are creating the literatures. Such maps are possible only through bibliometrics.

In short, historians and sociologists who want to display scholarly fields through means other than prose have not, until recently, been able to go beyond their own impressionistic diagrams. That they can now add citation mapping to their traditional methods seems a considerable advance.

## A Co-Citationist on Edge

What, however, is the epistemological status of the maps? They are, indisputably, composite views, informed by the citing behavior of many individuals. In reflecting the actions of the many, do they yield a view of a field that differs from that of a qualified observer? If so, how do we decide which view is right, which should be preferred?

The British sociologist of science David Edge has asked such questions in two critiques, (1977, 1979) of the citationists' work. His arguments, largely unanswered to date, have had some impact. For example, Cronin (1984, p. 27) credits Edge with raising "epistemological and methodological questions, which are responsible for hairline cracks in the conceptual superstructure" of citation analysis. As of late 1989, the two critiques have been cited more than 80 times in the journal literature. It is, therefore, worth examining Edge's criticisms in some detail as a means of understanding the epistemological status of co-citation studies, particularly co-cited author studies, more deeply. (He wrote before the latter per se had emerged, but his remarks apply at least as strongly to them as to the original work by Small, Griffith, and others.) Edge combines a fair statement of anticitationist views with some misconceptions that, if shared, may be useful to refute. My own answer to the epistemological questions raised above will be presented in the next section.

The 1977 essay is called "Why I Am Not a Co-Citationist." A 1979 expansion of the same work is "Quantitative Measures of Communing in Science: A Critical Review." In the latter, Edge describes several objective (i.e., countable) indicators of communication ties: citations, co-citations, acknowledgments of "trusted assessorship," coauthorships, and apprenticeships. Concentrating on citation and co-citation analysis, he offers two main objections:

> First, that quantitative methods, in their reliance on the published literature, may be perpetuating a "rationalized" account of the scientific processes they are attempting to measure— an account which systematically (and hence reproducibly) obscures key features of those processes. And second, that, in offering an "overall objective" view of science "as it is," such methods imply an inappropriately positivist and realist approach, and shift attention from the dynamic perspective of the scientists themselves: accounts derived from quantitative methods are intended to "*correct*" the "partial" perceptions of participants.
>
> * * *
>
> Essentially, [citation analysts'] "strong" claim is that in transcending the "limited, subjective and biased" perspective of individuals, and in giving some "public, aggregated, objective and unbiased" account, these measures have, as it were, a

*preferred logical status.* They are more "objective," more "reliable"; not only can they "correct" participants' accounts, but they can define what really is (or was) the case, and can arbitrate between conflicting accounts; and so on. (Edge, 1979, pp. 108-109; emphasis in original)

Edge's tone might lead one to think the citationists had indeed made the claims he attributes to them, and rather arrogantly too. But, in fact, his own quotations from their writings—presumably the strongest evidence he could find—show nothing of the sort. The "strong" claim and the apparent paraphrases are his own compositions. Certainly no proponent claims that citation analysis has "preferred logical status"—note that Edge is not quoting there— and none has ever proposed, on the basis of citations, to correct scientists' subjective accounts or to define "what really was the case" outside citations themselves. In an early attempt to use ISI citation data to trace the history of a line of research, Garfield, Sher, and Torpie (1964) expressed the belief that a time-ordered citation network corroborated Isaac Asimov's account of the discovery of the structure of DNA. They understandably looked at the network to see whether it revealed intellectual linkages that Asimov had missed, as would any historian examining a source of evidence not considered by another. (It did.) But that was in the spirit of *enriching* a conventional account rather than *superseding* it. (See Pickering & Nadel, 1987, in which a historian and a bibliometrician, respectively, collaborate to enrich the former's earlier account of the charm hypothesis in high-energy physics.) At most, citationists have, in effect, said to historians, "Here is some evidence from the literature of a connection you may have missed," which is far from the mode in which Edge implies they operate.

There are actually two kinds of citation analysis that Edge criticizes. Because they are different, his arguments call for different rejoinders.

One kind, in the manner of Garfield, Sher, and Torpie, is the creation of networks of individual papers (for example, A cited B, who in turn cited C) to study objective intellectual chains. According to Edge, citationists would hold each citation link to be *proof of influence,* even in the face of protestations to the contrary by the scientists involved. In fact, there is nothing to indicate that citationists believe that. Many relationships other than intellectual influence are reflected by citations, and some influences are not captured by citations at all, as the citationists themselves point out. Nor are they committed to giving a citation account greater epistemic standing than what scientists themselves say. Citationists believe, with Edge (1979, pp. 110-111), that, "if . . . the citation picture is to be accepted as the most accurate available representation of the 'real' events, it can only be because it is well supported by *other* evidence." That is why there have been repeated attempts to validate citation studies by comparing them with histories or perceptions obtained by other means, such as Asimov's. (Small & Greenlee, 1980, check their co-citation "snapshot" of recombinant DNA research against a historical account in *Scientific American*.) Edge (1979, p. 110) pursues this as if it were a telling inconsistency: "If citation methods are advocated on the basis of some *a priori* preferred status . . . why should it be necessary to 'validate' such studies at all?" The answer, although not what he intended, is obvious. They are given this status only by a straw man, not the citationists.

A good example of straw-bashing comes from his 1977 essay, which was published with a paper by Griffith, Drott, and Small (1977) on the assumptions underlying their own work in co-citation. Edge (1977, p. 15) writes:

When Griffith, Drott, and Small state, with emphasis, that ". . . *the investigator should use all means at his disposal to determine the degree of consensus within the relevant community represented by a citation count and the nature of that consensus* . . ." they are abandoning the notion of a preferred logical status for citation methods.

Actually, they are abandoning nothing, because they had never claimed this status in the first place. They are merely being sensible and calling for a multimethod validation of citation studies or a multimethod approach in general. Consequently, Edge himself notes that they differ with him only in assigning citation studies relatively more weight than he does.

The second kind of study criticized by Edge—co-citation analysis—has had more exemplars than the kind by Garfield, Sher, and Torpie. Even so, in distinguishing it from "straight" citation analysis, Edge gives a misleading account of its nature:

In citation analysis, the citing of B by A is taken to reflect an influence of B on A. But in cocitation analysis, the only assumption is that the citing of B and C together by A implies that, in A's perspective, *the work of B and C are related*. In other words, cocitation "maps," strictly speaking, reflect only the perceptions of *authors* [i.e., citers—HDW]. However, co-citation analysts do not use the technique to explore variations in the perceptions of scientists: rather, they act as if a co-citation of B and C by A was evidence that *B and C are related by communication ties*, and that authors 'clustered' by cocitation can be held to have been established, by an objective method, as *interacting groups*. (Edge, 1979, p. 105; emphasis in original)

To take the lesser misconception first, a co-citationist would not hold that the work of B and C are necessarily related merely because A cites them in the same work. It is the *piling up* of co-citations—the fact that their count over time exceeds a certain threshold—that indicates a relationship. Literally millions of works have a co-citation count of one, but the count is not going to exceed that for most of them because subsequent writers do not *recurrently* see them as related.

The greater misconception is that co-citationists simply *assume* communication ties or personal interaction to exist among clustered authors. As it turns out, heavily co-cited authors often *do* have personal communication ties, and clusters often reflect "schools of thought" with interacting members. That has been one of the interesting empirical results of co-citation studies, an example of which will be given shortly. But no one believes that cited authors in clusters are *necessarily* in personal communication. (Or were, in the case of the dead.) The relationship that holds within a cluster is generally *perceived similarity of subject matter or methodological approach in published and cited works*. (The perceivers, Edge correctly notes, are the citing authors.) Automatic clustering of co-cited authors is, in the main, just another form of automatic subject classification, an endeavor long familiar in information science. People clustered because of similar works may indeed have personal communication ties as a further relationship, but that is something that has to be independently established; it is not taken as a "given" by co-citationists.

The point may be illustrated with Edge himself as a co-cited author. As it happens, he was one of 71 mapped in the loose-knit field called "studies in science, technology, and society," as reported in White and Griffith (1982). The raw data were co-citation counts from the online Social Scisearch file of 1972-1980. Strictly on the basis of these counts, a hierarchical clustering routine put Edge in a cluster ordered exactly as follows:

Gerard Lemaine
Robert McGinnis
David Edge
Michael Mulkay
John Law
Hilary Rose
J. D. Bernal
Roy MacLeod
D. S. L. Cardwell
Paul Forman
John Ziman
Jerome Ravetz
Barry Barnes

This cluster is highly homogeneous. Not only are its members all (relatively) nonquantitative social historians or sociologists of science, they are almost all British (or U.K. based). Also, several have published on the emergence of scientific specialties. The co-citation technique accurately separates them from (a) their British colleagues with other disciplinary perspectives, such as the economist Christopher Freeman, (b) nonquantitative *American* social historians and sociologists of science, and (c) other clustered scholars who study science in different ways, such as philosophers, science policy analysts, and bibliometricians. Details of fine structure within the cluster are interesting: Note, for example, that Edge is placed next to Michael Mulkay, his coauthor on the book *Astronomy Transformed*, and not far from Roy MacLeod, his coeditor on the journal *Social Studies of Science*. (Additional fine structure is discussed in White & Griffith, 1982.) Thus, although I am not personally acquainted with anyone in the cluster, I know that Edge has communication ties with at least two of them and very likely more. But I would not conclude that I had isolated an "invisible college" with communication linkages among all members or that I had an accurate and complete picture of "what really was the case" in social relationships such as one person influencing another.

I am, therefore, surprised by what Edge sees in the citationists: a tendency to insist that the evidence from the published literature overrides any other sort of evidence and dictates the "true nature" of specialty boundaries and interacting groups of scientists. He even implies that citationists want to use evidence from the published literature to determine legitimate problems for sociologists of science like him to study. To repeat, there is nothing in what the citationists write to warrant this caricature. It is true that they use algorithms on publicly obtainable data from large, interdisciplinary files to derive their raw counts and to create their maps and clusters. In this sense, they rightly claim that their methods are objective, automatic, replicable, and so on and that their perspective, as far as the connectedness of writings is concerned, is "broader than can be achieved by any individual scientist." But they do not claim that their methods render human judgment unnecessary or vitiate the traditional "subjective" methods of interviewing people and reading primary documents. If co-citationists look for communication ties among authors after clustering them—for example, by interviewing the real people involved—it is not because they think clustering is the only or the best way to uncover scientists' social circles, it is to show that the cognitive structure revealed by co-citation is reinforced by social structure. The maps are essentially a new kind of graphics for revealing *intertextual* relationships. They may or may not reveal *interpersonal* ties; if they do, the ties may take many forms.

The living scientist, the living research group with their everyday problems, are the primary reality of science for Edge, and he is unhappy with the notion, put abroad by Derek Price and others, that science is equivalent to *published scientific papers* or to the process of *formally publishing results in journals*:

> The tendency to characterize "science" in terms of this formal process, and to employ methods designed to analyze the formal literature, "obscures key features" of scientific research. It diverts attention from "the soft underbelly": worse, it proposes that the *informal* should be understood in terms of insights gained by the study of the *formal*. I submit that this is to reverse the priorities of explanatory logic. Explanations of

scientists' behaviour in the informal domain should surely be
extended so as to include within their scope the formal aspects—including the relatively trivial behaviour of adding citations to papers. (Edge, 1979, p. 115; emphasis in original)

One of the authorities he quotes at length on the importance of
informal communication in science is Belver Griffith. Ironically,
Griffith is also an arch-co-citationist. I suspect, nonetheless, that
those doing citation and co-citation studies agree with Edge's stated
priorities; his quarrel is with an imaginary opponent. For my part,
I am sure that no citation or co-citation study of the emergence of
radio astronomy as a scientific specialty could be as rich as *Astronomy Transformed*, the book on the British radio astronomers he
wrote with Michael Mulkay. Whatever their merits, the citationists
cannot capture the intellectual complexity or the human drama of
science. Theirs, in the dry phrase of the Library of Congress classification scheme, is an "auxiliary science of history," and one can
scarcely imagine making a book-length narrative, let alone a play
or a movie, from anything they do. Edge notes that he makes modest
use of citation data in *Astronomy Transformed* to trace certain social
and intellectual connections. I think most citationists would find the
use there to be quite sensible and would simply hope that bibliometric methods could be added to those already widely practiced by
historians and sociologists—interviewing and critical reading.

## Limitations and Strengths

So is this to admit, finally, that there are "hairline cracks" in what
the citationists have built? Not at all—merely to acknowledge limitations. I would add, moreover, that one can get a better idea of the
limitations of citation analysis from those who practice it than from
their critics.

Let me be specific about co-cited author maps. In revealing the
subdivisions of a field, the maps have a well-known limitation: They
are only as good as the analyst's choice of authors. Ideally, one would
like to comb an entire ISI database so as to find and use all authors
who meet a certain threshold of co-citation with each other. Because,
in the foreseeable future, this will be too expensive for persons
outside ISI, the maps depend very much on the analyst's judgment

of who should be included. They are in truth a kind of art form—with all that connotes, for good or ill.

Another well-known limitation is that the maps are never "up to the minute." Because of normal lags in publication cycles, it often takes at least two years for one published work to be cited by another. Several more years may elapse before the citing work passes into the data of a co-citation study. By this time, the cited work is even older, and it is the latter that, as part of an oeuvre, is mapped. The map itself takes time to publish. Thus, when we speak of "citers' perceptions of authors," we really mean authors as they were some years ago. We see them *now* as they were *then*, rather like stars whose light takes years to reach us.

Putting these two limitations together, we arrive at reasons why a person who knows a particular field well might disagree with a map. First, the map may omit authors the insider views as essential. Here the disagreement is with the mapmaker's judgment sample. Perhaps the surest way to settle this argument is to remap the field with the proposed additions and see whether it makes any difference. Second, the map may fail to reflect the insider's knowledge of what authors (as persons) are doing *now*—where their most recent publications and shifts in interest have led them. In the latter case, one can only say, "Wait five years," and hope that citers will register the changes. An attractive feature of co-citation studies is that, over suitable periods, the maps mirror changes in the patterns of co-citation counts: Some author points will shift relative to others.

Given this dynamism, the maps (or other sorts of synoptic displays) are a tool for doing intellectual history. But the history of what? The maps actually render a set of connections given *by the literature*—aggregate data for which no one person is responsible and on which individual citing behavior has small effect. As such, they represent *the history of the consensus* as to important authors or works.[6] This may be compared with connections made by a qualified observer and judge—the typical historian or anyone with insider's knowledge of a field.

We come again to the postponed question of their epistemological status. Earlier, it was asked: What if the maps yield a view of a field that differs from that of a qualified observer? If they do, how do we decide which view is right, which should be preferred?

In any such case, the status of the maps is neither preferred nor nonpreferred a priori; it must be decided in light of the claims being made and the overall evidence brought to bear. Often the consensual map and the observer's judgment will, I think, agree. But in determining the intellectual history of a field, there are times when one might prefer the maps to one person's opinion because they actualize the notion of a consensus with better data. That is the test: Who has the better evidence toward a claim? If, for example, someone claimed that by 1980 Claude Shannon's work was central to information science, Figure 5.1 could be taken as strong historical counterevidence. On the other hand, there are times when interviews (or reading) can uncover what citations fail to show. If a scientist had a meager publication or citation record, so as to be placed far from the center of a map like Figure 5.1, it might be possible to demonstrate his or her centrality on other grounds. Edge makes such a case for the Australian radio astronomer J. L. Pawsey, and, in that instance, his account may be preferred (Edge, 1979, pp. 126-127).

There are several cases on record in which an independent citation account and a judgmental account of the same field have given wholly different results. On reflection, this should not surprise us. Citation analysis is both new and controversial. Even writers who have heard of it do not necessarily try it out or attune their thinking to it; and, of course, most persons go solely on their own impressions when they write. For example, many readers might organize the field of information science differently from Figure 5.1, perhaps to the point of giving primacy to authors and specialties not on the map. Judgments as to importance, similarity, pattern, interesting connections, and so on may derive from premises so unlike those that inform co-citation analyses that it is idle to compare the works that result.

The point, instead, should be whether co-citation maps like Figure 5.1 are validated by independent observations made on similar grounds. On that score, the maps perform well. I have not personally met any qualified observer for whom they lacked face validity, implying that, although people may not spontaneously organize a field as shown, they *recognize* a meaningful organization when they see one. Other co-citationists have had the same experience. But there have also been more formal validations. Keen (1987) accepted Culnan's (1986) factor analysis of co-cited authors in MIS as one basis for partitioning and reviewing the field of management information systems research. Lenk (1983) examined whether highly co-cited information scientists from White and Griffith (1981a) were also co-nominated when their colleagues were asked to name salient figures; he found a high degree of congruence. McCain (1986b) compared co-cited author clusters in both macroeconomics and genetics with clusters made after experts sorted the same authors on the basis of perceived similarity. Again, the results were highly congruent, and the differences that emerged were explicable. In a mapping of the field of human judgment and decision making (White & Griffith, 1981b), the computer's placement of 14 key authors along the horizontal axis duplicated almost exactly their placement on a unidimensional diagram (running from "psychology" to "economics") made by the psychologist Kenneth R. Hammond some years before (Hammond, McClelland, & Manpower, 1980). The six specialty groupings on this axis matched Hammond's perfectly. Similarly, a mapping of the social indicators movement (White, 1983) independently placed key writers and specialties as they had appeared in earlier historical reviews by Mullins (1973) and Rossi and Gilmartin (1980). These are some recent validations, less known than those of the late 1970s, which established the usefulness of article co-citation mapping despite its limitations (Mullins, Hargens, Hecht, & Kick, 1977; Sullivan, Koester, White, & Kern 1980; Sullivan, White, & Barboni, 1977).

De Mey, in an interesting critique of citation studies (1982), implied that a field already diagrammed by an expert could be mapped on the basis of co-citations and the results compared. His examples are the fields of artificial intelligence, as diagrammed by Newell (1973), and the study of comprehension, diagrammed by Lachman, Lachman, and Butterfield (1979). Another possibility is cognitive science: The diagram of its interrelated disciplines in Gardner (1985) strikingly resembles one created from co-citation data by White and Griffith (1982) for interdisciplinary studies of science, technology, and society. (The latter exemplifies a diagram made with better data than the one in Gardner.) The experts' diagrams are labeled with names of subjects rather than authors, and the two from De Mey contain date markers to show the historical evolution of the field; so there would be technical problems in making the maps fair equivalents. (Small & Greenlee, 1980, noted that their map picked up the ahistorical relationships of collagen research rather than its chronological development.) Nevertheless, the prospect of "comparative mapping" is intriguing, and there may be even better diagrams to work with of which the reader is aware.

## A Sketch of Results

I conclude with a sketch of findings from author co-citation studies to date. White and McCain (1989) review these studies within the broader context of bibliometrics.

- Authors (oeuvres) are a viable unit of analysis standing between the better-known units in citation and co-citation studies—articles on the one hand and journals on the other.
- Co-cited author searching—whether of single pairs of authors or of groups of pairs—is an effective technique for *subject retrieval* when carefully used. It usually retrieves "hits" not findable through conventional subject searches.
- Clustered authors on author maps have high potential for fruitful retrievals when systematically paired.
- Author maps reveal the "cognitive" or "intellectual" structure of a field by showing the consensus of citers as to important contributors and works.
- Author maps show who is central and who is peripheral to a field.
- The maps show who is central and who is peripheral *within clusters* representing specialties or schools of thought.
- Optionally, as an indicator of eminence, maps can include the mean number of co-citations an author has received. (This is rather like an indicator of magnitude on star maps.) Such means correlate well with subjective impressions of eminence. (McCain has an example in her chapter.)
- The maps show central and peripheral specialties (clusters of authors) within a field.
- The maps show broad dimensions on which clusters are arranged. Usually one of these can be interpreted as a subject dimension and another as a "style of work" dimension. A qualitative-quantitative polarity often appears. In a field that is quantitative overall, the dimension may reflect relative commitment to mathematical formalization.
- The knowledgeable interpreter of a map may see much to explicate in the fine structure of author points: for example, common nationality, temporal conjunctions, teacher-student relationships, collegial and coauthor relationships, or common philosophical orientations.

- Most authors show considerable stability in mapped positions over, for example, five-year intervals. The same stability characterizes most authors in multiperiod factor analyses.
- If a mapped author moves markedly in position over time, the reason may be (a) that he or she has taken up a new research area as a deliberate personal choice, and this is perceived by citers, or (b) that, independent of personal choice, the author is perceived in a new way by citers—some different aspect of his or her work becomes recognized and cited.
- Authors in clusters can be interpreted as and translated into subject terms naming the clusters (see White, 1989).
- Authors in clusters may have communication ties as persons as well as common subject matter or methodology. In certain fields, there may also be personal communication ties *across* clusters.
- When factor-analyzed, some authors load across more than one factor; others on one only. This can be interpreted as their "pervasiveness" in a field.
- Intercorrelations of factors (from oblique factor analyses) indicate the strengths of connections among different specialties of the same field.

## A Final Note: Toward Reviews

Although many of its separate steps are algorithmic, co-cited author analysis is still labor-intensive and time-consuming. *If* it could be more easily done—that is, if the separate steps could be integrated as one smooth-flowing, economical machine process—its practical applications in subject retrieval and in mapping scientific or scholarly fields would lead to wide use. The two applications meet, for example, in the preparation of reviews of literatures, a widely practiced form of scholarly writing. In recognition of this potential, the Institute for Scientific Information has twice launched its *Atlas of Science*, first as co-cited article maps with reviews of the co-citing ("research front") papers, then as reviews of the latter without maps. Small (1986) describes the exciting prospect of algorithmic synthesis of review articles or "specialty narratives" using co-citation cluster data as a starting point. But the *Atlas of Science* technology, however admirable, remains largely under ISI's control. What we need is a technology that would rapidly allow reviewers anywhere to create their own maps, using known key authors as input, and to retrieve the "research front" papers that co-cite those authors. As I wrote some years ago (White, 1983, p. 312): "Cocited author maps help verify 'natural' groupings of the literature (the clusters) upon which sections of the review can be based. Moreover, if included as graphics with published reviews, they illustrate relationships and offer discussion points that otherwise might be missed." The separate pieces of a "reviewer's technology" existed then, and they do now, but no one has yet brought them together.

## Notes

1. In White and Griffith (1982), a factor analysis produced seven factors in the field "studies of science, technology, and society": philosophy, social history, specialty structure, social psychology, communication, policy studies, and economics. The eminent Karl Popper loaded strongly on *one* (philosophy), and the equally eminent Robert K. Merton loaded strongly on *six* (all but economics). The interpretation was that Popper has a highly crystallized identity, whereas Merton is a more diffuse, pervasive influence.

2. Figure 5.1 does not include computer-derived cluster boundaries around the authors, but the clusters are plain. To the left are the scientific communication group (including citationists who use ISI data), centered on Derek Price and Eugene Garfield. To the right are the information retrieval formalists, centered on Gerard Salton. In the center, linking the two groups, are traditional bibliometricians, such as S. C. Bradford, William Goffman, Robert A. Fairthorne, and B. C. Brookes. Authors such as Manfred Kochen, B. C. Vickery, Donald W. King, Tefko Saracevic, Don R. Swanson, Patrick Wilson, F. W. Lancaster, and Charles Meadow are general interpreters of information science, but all are pulled toward the "retrieval pole" rather than the "science communication pole." Nicholas Jardine, a mathematical classificationist, has worked with C. J. van Rijsbergen. George K. Zipf and Claude Shannon are precursors (added for historical perspective). M. D. Line, Alexander Sandison, John Martyn, and Ben-Ami Lipetz have ties with both the bibliometricians and the citationists; they also share an interest in practical library studies.

3. A nonexhaustive list of examples, with identifications of each study by subject, includes Hilgard (1963) motivational psychology; Rosengren (1968) Scandinavian and world literary figures; Russett (1970) international relations; Mullins (1973) various sociological specialties; Cole and Zuckerman (1975) sociology of science; Cole (1975) sociology of deviance; Mullins (1975) causal modeling; Edge and Mulkay (1976) radio astronomy; Freidheim (1978) theoretical sociology; Cole, Cole, and Dietrich's (1978) sociology of deviance, sociology of science, nuclear and particle physics;

Oromaner (1981) various sociological specialties; Murray (1982) cognitive anthropology; and Blashfield (1984) neo-Kraepelinian psychiatry.

4. An incomplete list of examples, focusing on the work of Small, includes Garfield, Sher, and Torpie (1964) structure of DNA; Price (1965) general science; Small (1973) particle physics; Small and Griffith (1974) physics, biomedicine; Griffith, Small, Stonehill, and Dey (1974) biomedicine; Small (1977) collagen; Sullivan, White, and Barboni (1977) weak interactions; Mullins, Hargens, Hecht, and Kick (1977) reverse transcriptase, Australia antigen; Garfield, Malin, and Small (1978) general science; Small and Crane (1979) particle physics, psychology, economics, sociology; Garfield (1979b) general science; Sullivan, Koester, White, and Kern (1980) particle physics; Small and Greenlee (1980) recombinant DNA; Crawford and Crawford (1980) psychiatry; Nadel (1981) superconductivity; Small (1981) information science; Marshakova (1981) Soviet information science; Griffith and Small (1983) social and behavioral sciences; Nadel (1983) superconductivity, weak electromagnetic unification; Small (1984) collagen; and Small and Greenlee (1986) collagen.

5. This stream includes White and Griffith (1981a) information science; White and Griffith (1981b) human judgment and decision making; White and Griffith (1982) studies of science, technology, and society; McCain (1983) macroeconomics; Lenk (1983) information science; White (1983) social indicators movement; Hopkins (1984) causal modeling, ethnomethodology; McCain (1984) macroeconomics; Culnan (1986) management information systems; McCain (1986a) genetics and (1986b) macroeconomics, genetics; and Culnan (1987) management information systems.

6. It is not an *explicit* consensus, to which people have knowingly given assent, but an *implicit* one, a social construct like "a climate of opinion" or a "market," and perhaps all the more powerful for that. Small (1978, 1979, 1980, 1986) has argued that it approximates the Kuhnian paradigm. He believes that contextual analysis at the level of co-cited articles (not oeuvres) will allow us to replace bibliographic data with actual knowledge claims and thereby show the substantive content of the paradigm. De Mey (1982, p. 130) concedes that such structured knowledge is *part* of a cognitive paradigm, but not all: "To go beyond the structural stage, we need to comprehend the kind of partial knowledge that shapes expectations and provides directionality to search. Understanding those aspects of knowledge related to what is sometimes called *tacit* knowledge is essential to understanding what paradigms are."

KARL ERIK ROSENGREN

# 6. Who Carries the Field?
## Communication Between Literary Scholars and Critics

There are three types of criticism: journalistic, essayistic, and academic. Together with other groups of actors in the literary field, the three types of critics cooperate and compete in establishing and maintaining the field. All criticism is carried out against the background of a shared frame of reference, which may be empirically studied by means of the "mentions technique," building on mentions, or references to authors in the various types of criticism. By means of this technique, the size, structure, and composition of the literary frame of reference and its hierarchy of fame may be studied with some precision. This chapter presents results from a study in which the role of Swedish essayists and academic critics is assessed during the period from 1900 to 1950. They reshaped a hierarchy of fame received from the journalistic reviewers of the 1880s, in their turn relaying it to the journalistic reviewers of the 1960s and 1970s. The results show that current journalistic criticism exerts a considerable influence on the academic and journalistic criticism of later generations. Part of the task of today's journalistic critics thus is to shape the literary frames of reference for future academic critics.

## Theory and Methodology

### Theoretical Considerations

Culture exists and manifests itself in more worlds than one: the worlds of ideas, perceptions, actions, and artifacts (see Popper & Eccles, 1977). As a consequence of its differential modes of existence,

AUTHOR'S NOTE: This chapter is the outcome of a project made possible by a follow-up grant from the Bank of Sweden Tercentenary Foundation, Stockholm, to the literary subproject within the Swedish Cultural Indicators Research Program, funded for many years by the same foundation. The author wishes to express his sincere thanks to Ulla Johnsson-Smaragdi, who produced the LISREL model, and to Maria Elliot and Birgitta Henderson, who collected the new empirical data used in the study.

culture is partly autonomous—developing, growing, and declining according to its own laws—and partly dependent on the social positions of its creators and carriers and on the social systems surrounding them. This is so regardless of whether by *culture* we mean high culture or low culture or the overall culture of anthropologists and sociologists. It holds true for culture in toto and for cultural subsystems such as literature (Rosengren, 1984, 1985a, 1988).

The social aspects of literature have been recognized at least since Madame de Staël. In recent years they have been stressed over and over by scholars and researchers as different as, for instance, Bourdieu (1983), Clark (1982), Griswold (1983), Hirsch (1981), Mann (1983), Rees (1983a), Schmidt (1988), Tuchman and Fortin (1984), Verdaasdonk (1983), and Viehoff (1988). The social aspect of literature is relevant in every phase and mode of literary creation, distribution, and consumption. But it is especially visible, perhaps, in literary criticism: the process in which literary products are recognized as such; the process in which they are continuously interpreted and evaluated, rediscovered, reinterpreted, and reevaluated.

The centrality of literary criticism in the literary institution has been recognized for a long time (Escarpit, 1968, p. 419). During the last 20 years or so, various aspects of literary criticism have been studied by means of strictly empirical methods applied within different theoretical frameworks (Faulstich, 1977; Kepplinger, 1975; Rees, 1983b; Rosengren, 1968, 1983, 1987; Schmuck, 1981; Segers, 1978, 1989; Verdaasdonk, 1983; Viehoff, 1976).

It is often maintained that there are at least three different types of literary criticism: journalistic, essayistic, and academic criticism, carried out primarily in the daily press, in magazines, and in books and scholarly journals, respectively (Rees, 1983b, p. 398; Rosengren, 1983, p. 22). The three types of critics—scholars, "semischolars," and journalists—cooperate and compete with and between themselves as well as with other groups active within the literary institution, or "field," as it is sometimes called (Bourdieu, 1983; Rees, 1983a).

Among the three, journalistic criticism—the day-to-day reviewing of new literary books—has the lowest status. Nevertheless, the daily reviewers have one important advantage. They are the first gatekeepers to meet the literary work of art after its publication. It is true that the readers and editors of the publishing houses come before them (Coser, Kadushin, & Powell, 1982), but it is also true that the essayists and historians arrive at the scene later on—

sometimes very much later. To what extent are the literary frames of reference and canons of tomorrow's scholars shaped by the journalistic reviewers of today? Our own literary frame of reference was handed down to us at school, by teachers and textbooks. To what extent was it originally shaped by the journalistic reviewers of yesterday?

Questions such as these have only seldom been treated empirically, one reason probably being the size of the empirical data to be collected and sifted to find the facts and answer the questions; another reason being the lack of an adequate methodology. As it happens, however, there is a technique of content analysis well suited to answer such questions, the "mentions technique" developed by Rosengren (1968, 1983, 1987).

## Methodological Considerations: The Mentions Technique

Like other forms of scholarly and nonscholarly criticism, reviewing is carried out against the background of a shared frame of reference, a set of common ideas: cognitions and values. Both values and cognitions are connected with various authors and writers and with groups or categories of authors and writers who represent and exemplify them. An important element of the literary frame of reference, therefore, is the "lexicon" of authors and writers available to critics and reviewers: the stock of classic and modern, minor and major, poets and writers whose *oeuvres* embody the literary tradition and its present-day continuation. Indeed, that lexicon is so central to the literary frame of reference that its various characteristics are also characteristics of the literary frame of reference. The lexicon then can be used as a proxy for the literary frame of reference. In what way could we empirically study that lexicon of authors and writers?

In their reviews, reviewers of literature often mention, refer to, or allude to writers other than the one under review. Such cases will here be called "mentions." A *mention* may be regarded as an expression of an association made by the reviewer. It is a commonplace observation often made by historians of literature that if, during a given period of time, a given writer is often mentioned, it may be inferred that he or she has some topicality during that period (see, for instance, Ahlenius, 1932, p. 200; Jensen, 1961, p. 225; Shils,

1981, p. 150). Knowledge about all this has been common for quite some time but it has seldom been used systematically. The mentions technique, however, uses this knowledge, and works as follows.

If a mention may be regarded as an expression of an association made by the reviewer, and if the mentions of one specific writer can be used as an indicator of the topicality of that writer, all the mentions made in all reviews of the daily press in a country during a given time period (or a representative sample thereof) may be regarded as an expression of the lexicon of authors and writers available to the reviewers and constituting a central element of the literary frame of reference of that period. By means of the mentions technique—which offers large quantities of easily identified and characterized units of measurement—the size, age, geographical composition, structure, and rate of change of the reviewers' frame of reference can be reliably and validly measured and related to other phenomena within, and outside of, the literary system.

The mentions technique may be regarded as an application of psychological association theory (Deese, 1965) to literary sociology. In terms of bibliometrics, it is a special case of citation analysis, originally developed independently of that technique (Rosengren, 1961). (For recent citation studies, see, for instance, Splichal, 1989, as well as several chapters in this volume, especially the chapter by White.) The mentions technique also admits the study of "co-mentions," corresponding to what in chain citation analysis has become known as the co-citation technique, an aspect that will not be dealt with here. A number of results reached by means of co-mentions analysis of Swedish literary reviews were presented in Rosengren (1966, 1968, 1983).

The mentions technique has been applied to Swedish literature of the 1880s and the postwar period by Rosengren (1966, 1968, 1983, 1985b, 1987), to literature and film by Rosengren and Arbelius (1971), and to theater reviewing by Melischek (1984). Rosengren's work has been discussed, criticized, and used by, for instance, Aspelin (1975), Freeman (1986), Gaiser (1983) Kepplinger (1975), Sammons (1977), and Zima (1977).

Obviously, the reviewers' frame of reference as here conceived is an important element of the literary institution. More specifically, it could be regarded as an element of the "horizon of expectations" (*Erwartungshorizont*), that central but elusive phenomenon of German reception aesthetics within which literary reception is assumed to take place (Jauss, 1970; see Faulstich, 1977; Groeben, 1977; Segers, 1978; Viehoff, 1976). The empirical study of the reviewers' frame of reference thus conceived should also be of considerable interest to that time-honored discipline of comparative literature (*Vergleichende Literaturgeschichte, Littérature comparée*) as well as to its latter-day version, "intertextuality studies," and to studies of the concept and phenomenon of "tradition" so central to various schools of literary history and literary criticism (Shils, 1981; Wiemann, 1977).

Mentions may also be regarded as a means of relating characteristics of the literary system to other cultural subsystems of society. They may be used to produce a number of "cultural indicators" within the literary field to be related to cultural indicators from other fields and sectors of society and, finally, also to social and economic indicators (Melischek, Rosengren, & Stappers, 1984; Rosengren, 1981, 1984, 1985b, 1988).

In this chapter the mentions technique will be applied to the Swedish literary institution of the 1880s and the postwar period. It will be used to study an important aspect of literature: its change and continuity over time, and the role played in that process by the three types of literary criticism mentioned above. Although specific in time and space, the results gained by means of the mentions technique will prove of general interest to our understanding of the way scholarly and journalistic critics interact, cooperate, and compete over decades and centuries in shaping our present and future literary frames of reference. They will provide some answers to questions old and new about scholarly and semipopular communication within the literary field.

## Sources and Data

This study builds on two types of sources. One type of source material stems from representative samples of reviews of literary books published in leading Swedish newspapers during the periods 1876-1892 and 1953-1976. The two periods chosen represent important periods of change in the history of Sweden and her literature. The 1880s were the period of the "Modern Breakthrough" in Swedish literature (Gustafson, 1961; Rossel, 1982), while in the 1960s Sweden underwent much the same social and cultural upheaval as many other western countries did.

In the samples of reviews, all mentions found have been registered and categorized in a number of ways, some of which will be discussed below. These mentions then are taken to represent the literary frame of reference of the journalistic critics of the two periods.

Usual checks of reliability and representativeness of the mentions data have been undertaken. Because of the relative simplicity of the mentions technique, reliability is comparatively high. Technical details about the journalistic mentions material, data collection techniques, sampling procedures, sample sizes, reliability, specific techniques of analysis, and the like may be found in Rosengren (1968, 1983, 1987).

In addition to the reviewers' mentions material, another type of empirical data will be used in this study. These data concern the two types of criticism other than journalistic criticism: essayistic and academic criticism. The idea with this additional type of material, of course, is to facilitate an analysis of the communication, interaction, and competition between the three types of critics: scholars, "semischolars," and journalists.

Literary essays published in leading Swedish literary magazines between roughly 1895 and 1950—that is, between the two periods studied by means of the mentions technique—were scanned for mentions according to the rules previously used for mentions in the literary reviews of the daily press. So were histories of literature published in Sweden during the same period. Histories of literature were divided into two types: histories of Swedish literature and general histories of literature. We thus got three additional types of mentions: mentions in literary essays, in histories of Swedish literature, and in general histories of literature. We only collected mentions of authors and writers belonging to the literary cohort of realists and naturalists previously made the object of a special study, all born between the years of 1825 and 1849 (see Rosengren, 1985b, 1987, and the section below, "Time and the Literary Frame of Reference").

By definition, mentions appear in texts in reference to authors other than the ones who are the primary objects of the texts. We also measured the volume of texts—essays, articles, chapters, and so on—explicitly and directly dedicated to each writer and author belonging to the same cohort, in the same literary magazines and histories of literature, during the same period of time. In the histories of literature, the volume was measured in column or side centimeters. Because of the highly varying formats of the essays and the magazines publishing the essays, the "volume" of the essays was rated by means of a simple points system, intended to standardize the variation in the format. Volume was summated over the various essays and histories, and separately for essays, Swedish histories, and general histories.

In addition to the essays and academic histories of literature, we also measured the volume dedicated to measures of our cohort in a number of Swedish textbook histories of literature. In these books the mentions were so few that we decided to refrain from including them in our analysis.

Volume, of course, measures something else than mentions. Volume measures an important aspect of that literature that is referred to, interpreted, and understood in terms of the various literary frames of reference. The amount of attention (volume) given to an author is partly a result of that author's position in the "hierarchy of fame" (see below) of literary frames of reference in earlier periods. In its turn, it affects his or her position in the frames of reference in periods to come.

Presumably volume is much more a matter of choice, much more reflective of normative and educational considerations than the mentions—manifestations as the latter are of partly uncontrolled associations stemming from the literary frame of reference. Indeed, it is precisely because of this difference that it is so interesting to compare the results of the two types of measurements.

The choice of magazines and histories of literature to be analyzed was made on the basis of the general knowledge available to the project members and on literature in the field. Coder reliability was very high (in the .90s). Further technical details about this set of data, as well as lists of the books and journals analyzed and so on, may be found in Rosengren (1987).

# Time and the Literary Frame of Reference

## "Temporal Ecology"

Time is an integrating element in many or most literary studies. The first thing to note about time and the literary frame of reference as here conceived is that there is a considerable range of variation along the dimension of time in the frame of reference. At the time of the mention of a given writer in a literary review, 30 years may have elapsed since the birth of the writer, or 300, or 3,000. What can we tell about the distribution of the mentions over this huge span of time, about the "temporal ecology" of the literary frame of reference? This question has already been discussed at some length (Rosengren, 1968, 1983, 1985b, 1987).

Suppose that all mentions in literary reviews in the daily press of a given country and in a given period of time were characterized with respect to the literary period in which the mentioned writer lived and worked (operationalized as the year of birth of the writer in question). How would the mentions be distributed over the different literary periods? That is, in a given year—say 1890 or 1990—what proportions of the frame of reference would be dedicated to writers from the various periods recognized by traditional literary history: Antiquity, the Middle Ages, the Renaissance, and so on?

Figure 6.1 offers an answer to that question. It provides a historical atlas of the Swedish literary frame of reference during the nineteenth and twentieth centuries. We can see the various literary traditions waxing and waning in the literary frame of reference, sometimes slowly but often at a very quick pace.

The curves represent well-known theoretical measures of growth and decline (S-curves, exponential decay; see, for example, Chatterjee & Price, 1977) calculated from the large empirical mentions materials described above (mentioned in literary reviews of the daily press). The fit between the empirical data and the theoretical curves is quite satisfactory.

The curves show the very regular growth and decline of several important literary traditions in the reviewers' literary frame of reference; for instance, those of the romanticists (born 1749-1798), naturalists (born 1825-1849), and modernists (born 1875-1896). We

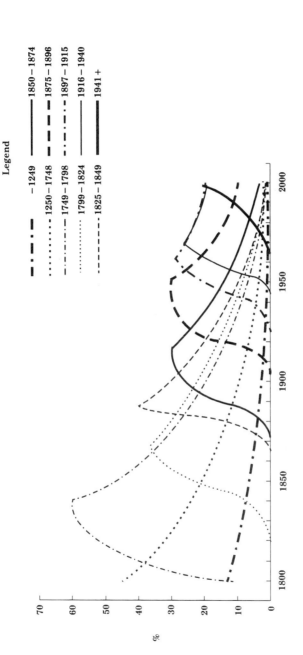

**Figure 6.1.** The Swedish Literary Frame of Reference During two Centuries: Curves of Growth and Decline for 10 Author Cohorts

also see the continuing decline in the reviewers' frame of reference for several literary traditions from Renaissance, Baroque, and Classic periods, as well as the growth and ensuing decline of more contemporary cohorts of writers. (For a detailed discussion of the labels of the cohorts and the demarcation lines between them as well as the character of the theoretical curves and the relationship between the empirical data and the theoretical curves and so on, see Rosengren, 1983, pp. 65 ff.)

The regularity of the processes of literary growth and decline is striking. It must be within the overall regularity of the waves of literary growth and decline that scholars and journalists have to cooperate and compete over the power to shape the concrete details of the literary frame of reference. The waves seem to roll on more or less according to their own pattern, but they are composed of the names selected by the reviewers.

### "Hierarchies of Fame"

Whose names will be used to build the growing waves of today's frame of reference? Whose names will be given a chance to reach the immortality—such as it is—of future frames of reference? To what extent were the names from earlier periods, that are still mentioned today, already selected by the reviewers of their own times?

The latter question was given an answer in Rosengren (1985b). In that study the cohort of mainly realist and naturalist writers (born 1825-1849) was followed in some detail as it appeared in the frames of reference of journalistic reviewers in the two periods of 1876-1892 and 1953-1976. This is the cohort over which the reviewers of the 1880s must have had the greatest influence, for, temporally, it was their own.

Figure 6.1 shows that there has been a heavy reduction of the relative size of the cohort in question (see Rosengren, 1983, p. 85). There has also been a heavy reduction in absolute terms. The naturalists had their day of glory. Now they are approaching oblivion asymptotically, just as other cohorts are and will. This is a macro process. How does it affect the fate of the single author of a given cohort?

To answer that question, the mass of mentions collected were first ordered yearwise, after the year of the mention. For each year of the two main periods of study, ranking lists of writers mentioned 1, 2, 3, . . . n times were compiled. Formally, these ranking lists show striking similarities to the type of ranking lists obtained when words in texts are ordered according to their frequency of occurrence (see, for instance, Mullins, 1976; Munch-Petersen, 1981), a fact that offers some food for thought. Substantively, the ranking lists may be called hierarchies of fame. They show which authors occupy a leading place in the frames of reference of the reviewers and which ones have to be satisfied with more modest approximations. Comparisons between hierarchies of fame from different years give us a notion of their development over time within reviewers' frames of reference.

The first two columns of Table 6.1 offer the names of the authors in our cohort found at the top of the literary hierarchies of fame of journalistic reviewers in the two periods under study. The striking thing when comparing the hierarchies of fame of our cohort during the two periods is that, in spite of the dynamic absolute and relative developments during and between the periods under study, the similarity between the hierarchies of fame of the two periods is so obvious. At the top of both lists we find much the same names, in much the same order: Ibsen, Strindberg, Zola, Rydberg, and so on. Our cohort has been heavily reduced, both absolutely and relatively. Yet it seems to be represented by much the same names appearing in the literary frames of reference in much the same order today as they did in the 1880s.

If that is so, the power of the reviewers of the 1880s has been considerable. They seem to have had power not only over their own literary frame of reference (and thereby, indirectly, over that of their contemporaries) but also over parts of the literary frame of reference of our own time. Our hierarchy of fame is similar to theirs. They have wielded power over us then. It is possible to arrive at more precise estimates of the strength of that power.

Measuring similarities of this type is a tricky question, however, and there are several options (see Rosengren, 1968, pp. 102 ff., 1983, pp. 172 ff.). Comparing the hierarchies of fame of the two periods, and also those of subperiods of the period 1876-1892, I ended up with correlations in the .50s and .60s (Rosengren, 1985b). According to these results, then, between one-quarter and two-fifths of the variation in the hierarchy of the naturalist cohort surviving into the

**TABLE 6.1**
Most Mentioned Authors of the Cohort Born 1825-1849, in the Leading Daily Press in Sweden and in Essayistic and Academic Criticism

| Mentions Daily Press Literary Reviews of Two Periods (per thousand) | | | | 1895-1950: Mentions (per thousand) in | | | | | |
| --- | --- | --- | --- | --- | --- | --- | --- | --- | --- |
| 1876-1892 | | 1953-1976 | | Essays | | Swedish Histories | | General Histories | |
| 38 | Ibsen | 17 | Strindberg | 139 | Strindberg | 191 | Strindberg | 176 | Zola |
| 23 | Zola | 5 | Tolstoy | 117 | Ibsen | 92 | Nietzsche | 128 | Taine |
| 22 | Björnson | 4 | Ibsen | 91 | Björnson | 89 | Rydberg | 60 | Tolstoy |
| 21 | Strindberg | 3 | Rydberg | 66 | Brandes | 87 | Ibsen | 59 | Ibsen |
| 16 | Kielland | 3 | Zola | 65 | Nietzsche | 82 | Snoilsky | 53 | Nietzsche |
| 14 | Brandes | 2 | Mark Twain | 46 | Rydberg | 60 | G. Brandes | 43 | Bros. Goncourt |
| 13 | Snoilsky | 2 | Nietzsche | 37 | Tolstoy | 49 | Wirsén | 38 | D. G. Rosetti |
| 8 | Edgren | | | 34 | Zola | 47 | Björnson | 28 | Verlaine |
| 8 | I. P. Jacobsen | | | 24 | E. Key | 28 | E. Key | 27 | Swinburne |
| 8 | V Rydberg | | | 22 | Kielland | 26 | Edgren-Leffler | 20 | G. Brandes |
| 7 | Bret Harte | | | 21 | Snoilsky | | | 18 | Daudet |
| 7 | Daudet | | | 20 | Taine | | | 18 | Lasalle |
| 7 | Wirsén | | | 20 | Verlaine | | | 18 | Strindberg |
| <7 | 181 authors | <2 | 44 authors | <20 | 86 authors | <26 | 86 authors | <18 | 83 authors |

118

literary frame of reference of our times seems to be due to influence from the reviewers of the 1880s. That influence seems to have been considerable.

Nevertheless, the better part of the variation in the present hierarchy of fame of the cohort under study (between three-fifths and three-quarters) must have origins other than those emanating from yesterday's reviewers. Foremost among such other sources of influence we must count the influence from 100 years of scholarly and semischolarly as well as academic and essayistic criticism, as well as the discretion exercised by today's reviewers themselves. The hierarchy of fame of today's reviewer is the result of a number of cooperating and competing influences then. Is it possible to discern with any precision the strength of some of these different influences? Is it possible to say whether today's hierarchy of fame is more the result of the influence of essayists and historians of literature than the influence of earlier reviewers? Such are the questions to which we now turn our attention.

## Scholars, Essayists, and Journalists

We have already noted that there are three types of critics: journalistic, essayistic, and academic. Until now, we have been dealing only with the reviewers, but we have mentioned the fact that the literary frame of reference of today's journalistic critics must have been partly shaped by journalistic critics of previous generations, partly by essayists and scholars, academic and semiacademic critics and historians of literature. Figure 6.2 offers a theoretical model of this interplay between our three types of critics.

According to the model, journalistic criticism influences the scholarly criticism of essayists and academics, which, in turn, influences the next generation of journalistic critics, and so on. In this section we will present and discuss some data and results that will gradually lead up to an opportunity to test the model empirically.

### Hierarchies of Fame Among Scholars and Journalists

Table 6.2 as well as the last three columns in Table 6.1 offer the hierarchies of fame for the cohort under study as they appear among essayists and academic critics and their followers, the authors of

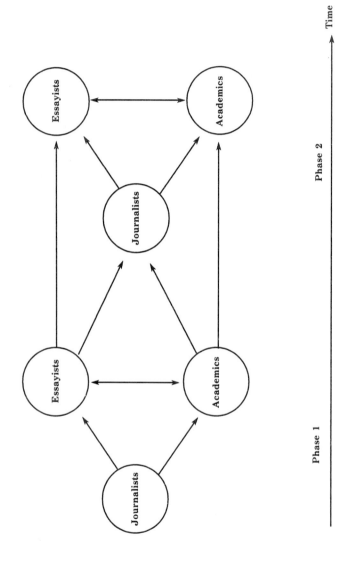

**Figure 6.2.** Theoretical Model of Reciprocal Influence Between Journalistic, Essayistic, and Academic Literary Critics

TABLE 6.2
Volume Dedicated to Authors of the Cohort Born 1825-1849 (per thousand)

| | Essays | | Swedish Histories | | General Histories | | Schoolbooks |
|---|---|---|---|---|---|---|---|
| 167 | Strindberg | 436 | Strindberg | 93 | Zola | 385 | Strindberg |
| 79 | E. Key | 184 | Rydberg | 84 | Tolstoy | 362 | Rydberg |
| 79 | Rydberg | 145 | Snoilsky | 65 | Swinburne | 161 | Snoilsky |
| 77 | Snoilsky | 43 | Edgren-Leffler | 49 | Taine | 27 | Edgren-Leffler |
| 71 | Ibsen | 41 | Wirsén | 47 | Anatole France | 27 | Wirsén |
| 60 | Björnson | 25 | P. Wikner | 44 | Nietzsche | 5 | Björnson |
| 54 | Brandes | 15 | E. Bäckström | 43 | D. G. Rosetti | 5 | E. Bäckström |
| 43 | Nietzsche | 14 | J. J. Wecksell | 38 | C. F. Meyer | 5 | Ibsen |
| 34 | J. Lie | 34 | Bros. Goncourt | | | | |
| 31 | H. Höffding | 32 | Daudet | | | | |
| 26 | Kivi | 31 | T. Hardy | | | | |
| 23 | Drachmann | | | | | | |
| 23 | Tolstoy | | | | | | |
| < 23 | 23 authors | < 14 | 54 authors | < 31 | 82 authors | < 5 | 23 authors |

textbook histories of literature. Two types of data have been used: mentions data (Table 6.1) and amount of attention as measured by the volume dedicated to each author (Table 6.2). (For lack of enough cases, mentions data have not been used for the textbook material.) Both tables offer per-thousand figures of the total amount of mentions or volume given to the cohort under study.

The basic characteristic of all the hierarchies of fame presented in the two tables is their similarity. In spite of the highly different environments reflected by them, and in spite of the fact that they represent two very different types of measurement, it must be admitted that it is much the same names that appear in much the same order in the various hierarchies. (The complete lists would have strengthened this impression, had space permitted us to publish them; they are available from the author on request.)

Once this is said, however, it must also be said that it is not very difficult to find differences between the various hierarchies of fame—systematic differences that are due to the environments and methods of measurement having produced them.

One of the differences already discussed in connection with Table 6.1 also turns up in Table 6.2. The 200 authors of the cohort being mentioned in the reviews of the 1880s are heavily reduced in all the columns of the later tables (at the same time as some new names have been added by the essayists and academics). This is the inevitable consequence of the macro development of the whole literary frame of reference as depicted in Figure 6.1. Quite naturally, the number of names is lowest in the textbooks, which present only the barest outline of the lives and letters of the cohort's many authors.

At the same time, the concentration of names at the top of the hierarchies is much heavier in essayistic and academic criticism than in journalistic criticism. Especially in the Swedish histories and their minor companions, the textbooks, the concentration is enormous. More than 40% of the space dedicated to the cohort in the histories of Swedish literature is given to Strindberg, and that proportion is not much smaller in the textbooks. There are at least two reasons for this difference.

In the first place, histories of Swedish literature by definition give most of their space to Swedish authors, paying only scant attention to literatures and authors outside Sweden. Second, both textbooks and histories of literature are partly normative, expressing by the amount of space and attention given to them the value of authors who, for historical, aesthetic, moral, or other reasons, are considered to be especially important. As it happens, Strindberg's contemporaries in Sweden are considered to be rather insignificant.

A salient difference between the various hierarchies of fame, related to the one just discussed, is the proportion of Swedish and non-Swedish names. Again there are great differences between histories of Swedish literature, on one hand, and the essays and the histories of general literature, on the other—for obvious reasons. Non-Swedish names are somewhat more frequent in the Swedish histories than vice versa, a difference reflecting the differential role played by Swedish literature in world literature and by foreign literatures in Sweden. (These tendencies are especially pronounced at the top of the hierarchies. Stepping down the ladder, we find the difference to be much less noticeable.)

Yet another difference, the difference between lists based on mentions and lists based on volume, has more theoretical implications. We have already mentioned that volume measures something other than mentions measure. The amount of attention (volume) bestowed upon authors in essays and histories of literature is an expression of their status in the literary thought prevailing among scholars and essayists (Assmann & Assmann, 1986-1987; Gaiser, 1983). The status of authors—here operationalized as the amount of attention (volume) given to them—is partly a result of their position in the hierarchy of fame prevailing among journalistic reviewers active in earlier periods. In its turn, it supposedly affects their position in journalistic reviewers' frames of reference in periods to come.

To study the interplay between academic scholars and journalistic reviewers more systematically, however, we must leave verbal comparisons between the top names of the different hierarchies of fames and turn to systematic and quantitative comparisons between the complete lists.

## Similarities and Dissimilarities

How do journalistic, essayistic, and academic critics interact and compete in shaping today's literary frame of reference? To answer that question—which lies at the heart of our study—we must know how similar or dissimilar the frames of references of the three different types of critics are to each other. (Similarity is not enough, of course, but it is at least a beginning.)

As above, we start by measuring the similarity by means of simple Pearsonian product-moment correlations between the hierarchies of fame, the most prominent of which have been presented in Tables 6.1 and 6.2. A large number of such correlations were presented in Rosengren (1987). Space does not permit us to discuss them all here. Suffice it to say that the closest similarity (represented by the highest correlation, .89) is found between the hierarchies of fame based on mentions in Swedish histories and mentions in essays. Essayists and historians of literature working during the same period (1895-1950) seem to have frames of reference that are very close to each other. The two next highest correlations (.82) are found between, on one hand, the hierarchies of fame of nineteenth-century reviewers and essayists and, on the other, Swedish histories and twentieth-century reviewers. On the basis of these correlations, it is not too difficult to imagine essayists and historians forming a bridge between nineteenth- and twentieth-century reviewers, much as the model in Figure 6.2 suggests. We will return to this problem, however, in the following sections.

Including now in our arguments also the similarity between the measures of volume, we find both the highest and the lowest correlations in the whole matrix. The textbooks show very close similarity to Swedish histories in the volume given to the various authors of our cohort (.94), and very little similarity (.08) with the general histories, with respect both to volume and to number of mentions. Quite naturally, histories of Swedish literature (and also, although to a less extent, Swedish essayists and reviewers) concentrate on Swedish authors, although—even in Swedish general histories of literature—Swedish authors must of necessity play a much more modest role, if any at all. This is a general problem, which called for analyzing Scandinavian and non-Scandinavian authors separately.

Such analyses show that, when compared with themselves, Scandinavian authors are ranked much the same way in the hierarchies of fame of the general histories as they are in, say, histories of Swedish literature. So are non-Scandinavian authors. The difference lies in the relationships between Scandinavian and non-Scandinavian authors in Swedish histories. There Scandinavian authors are generally given high ranks; in general histories, low.

## Causal Analysis

In the previous section we have discussed the similarity between the frames of reference of various groups of journalistic, essayistic, and academic critics. But the observation of similarity or dissimilarity is only one step toward the problem we are really trying to come to grips with—the interplay and competition between the three types of critics. To what extent is the literary frame of reference of today's reviewers influenced by that of yesterday's reviewers, and to what extent is such an influence, if it exists at all, relayed by the essayists and academics active between 1875 and 1950, that is, by the scholars and semischolars working after the nineteenth-century reviewers but before the reviewers of our time? To what extent do these scholarly critics exert an influence of their own on today's reviewers?

To answer such questions, similarity and dissimilarity are not enough. We must do two things: introduce the element of time and proceed from bivariate to multivariate techniques of analysis.

The problem of time is not too difficult, given the design of our study. Indeed, we have arranged our data so that the time sequence between the three types of literary critics and their frames of reference is fairly clear, with the reviewers of the 1880s coming first, followed by essayists and academics active from 1875 to 1950, and, finally, the reviewers of the period 1953-1976.

Under these conditions, it is meaningful to ask how much of the variation in the hierarchy of fame of twentieth-century reviewers' literary frame of reference may be explained by means of the frames of reference of previous reviewers, essayists, and academics, and by the attention (measured in terms of volume) given by essayists and academics to the different authors of our cohort. A statistical technique appropriate for finding answers to such questions is multiple regression (Chatterjee & Price, 1977).

Regressing the hierarchy of fame of the twentieth-century reviewers simultaneously on all the other variables listed in Tables 6.1 and 6.2, we get a notion of how much variance in that hierarchy is explained by the variance in the other lists of names (based on mentions and measures of volume). This was done in Rosengren (1987). Combining in the best possible way all the independent variables in a stepwise multiple regression, starting with the nineteenth-century reviewers (because, temporally, they come first), and then introducing the single variables in order of explanatory power, we find that, together, the two variables "nineteenth-century reviewers" and "volume in Swedish histories" explain 79% of the variance in the hierarchy of fame of our cohort in modern reviewers' frame of reference. By adding mentions from the essayist, we reach 84% of explained variance. The remaining 6% of the explained variance is divided between the other five independent variables.

By combining three powerful variables then, we may explain more than four-fifths of the variance in the hierarchy of fame of our cohort in modern reviewers' literary frame of reference. Characteristically, the three variables tap all of journalistic, essayistic, and academic criticism as well as volume of Swedish histories and names from essays dealing with both Swedish and foreign authors.

## Toward an Empirical Model

In the previous sections we have tried to assess the influence exerted by journalistic, essayistic, and academic criticism from the end of the nineteenth to the middle of the twentieth century on the hierarchy of fame in modern reviewers' literary frame of reference. Our efforts have been directed by the model represented in Figure 6.2. But the type of analysis undertaken has not allowed us to say anything precisely about the structure of the network or the structure of influences depicted by the model, only about the proportions of variance in the fame hierarchy of the modern reviewers explained by the different groups of literary critics preceding the modern reviewers. That is more than we knew before, of course, and, as far as it takes us, it is interesting enough. But it does not cover all the things that the model in Figure 6.2 asks us to do.

What is missing is more structure in the data. What is missing is coefficients on the arrows of Figure 6.2, telling us precisely the strength of the direct and indirect influence exerted by all the model's independent variables (the different hierarchies of fame of the early journalistic, essayistic, and academic criticism) on the dependent one (the hierarchy of fame of the modern reviewers).

In order to obtain such knowledge, we will leave the multiple regression technique and turn to structural equation modeling by means of LISREL (Jöreskog & Sörbom, 1989; see Saris & Stronkhorst, 1984). These techniques are rather new. In spite of very rapid development, they also continue to be rather expensive in terms of man-hours and computer time. Yet their power is such that they can provide answers to questions that, before their entrance upon the scene, must often have been left unanswered. They have been increasingly and successfully used in sociology and communication studies (see, for instance, Rosengren & Windahl, 1989).

In a future study the data discussed in this study will be analyzed by means of the LISREL technique. A first attempt in that direction was presented in Rosengren (1987), but for technical reasons the model did not reach a satisfactory level of probability. It did show clearly, however, that essayists and academic critics do indeed relay the influence from the early reviewers' frame of reference to that of contemporary reviewers.

## Concluding Discussion

By means of the mentions technique, in combination with various multivariate techniques of statistical analysis, we have investigated a century-long interplay of three types of literary critics. Concentrating on one cohort of authors—those born between 1825 and 1849, consisting mainly of realists and naturalists—we have found that this cohort's hierarchy of fame in the modern reviewers' literary frame of reference is very similar to the hierarchy already established by the nineteenth-century reviewers.

Those reviewers then have been able to stretch a long arm of influence over the three-quarters of a century separating them from their modern colleagues. They have done this mainly by influencing the other two types of literary critics included in our study, the scholars—essayists and academic critics working in the long period between nineteenth- and twentieth-century reviewers. A main role of these essayists and academics has been to relay the influence from the nineteenth- to the twentieth-century reviewers. They have also exerted an influence of their own, however, on the modern reviewers' frame of reference.

The joint influence from these three types of literary critics is so strong that very little variance in the cohort's hierarchy of fame with the modern reviewers stems from these reviewers themselves, say, one- or two-tenths. The power of yesterday's reviewers, essayists, and academics over today's reviewers is strong indeed.

It could be argued, of course, that the similarity between the various hierarchies of fame is the result not of an influence exerted by one group of literary critics over another but of qualities inherent in the authors of the cohort under study and in their *oeuvres*. If that is so, however, the highly divergent degree of similarity between the various hierarchies of fame becomes difficult to explain. It is more reasonable to assume that at least a large proportion of the beauty and power of a literary work lies in the eye of the beholder, in the minds of the readers, and thus is to a large extent socially determined rather than determined exclusively by qualities inherent in the literary work of art (see, for instance, Jensen & Rosengren, 1990; Rees, 1983a, 1985; Svensson, 1985; Verdaasdonk, 1983).

It is a reasonable assumption that this process of social determination starts as soon as the literary works of art come into contact with the readers of the publishing houses, getting an increased impetus when they have been published. That is what gives such a position of power to the journalistic reviewers, the first gatekeepers to meet the literary work of art after its publication. (The judgments and opinions of the reviewers, of course, in their turn are determined to a large extent by the climate of opinion and culture prevailing in the surrounding society; see Rosengren, 1983, 1985a, 1985b, 1988.) Our study has shown that, once this process of determination has made its first round through the three types of literary critics, very little seems to be left for later generations to determine—whether scholars or journalists.

What actually is left to later generations of critics, then? At least three things, it would seem.

The first thing they can do, and presumably do every so often, is to enlarge upon the reasons for which this or that author occupies this or that position in the hierarchy of fame. Such activities could be written off as post hoc rationalizing, but that would probably be far too rash a verdict. It may be wiser to look upon them as processes of enriching a literary heritage, cultivating it and handing it over to later generations.

The second task for later generations of critics is to undertake whatever adjustments in the literary hierarchy of fame may seem necessary and possible as consequences of the activities of enriching and cultivating the literary heritage. Our study has shown that this type of activity probably has rather limited effects, even if isolated cases of drastic reevaluations may be found (see Rosengren, 1985b, Table 2). Granted that, from time to time, it may be adjusted here and there, the hierarchy of fame of a given cohort of writers seems to be something very stable, something to be handed down through the centuries more or less unchanged.

What every generation of critics can do, however, is to establish the hierarchy of fame of their own generation of writers. That is the task begun anew by every generation of journalistic reviewers and followed up by every generation of more scholarly critics: essayists and academics. Indeed, that is the primary task of literary criticism, calling for all three types of critics: journalistic, essayistic, and academic.

As far as we can tell from our data, the three groups of critics seem to be sharing the important task in a rather brotherly fashion: The journalists have about a third of the determining power; the essayists possess a little less; and the academics, somewhat more. In this process, however, later generations are the losers. These possess only one- or two-tenths of all the power exercised over literary cohorts of the past. As long as the process rolls on, however, the future will be theirs.

Today's hierarchies of fame were invented by yesterday's critics. The facts about these hierarchies are discovered today. Future hierarchies of fame are invented by today's critics. The facts about them will be discovered tomorrow.

DON R. SWANSON

# 7. The Absence of Co-Citation as a Clue to Undiscovered Causal Connections

The relationship between citation pattern and logical structure in scientific literature is of central concern in this chapter. The chapter shows how a process of literature synthesis can in principle lead to the discovery of previously unknown causal connections. That process is based on identifying two literatures that are not co-cited and that do not cite each other but that are implicitly related by the logic of their respective arguments. Three examples of such structures in the biomedical literature are summarized here. For the first two examples, supporting clinical and laboratory evidence was subsequently published independently, thus adding weight to the claim that new connections can be brought to light by assembling published pieces that might not previously have been brought together.

## The Significance of Logically Related Noninteractive Literatures

Scientific articles can be organized into clusters, or "literatures," within which common problems and topics are addressed, related arguments are advanced, and articles interact by citing one another. Although such clusters in general are connected internally by a network of citations, the clusters are defined here not in terms of that network but in terms of their substantive or logical content. Each cluster represents a specialized, problem-focused area of research—for example, research on some specific disease or aspect of a disease.

We can say that one literature "interacts" with another to the degree that articles in either literature cite articles in the other.

AUTHOR'S NOTE: This work has been supported by U.S. Department of Education grant RA039A80028 from the Office of Educational Research and Improvement—Library Research and Demonstration Program.

Co-citation may also be considered a form of interaction—that is, two literatures may be said to interact if one or more articles from one literature are co-cited with one or more articles from the other literature. Two literatures that have no articles in common have no authors in common, do not cite or refer directly to each other, and are not co-cited are said to be "noninteractive," or mutually isolated.

In addition to citation patterns, we shall be interested here in the "logical" connection that each article implicitly establishes with other scientific articles. Some of these connections are made explicit within each article and are accompanied by appropriate citations. I shall show, however, that there may exist many implicit logical interarticle connections that are unintended and not marked by citations and that such implicit unmarked links can potentially become a source of new scientific knowledge.

The word *logical* here is used informally; a "logical connection" is formed by statements that are related by scientific reasoning or argument, particularly reasoning about causal relationships. If two literatures are linked by arguments that they respectively put forward—that is, are "logically" related or connected—one would normally expect them to cite each other. But let us suppose, in the following argument, that two such literatures were developed independently of each other and that no author in either group cited, or even knew about, the other literature. The fragmentation of science into a large number of highly specialized areas and problems suggests that this supposition is not implausible.

Notwithstanding such mutual isolation, it is not difficult to see how, in principle, the respective arguments put forward within the two literatures might nonetheless be unintentionally linked or related. Suppose, for example, that one literature establishes that dietary factor A influences the structure of certain cell membranes and that a second literature establishes that the same changes in membrane structure influence the course of disease C. Presumably then anyone who reads both literatures could conclude that dietary factor A might influence disease C.

If any researchers had ever examined a possible relationship between A and C, it is plausible to suppose that, in writing about their work, they would have cited at least a few articles from each of the two corresponding literatures—that is, they would have co-cited the two literatures. The absence of co-citations on the other hand would suggest the possibility that no one had ever before considered the two literatures together, at least not seriously enough to mention the fact in print. The intriguing question is, therefore, whether in that case anyone at all is in a position to see that there are good reasons to think that A might influence C. A synthesis of the two noninteractive literatures in question would make such reasons immediately apparent. How a synthesis could be brought about, however, is not obvious, for no one reading one literature would be led by reference citations to suspect the existence of the other. Moreover, a subject search on cell membrane structure would require, first, that the searcher know in advance that it might play a key intermediate role and, second, that its literature is small enough to assimilate in its entirety. Neither assumption is considered here to be warranted.

One might still suppose that the two premises, "A influences B" and "B influences C" (where "B" stands for cell membrane structure), could be learned from some published source other than the two literatures mentioned above. But such an argument merely shifts the problem to two new literatures, a complication that can be avoided by assuming, for the sake of this argument, that each of the two original literatures corresponding to the AB and BC relationships, respectively, is essentially "complete."

The ABC syllogism can be considered as a simple model or paradigm but is not the only structure of interest. B itself, for example, might involve a multistep process (Small & Garfield, 1989). Indeed, in principle, any chain of scientific reasoning in which different links appear in noninteractive literatures may entail undiscovered, potentially new connections.

I have called attention in the foregoing discussion to two conceptually distinct relationships that might exist between two literatures—first, the idea that they may be noninteractive and, second, that they may be related by the logic of the arguments that they respectively contain. Neither relationship by itself is necessarily of much interest, but two literatures that are both noninteractive and yet logically related may have the extraordinary property of harboring undiscovered causal connections.

There is, of course, no way to know in any particular case whether the possibility of an AC relationship has or has not occurred to someone or whether or not anyone has actually considered the two literatures on A and C together. However, it is possible, and of great interest, to determine whether there is any printed evidence indicating that such is the case. Our direct concern here is with public rather than private knowledge—with the state of the record produced rather than the state of mind of the producers.

## What Do Citations Mean?

For any single article, little general significance can be attached to the failure of the authors to cite certain references that others might think should have been cited. There is room for considerable difference of opinion on that score; authors' purposes and attitudes toward citations are numerous and varied. The "significance" of citations has generated much controversy and fascinating discussion by information scientists, sociologists, and others (Brooks, 1986; Cozzens, 1989; MacRoberts & MacRoberts, 1989; Small, 1986, 1987; Zuckerman, 1987, to mention only a few). However, if one takes as the unit of analysis a "complete" literature (in the sense earlier defined) that may consist of dozens or perhaps hundreds of articles that address the same topic or problem, then the absence of any interaction with a second literature is far more significant than any similar citation failure at the level of the individual article.

The direct citation of one literature by another can, incidentally, be seen as a special case of co-citation in which the citing article belongs to one of the two cited literatures. One need only assume that every article cites itself and so is included on its own list of references.

Irrespective of the intent, reasons, or motives that underlie citation behavior, the *effect* of a citation or a co-citation unequivocally is to link two papers and so provide an opportunity to form new combinations of concepts (Small, 1986) and new syntheses from which "recombinant ideas," such as the AC relationship, might emerge (Swanson, 1990b).

## Hypothesis Versus Knowledge

The question of whether an unnoticed, unintended, and undiscovered causal connection such as that between A and C can represent the discovery of "new knowledge" requires further clarification.

The AC relationship cannot become accepted or established as part of scientific knowledge until it has undergone a direct test. No matter how well established the premises, or empirical findings, that A causes B and B causes C, neither premise can be taken as certain. Moreover, A may be only one of several possible causes of B, and any one cause may itself be contingent on other factors, not all of which are necessarily known; and the same is true for the relationship between B and C. The apparent conclusion that A causes C must, therefore, remain hypothetical. Nevertheless, such a hypothesis on the face of it has a greater claim to plausibility, and a greater claim to merit a test, than it would if it were a pure conjecture unsupported by the AB and BC premises.

Thus, prior to a direct test, one can say of the AC connection at least that it represents the discovery of a promising hypothesis and is, therefore, a potential source of new knowledge. Usually we think of hypotheses as conjectures or inventions, and, so far as I know, no one has proposed any systematic "method" for the act of inventing. To claim that any kind of hypothesis can be "discovered" is at least unusual. The point of bringing together the AB and BC literatures, in any event, is not to "prove" an AC linkage but to call attention to a previously undiscovered connection that may be worth investigating.

## Objective Knowledge

To further clarify my terminology, I use the word *knowledge* throughout to refer to scientific or empirical knowledge—and in an objective sense ("recorded knowledge") rather than in the subjective sense of "what someone knows." The distinction between objective and subjective knowledge and the many ramifications of that distinction have been illuminated by Karl Popper (1972). He has proposed that there exists an abstract "world" of objective knowledge that consists of problems, theories, and other products of the human mind and that this world interacts with the world of subjective knowledge, which in turn interacts with the physical world. Whatever arguments may be brought forward for or against such an epistemology, at the very least it stimulates and lends legitimacy to a richly evocative set of metaphors. We can speak of assembling and synthesizing fragments of knowledge and of interacting with what we have constructed. Most important, Popper's abstract world of objective knowledge is open to exploration and discovery, for it can contain territory that is subjectively unknown to anyone. If it seems paradoxical to say that something human-created can be altogether unknown, consider the ontogenesis of the AC hypothesis: Prior to the time at which some person brought together and contemplated the human-created, mutually isolated AB and BC relationships, the unintended but implicitly existing AC connections could have been altogether unnoticed and unknown.

## Examples of Knowledge Synthesis

The foregoing discussion serves as an introduction to a series of journal articles, published elsewhere, that attempt to demonstrate more concretely just how, and in what sense, new knowledge might be gained through a synthesis of logically related noninteractive literatures—that is, by assembling pieces already published but perhaps never before put together. In each case, logical connections not previously noted in print came to light (Swanson, 1986a, 1986b, 1987, 1988, 1989a, 1989b, 1990b, 1990c).

Three examples, based on medical literature, have been developed. The first such published analysis identified one set of articles showing that dietary fish oils lead to certain blood and vascular changes and a second set containing evidence that the same changes might benefit patients with Raynaud's syndrome. (One can recognize in this description the previously mentioned ABC syllogism.) Yet these two literatures were noninteractive; neither literature mentioned the other or directly suggested what the two together imply—that dietary fish oil may benefit Raynaud patients (Swanson, 1986a, 1986b). This latter inference may be regarded as a successful prediction; two years after publication of the above analysis, the first clinical trial demonstrating such a beneficial effect of fish oil was reported by other researchers (DiGiacomo, Kremer, & Shah, 1988).

A second and similar example of literature synthesis, based on 11 indirect connections, led to a prediction that magnesium deficiency might be implicated as a mechanism or a causal factor in migraine headache (Swanson, 1988, 1989b). In response to the 1988 article, one physician reported prior clinical experience that supported such a claim (Weaver, 1989). One year following the 1988 article, other researchers reported additional supportive evidence based on nuclear magnetic resonance measurements of brain magnesium (Ramadan et al., 1989).

A third example involves literatures on somatomedins (insulin-like growth factors) and dietary arginine (Swanson, 1990b). My report of this third example includes a brief allusion to a new problem that could provide an interesting complement to the co-citation study of AIDS reported by Small and Greenlee (this volume). These authors illuminated the history of AIDS research through an analysis of logically related and highly interactive literatures. I have shown that there are potentially interesting logical connections between the literature on AIDS and the literature on somatomedins that arise from a mutual concern with states of severe malnutrition and emaciation (1990b). Yet the AIDS and somatomedin literatures appear to be mutually isolated in that they have no records in common, at least so far as one can determine through an online search. As of October 1989, there were almost 4,000 Medline records on somatomedins and nearly 20,000 that mentioned AIDS, but no records that mentioned both. A co-citation analysis must still be performed, however, before one can conclude that the two literatures are truly noninteractive, and a deeper analysis and review of the AIDS literature and the malnutrition literature is required to establish more explicitly the nature of the logical connections to which I have alluded.

## The Process of Finding Logically Related Noninteractive Literatures

The project identified above has pursued three goals: (a) to show in principle how new knowledge might be gained by synthesizing logically related noninteractive literatures; (b) to demonstrate that such structures do exist, at least within the biomedical literature; and (c) to develop a systematic process for finding them. The first two goals have been largely attained, as discussed above. I (1989a, 1989b) have reported some progress toward the third goal, but much remains to be done. In general, a quest for examples of these literature structures can begin with a problem—such as the problem of finding a cause or cure for some disease—and then proceed with a search for logical connections. Search strategies depend essentially on a trial-and-error process, aided by online searching, in which only noninteractive literature pairs are allowed to survive as candidates for further study. Numerous conjectures regarding logical relationships are explored briefly and then co-citation patterns are used as a means of eliminating all relationships based on interactive literatures.

It may be possible to reverse the process and begin by identifying noninteractive literatures, provided we redefine a "literature" as a co-citation cluster of some kind. One must then construct and describe the logic of the arguments in the literature for each cluster and go on to seek implicit connections between noninteractive clusters.

Whatever method is used, extensive reading and analysis of the medical literature is necessary, a process in which human judgment and knowledge is not likely in the foreseeable future to be replaced by algorithms or mechanisms. Bibliometrics can be a valuable tool but, as is the case with many other applications, only insofar as it can be brought into relationship with the substantive or logical content of the literature.

To say that a logical connection such as that between A and B has been "established" is, therefore, neither simple nor straightforward; a careful literature review is required, for, in general, one can draw such an inference only after taking into account many arguments, pro and con, as well as mutually corroborating evidence from a number of laboratories. Moreover, the simple structure of the ABC syllogism that I have presented as a model by no means reflects the complexity or range of actual problems encountered, and few logical or causal relationships are applicable under all conditions or are free of dispute. In none of the examples can one consider a single connection to be as significant as the mosaic formed by many connections. The objective in any event is not simply to draw mechanistic logical inferences but to enhance or simulate human perception of plausible hypotheses that appear to be worth testing.

The process I have described for exploring and reviewing the literature (Swanson, 1988, 1989a, 1989b) is intended to cut across specialties and would not be practical if expert knowledge of all specialties were required. Although lack of subject expertise may be a limitation in this kind of study, the form and structure of logically connected arguments are in general recognizable by scientists irrespective of their specialty, a point that may be of some importance to information scientists who attempt to conduct studies similar to those that I have reported.

The approach to literature exploration outlined in this chapter suggests that citation patterns should play a key role in research on futuristic knowledge-based systems. In this light, the extensive work on co-citation analysis and on the mapping of scientific specialties by means of co-citation clusters may be especially relevant and important (Small, 1973, 1979, 1980, 1986; Small & Griffith, 1974). Only through citations can we know which fragments of knowledge have been explicitly linked up and which have not. The increasing specialization and fragmentation of science that accompanies its growth confronts us with a potential explosion of implicit unnoticed connections and a challenge to develop compensating mechanisms of literature integration and synthesis (Kochen, 1974; Swanson, 1990a).

RONALD E. RICE

# 8. Hierarchies and Clusters Among Communication and Library and Information Science Journals, 1977-1987

Citations among the 77 core communication and library and information science journals, from 1978 through 1987, were network-analyzed to detect structural evidence for a possible increasing interdependence between the two disciplines. Results showed changes in hierarchies and clusters within, but not across, the two disciplines. Results indicate the existence of two distinct subdisciplines in communication research and three in library and information science. Related results indicate increasing cross-disciplinary citations since 1983, especially from communication research journals.

## Citation Patterns as Social Networks

This chapter considers bibliometrics as one example of a more general analytical approach—network analysis—and uses one kind of network analysis to identify whether structural changes have occurred in the flow of citations among the journals of two potentially related disciplines—communication research and library and information science.

Network analysis is the study of patterns of relations among a set of nodes. Network analysis has developed from a variety of

AUTHOR'S NOTE: This short chapter is part of a larger project conducted in collaboration with Dr. Christine Borgman. I would like to acknowledge the exceptional contributions of Diane Bednarski in collecting and organizing the citation data, Eric Wade and Dr. Douglas Shook for additional data collection, Dr. Shook and Ellen Sleeter for writing certain software utilities, Drs. Steve Borgatti, Lin Freeman, and Karl Reitz for providing network analysis software, the UCLA Academic Senate for partial funding of the data collection effort, and Drs. Borgman and Paisley for their helpful comments on an earlier draft.

sources, includes sociology, anthropology, small group communication, and network engineering (Burt, 1980; Rice & Richards, 1985). It may be said that network analysis was derived from theoretical and applied interests in forms of social structure such as the allocation of scarce resources (material goods, social status, and so on), formal relations (genealogies, organizational hierarchies, and so on), and informal relations (friendships, political coalitions, and so on).

The basic network dataset consists of measures of the strength (simple presence or absence, frequency, importance, and so on) of links (formal or informal relationships) shared by a set of N nodes either among themselves (thus producing an $N \times N$ matrix) or with respect to a common set of phenomena (thus producing a $N \times K$ matrix). These data may also be represented by a list of pairwise links, especially useful for large and sparse networks (see Small & Greenlee, this volume). Examples include the frequency of communication among friends, the dollar amount of trade flows among nations, the number of executives sitting on common corporate boards, or the number of co-occurrences of word pairs in one or more documents.

It is easy to see that author co-citation data are a special case of an $N \times K$ matrix (all the citations made by N authors in a database to K central authors) converted into a $K \times K$ matrix (where the cell values are the number of times each pair of those K central authors is cited by the N authors). It is also easy to see that citations made among N articles are a special case of the $N \times N$ matrix. Further, aggregating those N articles into their respective $N'$ journals creates a $N' \times N'$ journal-to-journal citation network matrix (e.g., Price, 1965). Indeed, the citation has been characterized as a particular form of "sociometric choice" (Garfield, Malin, & Small, 1978). Bibliometricians have begun to use formal network analysis concepts and methods in the study of national subfields (Smeenk & Hagendijk, 1989) and changes in co-occurrence of words in key words from articles about a particular subspecialty (Rossum, 1989).

Network analysis can provide descriptive and inferential insights into a wide variety of topics: (a) *roles* such as isolates, members of groupings, or bridges between groupings; (b) the existence and relative positions of those *groupings*; (c) *relationships* such as strength, direction, reciprocation, and stability; and (d) *structure* such as transitivity, hierarchies, and status rankings.

It is easy to see that bibliometric analysis of the flows of citations among journals is a special case of those more general sociological and organizational concerns: (1) Which journals represent various disciplines or provide channels for diffusion of scientific knowledge across the disciplines? (2) Which journals represent subdisciplines and how are those subdisciplines related? (3) Which journals receive proportionately more citations? (4) Do the disciplinary and subdisciplinary structures change over time, particularly in ways that indicate convergence or integration?

Indeed, these questions are particularly relevant to current concerns about scholarly communication within and between the disciplines of communication research and library and information science. The next sections summarize these concerns and apply network-analytic techniques to provide some preliminary answers.

## Communication Research and Library and Information Science: Integration or Isolation?

In the mid-1980s, the social science disciplines of communication research and library and information science began to show increased concern with issues of potential convergence and fragmentation both within and between the areas. In communication research, concerns focused on debates between quantitative and qualitative methods and on the relevance of sociological and cognitive theories. See, for example, the special issue of the *Journal of Communication* ("Ferment in the Field," 1983). In information science, concerns focused on cognitive approaches to information retrieval and storage and the relative emphasis of traditional librarianship and newer information science topics. In both disciplines, new media began to provide fertile opportunities to challenge and develop theories of communication and information processing (Rice & Associates, 1984) and scholars became more aware of the interdependence and resonances of the concepts of "information" and "communication" (Beniger, 1988). Finally, several edited handbooks and annual series have attempted to consolidate empirical and theoretical developments across the disciplines and their subdisciplines (Berger & Chaffee, 1987; Dervin & Voigt, annual series; Jablin,

Putnam, Roberts, & Porter, 1987; Ruben, annual series; Williams, annual series).

In spite of these concerns and the potential for integration within and between these two disciplines, there is doubt as to whether the deeper institutional structures of these disciplines (as opposed to side researchers or schools) are responding to, or even acknowledging these challenges. For example, Paisley (1986) and Miyamoto, Midorikawa, and Nakayama (this volume) note that both disciplines are extremely isolated in the wider arena of social science. Rice, Borgman, and Reeves (1988) show a rather stable cleavage between interpersonal and mass media research. Other articles in the special issue of *Human Communication Research* ("Symposium," 1988) suggest continuing cleavages in communication research, and isolation from other social sciences, due to historical origins, research focus, methodological preferences, and so on.

## Why Journal-to-Journal Citation Analysis?[1]

One deeper structural indicator of these possible changes, or inertia, is the patterns of citations made *by* articles among communication research and information science journals *to* articles in those journals. Journals are the primary formal channels for communicating theories, methods, and empirical results to the readers of those journals. Thus they may usefully indicate changing research fronts and disciplinary transitions (Brooks, this volume; Price, 1963). Journals are "a central institution of science. . . . [and authors'] public forums" (Doreian, 1985, p. 411). Conducting analyses at the level of the journal presumes that journals focus attention on related materials. This is especially true for "official" journals of associations, for journals that have titles explicitly indicating their content, or for journals that are known for particular emphases. Thus, although authors include citations in an article, and cite specific other articles, aggregating these citations at the journal level should reflect longer-term, more underlying changes or stabilities in the relationships within and between disciplines.

White (this volume) also argues that the large numbers and sources of citations to authors and articles found in datasets typically used in citation analysis should reduce the effect of differing citation motivations by individual authors. Using the journal as the unit of analysis should further minimize this particular threat to the validity of bibliometric analyses.

Further, journals are one level more general than "invisible colleges," which, although a useful construct (Price, 1963), has questionable empirical validity and requires knowledge of communication processes and content outside of institutional structures (Lievrouw, this volume; Mullins, 1973). As Paisley (1989a, p. 713) notes: "The [co-]citation network extends well beyond any individual researcher's knowledge of who is in the network and what type of research he or she does." Thus formal patterns of communication (citations aggregated at the journal level) are more appropriate for investigating disciplinewide and long-term changes than for studying individual authors or specialties (Lievrouw, this volume).

Finally, analysis of the flow of citations aggregated at the journal level fits into several of the cells suggested by Borgman (this volume) as characterizing bibliometrics. Variables analyzed by such studies include (a) producers, in the form of disciplines and subdisciplines, and (b) artifacts, in the form of citation patterns involving a defined set of academic journals. The research questions posed by such studies include both (a) characterizations of scholarly communication and (b) diffusion of ideas—as identified by roles, groupings, relations, and structure among formal disciplinary channels.

## Method

### Data

This section summarizes the particular journal-to-journal citation data used to illustrate some bibliometric applications of network analysis. As described elsewhere (see Note 1), the basic data include the asymmetric matrix of citations made to, and received from, all the journals listed as "core journals" in "communication" and in "library and information science" in the Institute for Scientific Information (ISI) *Journal Citation Report* for each year from 1977 to 1987 (then corrected for aberrant and changed journal titles). Table 8.1 lists the full journal titles and the abbreviations used in the figures.

TABLE 8.1
"Core" Communication and Library and Information Science Journals Included in the
Journal Citation Report, with Abbreviations Used in Present Analysis

| Abbreviation | Full Journal Title |
|---|---|
| Cen1 | *Central States Speech Journal* |
| Col2 | *Columbia Journalism Review* |
| Com3 | *Communication* |
| Com4 | *Communication Education* |
| Com5 | *Communication Monographs* |
| Com6 | *Communication Research* |
| ECT7 | *Educational Communication and Technology Research* |
| Hum8 | *Human Communication Research* |
| JBr9 | *Journal of Broadcasting and Electronic Media* |
| JC10 | *Journal of Communication* |
| JT11 | *Journal of Technical Writing and Communication* |
| JQ12 | *Journalism Quarterly* |
| La13 | *Language and Communication* |
| Me14 | *Media, Culture and Society* |
| Pu15 | *Public Opinion Quarterly* |
| Pu16 | *Public Relations Review* |
| QJ17 | *Quarterly Journal of Speech* |
| Sp18 | *Speech Communication* |
| Te19 | *Telecommunications Policy* |
| Wr20 | *Written Communication* |
| Am21 | *American Archivist* |
| AR22 | *Annual Review of Information Science and Technology* |
| AS23 | *ASLIB Proceedings* |
| Be24 | *Behavioral and Social Sciences Librarian* |
| BM25 | *Bulletin of the Medical Library Association* |
| Ca26 | *Canadian Journal of Information Science* |
| Ca27 | *Canadian Library Journal* |
| CR28 | *College Research Libraries* |
| Db29 | *Database* |
| Dr30 | *Drexel Library Quarterly* |
| Ed31 | *Education for Information* |
| El32 | *Electronic Library* |
| Go33 | *Government Information Quarterly* |
| Go34 | *Government Publications Review* |
| IF35 | *IFLA Journal* |
| In36 | *Information Age* |
| In37 | *Information Processing and Management* |
| In38 | *Information Technology and Libraries* |
| In39 | *Information Technology—Research Development Applications* |
| In40 | *Interlending and Document Supply* |
| In41 | *International Classification* |
| In42 | *International Forum on Information and Documentation* |
| In43 | *International Library Review* |

*(continued)*

TABLE 8.1 continued

| Abbreviation | Full Journal Title |
| --- | --- |
| JA44 | Journal of Academic Librarianship |
| JD45 | Journal of Documentation |
| JE46 | Journal of Education for Library and Information Science |
| Jo47 | Journal of Information Science |
| JL48 | Journal of Librarianship |
| JL49 | Journal of Library History Philosophy and Comparative Librarianship |
| JA50 | Journal of the American Society for Information Science |
| La51 | Law Library Journal |
| L&52 | Library and Information Science Research |
| Li53 | Library Acquisitions—Practice and Theory |
| L&54 | Library and Information Science |
| Li55 | Library Journal |
| Li56 | Library Quarterly |
| Li57 | Library Resources and Technical Services |
| Li58 | Library Trends |
| Li59 | Libri |
| Na60 | Nachrichten fur Dokumentation |
| Na61 | Nauchno-Tekhnicheskaya Informatsiya Seriya 1 |
| Na62 | Nauchno-Tekhnicheskaya Informatsiya Seriya 2 |
| On63 | Online |
| On64 | Online Review |
| Pr65 | Proceedings, American Society for Information Science |
| Pr66 | Program-Automated Library and Information Systems |
| Re67 | Review of Public Data Use |
| RQ68 | RQ |
| Sc69 | Scholarly Publishing |
| Sc70 | Scientometrics |
| Se71 | Serials Librarian |
| So72 | Social Science Information |
| So73 | Social Science Information Studies |
| Sp74 | Special Libraries |
| Wi75 | Wilson Library Bulletin |
| Ze76 | Zeitschrift für Bibliothkswesen und Bibliographie |
| Ze77 | Zentralblatt für Bibliothekswesen |

## Analysis

In order to portray information about roles, groupings, relationships, and structure in a parsimonious way, the matrices were
analyzed by the HRCHY network analysis program (Reitz, 1988).
The program defines groups on the basis of both hierarchy and
closeness.

Hierarchical relationships are determined by ranking the journals according to the total number of citations they receive; ties are broken by determining the total number of citations received by the journals that cite the tied journals. A journal that is "close" to a particular highly ranked journal will most likely be a member of the same grouping as the highly ranked journal. The symmetric measure of closeness is computed by first dropping any journal that does not cite, or is not cited by, at least two journals (including itself), then doubly normalizing the asymmetric citation matrix, resulting in each row and column summing to the number of journals in the remaining network. In effect, this controls for the obvious fact that some journals make or receive more citations in a given year simply because they have more issues and/or more articles (Doreian, 1985). Thus the sum of the final values in matrix cells $(i, j)$ and $(j, i)$ represents the closeness, or proportional degree of citation, between any two journals $i$ and $j$, controlling for differences in total citations both made to and received for each journal. It is a measure of "pure" structure.

Grouping journals into local clusters is performed by following the path of strongest closeness for each journal that has the locally highest status. Then two such local clusters are combined if the average tie between the two clusters is (a) greater than one and (b) the largest average involving each of the clusters. This continues until no more clusters appear.

The results from this method (a) take into account both status and closeness, (b) are not dependent on the overall network density (of journal-to-journal citation flows divided by the possible number of citation flows, which is $N \times [N - 1]$), (c) are not dependent on the overall size of the network, and (d) provide clusters that contain hierarchic groupings of ranked journals that are closer to each other than expected and than to journals in other clusters.

## Results

Due to space limitations, Figures 8.1 through 8.4 portray the hierarchies and clusters only for 1978, 1981, 1984, and 1987 (see Note 1). The vertical axis shows the ranking of journals based on citations received; the horizontal axis is arbitrary.

*(text continues on page 150)*

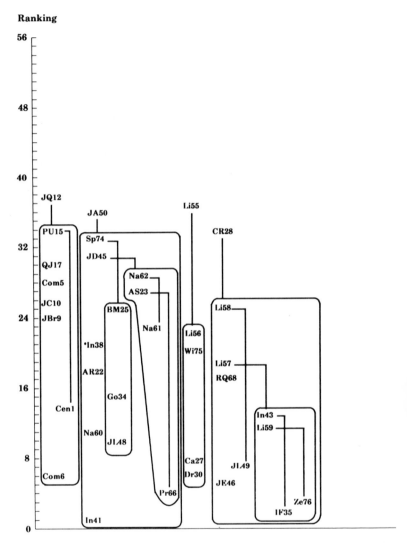

**Figure 8.1.** Journals Ranked by Citations Received and Clustered by Double-Normalized Citation Closeness, 1977

Ranking

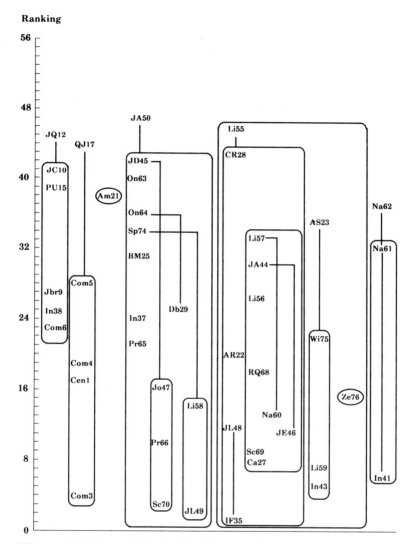

**Figure 8.2.** Journals Ranked by Citations Received and Clustered by Double-Normalized Citation Closeness, 1981

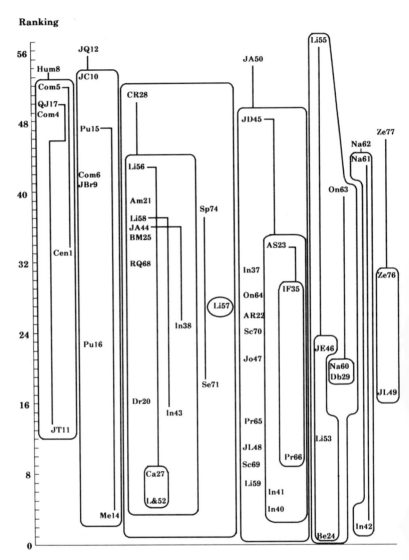

**Figure 8.3.** Journals Ranked by Citations Received and Clustered by Double-Normalized Citation Closeness, 1984

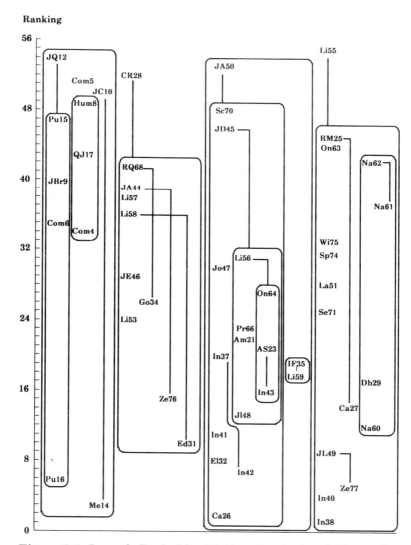

**Figure 8.4.** Journals Ranked by Citations Received and Clustered by Double-Normalized Citation Closeness, 1987

Over the four periods, the number of journals making citations to or receiving citations from at least two journals generally increased (38, 47, 57, and 55, respectively; also see point e in Note 1) as did the number of inclusive clusters (4, 8, 10, and 7). (Both measures declined slightly in 1987 due to the use of 1985 as our base year; see point b in Note 1.)

In 1978, "communication" was represented by a single cluster with a mixture of interpersonal and mass media journals, indicating a fairly simple and unified discipline, relative to the complete two-discipline network. *Journalism Quarterly* was the highest ranked of all the journals in the two-discipline network.

"Library and information science" was represented by three clusters, indicating multiple subdisciplines. The most numerous and complex cluster was headed by the *Journal of the American Society for Information Science*, commonly referred to as *JASIS* (JA50). The two other clusters were led by *Library Journal* (Li55) and *College and Research Libraries* (CR28), respectively. Throughout all the time periods, the *Journal of Documentation* (JD45) led its own subcluster but was slightly secondary to *JASIS*.

By 1981, communication had split into two subdisciplines, mass media (led by *Journalism Quarterly*) and interpersonal communication (led by the *Quarterly Journal of Speech*).

In library and information science, a number of new journals entered the ranks. Three major subdisciplines remained but within two clusters. *JASIS* (JA50) and *Library Journal* (Li55) continued their high rankings, with *College and Research Libraries* (CR28) increasing its ranking but this time placed within the *Library Journal* (Li55) cluster. A small third cluster was led by *Nauchno-Tekhnicheskaya Informatsiya Seriya 2* (Na62).

By 1984, the overall network had become more elaborate. The interpersonal (led by *Human Communication Research*, Hum8) and mass media (again led by *Journalism Quarterly*, JQ12) subdisciplines remained in communication. After 1981, *Quarterly Journal of Speech* (QJ17) lost its relationship of the interpersonal subdiscipline.

In library and information science, the overall structure continued to become more complex, with five distinct clusters or subdisciplines, three led by the major journals *College Research Libraries* (CR28), *JASIS* (JA50), and *Library Journal* (Li55) and two small clusters led by *Zentralblatt für Bibliothekswesen* (Ze77) and the Na62 subcluster.

By 1987, communication was clustered as one overall discipline, but the two major subdisciplines remained, led by *Journalism Quarterly* (JQ12) and *Communication Monographs* (Com5), along with a third subdisciplinary clustering led by *Journal of Communication* (JC10), which reported a wide diversity of research topics.

In library and information science, three disciplines have quite clearly emerged. *College and Research Libraries* (CR28) leads what might be called "library science," which includes scientific studies of practice and policy in academic and research libraries and some new trends in systems. Higher-status journals in this subdiscipline include *RQ* (RQ68), *Journal of Academic Librarianship* (JA44), *Library Resources and Technical Services* (LI57), *Library Trends* (Li58), and *Journal of Education, Library and Information Science* (JE46).

*JASIS* (JA50) leads what might be called "information science," which includes bibliometrics, information retrieval, and some historical interests. Higher-status journals in this subdiscipline include *Scientometrics* (Sc70), *Journal of Documentation* (JD45), *Library Quarterly* (Li56), *Journal of Information Science* (Jo47), and *Online Review* (On64).

*Library Journal* (Li55) leads what might be called "librarianship," which includes practice, training, news, and current topics. Higher-status journals in this subdiscipline include the *Bulletin of the Medical Library Association* (BM25), *Online* (On63), *Wilson Library Bulletin* (Wi75), *Special Libraries* (Sp74), *Law Library Journal* (La51), and several German documentation journals.

Generally, the journal-to-journal structure increased in complexity over the four cross-sectional mappings; not only the size but also the topography of intellectual space in the two disciplines changed. However, the portrayal of this space in 1987 shows that a fairly explicit hierarchic and clustered structure had emerged. The overall communication discipline consisted of the two traditional subdisciplines with *Journal of Communication* emerging as a possible bridge both between these and two other disciplines (see Rice, Borgman, & Reeves, 1988). The overall library and information science discipline consisted of three, rather than two, subdisciplines: library science, information science, and library practice.

## Discussion

In the context of this volume, this chapter is reflective; it uses bibliometric methods to study the disciplines most concerned with scholarly communication. It applied a general methodological approach (network analysis) to issues of interest to the audiences of this volume (potentially changing structures of scholarly communication) by inspecting formal relationships (indicated by journal-to-journal citation patterns) within and between the two primary audiences (information science and communication research).

The particular network analysis method used here is just one of many that analysts of scholarly communication might consider (see Rice & Richards, 1985). It has a variety of advantages, as noted earlier. However, it does seem to allow the variability in journal rankings (due to the addition of numerous new journals to the overall network year and to the naturally changing levels of citations within and among journals) to influence the results—see, for example, the shifting cluster membership of the lower-ranked library and information science journals. Finally, this method does not show whether the clusters are coming closer together in intellectual space. However, multidimensional scaling of the covariance matrix derived from the citation relationships within and among the primary aggregated clusters could be used to complement the present analyses (see Rice, Borgman, & Reeves, 1988). But results did show an increasing complexity in the hierarchic clustering of journal rankings in the four one-year periods of 1978, 1981, 1984, and 1987. Further, the top-ranked journals were consistent throughout, and the clusterings seem to be evolving into identifiable subdisciplines.

Indeed, we must conclude from these results that, although there *is* movement and change *within* disciplines, there is no significant change in cross-disciplinary clustering, based upon citations exchanged among the primary formal communication channel, the academic journal (but see point e, Note 1; there cross-citation has occurred since 1983, proportionately much more of it involving communication journals). As Pierce (this volume) notes: "If the separate bodies of knowledge of different disciplines provide strength, they are also a weakness." In this case, the structure of citation flows among journals has yet to change in ways that reflect some of the growing concerns both within and across the two disciplines of communication research and information science.

# Note

1. The extreme page limitations for this chapter prevent any discussion of the following important topics:

(a) the larger study (see Rice, Borgman, & Reeves, 1988);

(b) strengths, weaknesses, and assumptions in the use of citation data in general, and our particular solutions to various problems with the source journal citation data (obtained from the ISI *Journal Citation Report*; see Edge, 1979; Pierce, this volume; Rice, Borgman, Bednarski, & Hart, 1989; White, this volume);

(c) the need to combine analysis of citations with analysis of other aspects of scholarly communication such as cognitive maps of a discipline, actual lab and writing processes, informal use of multiple channels (such as telephone, electronic mail, and conferences), and experts' nominations (see Borgman, Lievrouw, McCain, Pierce, White—all this volume);

(d) detailed analyses of the relationships among the communication research journals (see Rice, Borgman, & Reeves, 1988);

(e) more detailed analyses of the trends in the overall journal-to-journal citation network and changes between the two disciplines (Borgman & Rice, in preparation);

(f) a wider discussion of network analysis methods, concepts, and issues in general (Rice & Richards, 1985) and specific advantages and techniques of network analysis for bibliometrics (Rice, Borgman, & Reeves, 1988); and

(g) prior research on journal-to-journal citation networks (Doreian, 1985; Rice, Borgman, & Reeves, 1988).

# PART III

# Empirical Studies

EVERETT M. ROGERS
CHARLOTTE A. COTTRILL

# 9. An Author Co-Citation Analysis of Two Research Traditions: Technology Transfer and the Diffusion of Innovations

Research on technology transfer and on the diffusion of innovations represents two scholarly traditions with a common interest in technological innovation. However, a modified author co-citation analysis shows that these two scientific specialties are relatively distinct. Possible reasons for this lack of academic convergence may be the disciplinary affiliations of the two sets of innovation scholars, their differing perspectives on the technological innovations that are the objects of study, and the distinct intellectual foundations from which the two research traditions have sprung.

The purpose of this brief chapter is to examine the interrelationships among the works of scholars in two research traditions: technology transfer and the diffusion of innovations. We utilize a modified author co-citation analysis to investigate the formal communication structures (expressed in scholarly publications) of these two specialties. This chapter is based on Cottrill (1987) and Cottrill, Rogers, and Mills (1989) but goes beyond our previous work in considering the contents of the publications in technology transfer and the diffusion of innovations that are analyzed here, so as to aid the interpretations of our statistical results.

## The Technology Transfer Tradition

*Technology transfer* is the process through which the results from basic and applied research are put into use. Originally, technology

157

was thought of mainly as hardware tools, but now we see that it almost always had a software aspect also, that may be incorporated, for instance, in the knowledge and skills that must accompany the hardware aspects of a technology. The software aspects of a technology provide an information base for a tool. The essence of technology transfer is thus the communication of information that is used for an instrumental purpose (Eveland, 1987).

Technology transfer is a two-way process, although in the past it has often been thought of in a more limited sense, as the movement of a technological innovation from universities and other organizations conducting basic research to private companies that commercialize the research findings in the form of a new product. Closer analysis of the technology transfer process, however, shows that it is usually a transaction, with information exchanged among the participants.

The issue of technology transfer has risen to an important place on the national policy agenda of the United States during the past decade due to fear of Japanese competition. In the 1980s, Japanese companies dominated U.S. markets for television sets, VCRs, compact-sized automobiles, and semiconductor memory chips. Analysts of this phenomena conclude that, although the United States has led in creating the important new technologies in these industries, Japanese companies have more effectively transferred or exploited these innovations in the form of new products as well as manufacturing these products with higher quality and selling them at a lower unit price. The U.S. national policy concerned with improving technology transfer has been expressed in the Stevenson-Wilder Technology Innovation Act of 1980 (Public Law 96-480), the National Cooperative Research Act of 1984, and the Federal Technology Transfer Act of 1986 (Public Law 94-502).

Most scholars of the technology transfer process view it as consisting of various stages. *Basic research* is defined as original investigations for the advancement of scientific knowledge that do not have the specific objective of applying this knowledge to practical problems (Rogers, 1983, p. 138). *Applied research* is investigation intended to apply scientific knowledge to practical problems. *Development* is the process of putting a new idea into a form that is expected to meet the needs of a potential market. *Commercialization* is the production, manufacturing, packaging, marketing, and distribution of a product that embodies a new idea. These four activities in the technology transfer process are usually thought to occur in sequence, starting with basic research and ending with commercialization, although certain of these stages may be skipped for certain new ideas.

When has technology been transferred? The technology transfer process can end at several different levels:

(1) when the receptor knows about the technology,
(2) when the receptor has put the technology into use in the receptor's organization, or
(3) when the receptor has commercialized the technology by incorporating it in the form of a new product.

These three levels of transfer effects are parallel to stages in the innovation-decision process (knowledge, decision, implementation, and routinization) that has been conceptualized in the diffusion of innovations, a research tradition closely related, conceptually, to the technology transfer tradition.

The technology transfer research tradition began in the 1960s with a series of investigations by scholars like Thomas J. Allen and Donald G. Marquis in the Sloan School of Management at MIT; Zvi Griliches, then in the Department of Economics at the University of Chicago, and later at Harvard University; Edwin Mansfield in the Wharton School at the University of Pennsylvania; and Alvin H. Rubenstein in industrial engineering and management at Northwestern University (Table 9.1). These scholars, working with various coauthors, investigated a technology as it moved over time through the process from research into commercialization. Usually these studies focused on one or a very few technological innovations. Often the research identified barriers or resistances to technology transfer on the part of the receptor organizations. Usually the early studies in the technology transfer tradition displayed a *pro-innovation bias*, an assumption or belief that the technological innovation under study was advantageous for the expected receptors and that it should be utilized widely and rapidly (Rogers, 1983). Much of the early work in this research tradition was sponsored by the National Science Foundation as part of a general intellectual interest in gaining an improved understanding of how scientific research results were put into practical use.

TABLE 9.1

Characteristics of Two Research Traditions: Technology Transfer and the Diffusion of Innovations

| Characteristics of the Two Research Traditions | Technology Transfer | Diffusion of Innovations |
| --- | --- | --- |
| 1. Main objects of study | Technology innovations | Technological innovations |
| 2. Date of founding | 1950s | 1940s |
| 3. Unit of analysis | Organizations or innovations | Individuals and, recently, organizations |
| 4. Perspective | Source (producer) oriented | Receptor oriented |
| 5. Main dependent variable | Transfer of a technology to a receptor organization | Adoption and use of an innovation relative to the time of adoption by other units |
| 6. Frequently used research designs | Case study of a technology through time | Cross-sectional surveys of adopters, who are asked to recall their innovation process |
| 7. Main findings | Success of the technology transfer process | (1) Characteristics of earlier and later adopters<br>(2) Characteristics of innovations with a slower and more rapid rate of adoption |
| 8. Disciplinary affiliations of scholars in the research tradition | (1) Economics<br>(2) business management, and<br>(3) various other engineering and social science disciplines | (1) Sociology,<br>(2) communication, and<br>(3) various other social science disciplines |
| 9. Nature of the process | Planned | Mainly spontaneous |

SOURCE: Based on Cottrill, Roger, and Mills (1989), Rogers (1983), and Cottrill (1987).

## The Diffusion of Innovations Tradition

Another research tradition that might be expected to be closely allied with work on technology transfer is the diffusion of innovations. An *innovation* is an idea perceived as new by an individual or organization or some other type of system (Rogers, 1983). Both research traditions of study here are centrally concerned with innovation.

The technology that is transferred in the technology transfer process is usually new to the receptors, although not necessarily so. The innovations studied in the diffusion of innovations tradition are usually technological innovations, although this need not necessarily be the case. In fact, a few of the several thousand diffusion studies completed to date have investigated the spread of a nontechnological idea, such as a political or religious philosophy (for example, transcendental meditation), or a nonmaterial idea, such as quality circles or a news event. So the two research traditions usually both study the communication of a technological innovation. However, these two scholarly traditions differ in a number of other important ways (see Table 9.1).

*Diffusion* is the process through which a new idea is communicated via certain communication channels over time in a system (Rogers, 1983). Although the intellectual roots of the diffusion research tradition can be traced back to the writings of the French scholar Gabriel Tarde around 1900, and to early British and German-Austrian anthropologists (called "diffusionists"), concerted empirical study of the diffusion research tradition attracted an increasing number of rural sociologists in the 1950s and then caught the attention of communication scholars, geographers, students of marketing and education, and a wide variety of other social scientists. By 1962, 405 diffusion publications were identified, and today there are approximately 4,000.

The typical diffusion study consists of a survey of adopters (and perhaps nonadopters) of a technological innovation or of several related innovations. The characteristics associated with earlier versus later adoption of an innovation are identified, along with the various communication channels utilized by adopters to gain awareness/knowledge of the innovation and to become persuaded to use it. Some attention is given by the diffusion tradition to the perceived attributes of an innovation and to other factors that are related to its relatively more rapid versus slower rate of adoption (see Table 9.1).

## Co-Citation Analysis of the Two Traditions

We conducted a special type of co-citation analysis of two samples of publications, one for each of the two research traditions. Our procedures, available in detail in Cottrill, Rogers, and Mills (1989), are summarized as follows:

(1) A starting list of about 20 seminal documents in each of the two traditions were selected on the basis of texts, reviews, and discussions with scholars in each of the two specialties. These starter documents tended to be highly cited by later publications.

(2) Additional publications entered the two samples on the basis of being linked by their citations to documents at the previous stages (three orders of remove from the starter documents were included). We utilized this snowball sampling design with citation data provided by the Institute for Scientific Information (ISI) *Social Sciences Citation Index*. We identified 1,232 diffusion of innovations documents and 799 technology transfer documents during the period of study, from 1966 to 1972. The two samples had 249 documents in common.

(3) We used a threshold of five or more citations to reduce the diffusion sample to 95 documents by 73 authors, and the technology transfer sample to 70 documents by 57 authors. The *oeuvres* (sets of work by an author) of 20 scholars were common to both research traditions.

(4) The two samples were combined to create a third dataset, which contained 110 oeuvres. This combined diffusion/technology transfer dataset was reduced to a symmetical matrix. The entry in each cell represented co-citation frequency, that is, the number of times the oeuvre in a row was cited with the oeuvre in the intersecting column.

(5) The degree to which each oeuvre was cited by each other oeuvre was computed in a kind of network analysis.

(6) A variety of types of cluster and factor analyses were computed to measure the relatedness of the two traditions, following a triangulation strategy of data analysis.

(7) The clusters were delineated on plots generated with an MDS computer program.

(8) To aid our interpretation of the clusters, a brief profile of each author was compiled on the basis of various "who's who" sources. The profiles and a literature review were used to identify each of the intellectual concentrations.

## What Did We Find?

(1) We found relatively little cross-referencing between the authors identified in the two research traditions. For example, during the period of study (1966-1972), the most highly cited authors in each tradition did not cite each other's work.

(2) The technology transfer research tradition is less coherent and less integrated than the diffusion of innovations tradition, even though both specialties are multidisciplinary in nature.

(3) Several subclusters were identified within each of the two traditions, and certain subclusters (for example, one concerning organizational innovativeness) were represented in both traditions. Diffusion studies of the adoption of innovations by organizations and technological transfer studies of organizations like R&D labs and companies had certain common elements, indicated by the citation of similar source documents.

Thus our co-citation analysis indicated the general separateness of the two traditions, even though certain points of intersection have occurred.

## Reasons for the Lack of Convergence

Given the common focus of both research traditions on technological innovation, why have the two sets of scholars not displayed a greater degree of convergence in their co-citation behavior? We interpret three possible reasons from the current data and from the historical and social context surrounding the two research traditions.

(1) *Disciplinary differences*. Scholars of technology transfer are predominantly (but not solely) economists and business management scholars. Naturally, their disciplinary affiliations structure the academic conferences they attend, the scholarly journals they read, their literature citation practices, and who they include in their invisible colleges. A similar structuring of intellectual relationships occurs for the sociologists, communication scholars, and other social scientists who identify with the research tradition on the diffusion of innovations. So the disciplinary differences between the two research traditions tend to separate them into two camps, with

little direct academic contact. When it does occur, such as at the occasional academic conference focusing on the broader issue of technological innovation (the last one held, to the extent of our knowledge, was an international symposium on technological innovation in 1986 in Venice, Italy), the two traditions find that they do not generally talk the same language.

(2) *Contrasting perspectives on innovation.* The two research traditions do not completely share an intellectual paradigm (a scientific approach to phenomena that provides model problems and solutions to a community of scholars). The two traditions focus on somewhat different variables, employ distinct research designs (especially in data gathering), and disagree in their basic perspective on the technological innovations under study. The technology transfer tradition tends to be source oriented, with scholars generally taking the viewpoint of those from whom the technology emanates, almost seeming to blame the receptor individuals and organizations for not utilizing the technology of study.

Further, the technology transfer tradition tends to identify economic and management factors as chief among the resistances to technology transfer. In contrast, the diffusion tradition tends to focus upon social variables as independent variables of study, as these scholars perceive the spread of innovations as essentially a social process, determined in large part by the structure of social relationships among the individuals and organizations composing the social system in which a technological innovation diffuses. To diffusion scholars, the spread of innovations is assumed to be more spontaneous, and the actors involved are seen as sense-making individuals whose subjective perceptions of the innovation of study are shaped largely by social influences. In contrast, scholars of technology transfer view the actors' behavior as somewhat more rational in nature and the technology transfer process as a relatively unplanned and ordered phenomenon, even though it may often be unsuccessful in the way it functions.

Further, the two traditions are interested in different aspects of innovation. Technology transfer is concerned with invention and discovery, development, commercialization, and production. In contrast, diffusion research demonstrates little interest in invention and the origin of innovation; instead, the diffusion tradition concentrates on the decisions of members of a system to adopt an innovation and how such behavior by one adopter influences the adoption decisions of others. So the marketing of an innovation is a central issue in diffusion studies.

The contrasting paradigms of the two research traditions are hardly surprising, given their different disciplinary composition.

(3) *Intellectual foundations.* The two traditions also stem from quite different academic ancestries. The paradigmatic study that has heavily influenced the diffusion tradition is the Ryan and Gross hybrid seed corn study (as explained previously, and detailed in, Rogers, 1983). Later diffusion studies, such as the investigation by Elihu Katz, James Coleman, and Herbert Menzel of the diffusion of a new antibiotic drug among medical doctors, or the investigation by Richard O. Carlson of the diffusion of modern math among schools, followed a research design and a theoretical format patterned after the Ryan-Gross prototype. Technology transfer scholars also followed their own paradigmatic studies, with each later descendant structured along the lines of earlier work.

Even when both of the two research traditions studied the same innovation (hybrid seed corn) as it diffused among the same kind of respondents (Midwestern farmers), the investigations were carried out along quite different lines, and scholars in the two traditions disagreed about the meaning of the results. Diffusion scholars criticized technology transfer scholars for concluding that farmers adopted hybrid seed corn in a highly rational manner, with the degree of profitability of the innovation explaining its rate of adoption at an aggregate level of analysis.

So once each research tradition based its ensuing studies upon scholarly examples of the past, the two continued to flow along different paths that did not cross.

HENRY SMALL
EDWIN GREENLEE

# 10. A Co-Citation Study of AIDS Research

A co-citation analysis of AIDS research is presented covering the years 1982 to 1988. Through the use of cluster strings and co-citation maps at various levels of aggregation, the development of the field is traced, including major findings and shifts in research emphasis. The implications of this case of a rapidly growing research area for the development of scientific fields in general are explored, in particular, the relation of changes in the bibliometric structure to changes in scientific knowledge and understanding.

It is difficult to think of a social and scientific problem more important than AIDS. The suffering AIDS has caused and the potential it offers for insights into basic biology are enormous. Our goal is to apply bibliometric tools to understand how new fields of research develop. With luck, we will someday be able to use this understanding to hasten such development (Swanson, 1987).

In the view of many sociologists of science, the scientific paper is the medium through which scientists stake out their claims to new knowledge (Gilbert, 1976). Citations to papers acknowledge the existence of these claims and provide a running commentary on them. By aggregating citations, we aggregate commentaries on earlier papers and provide a means for examining consensus in a field of science (Cozzens, 1988). The systematic application of bibliometric methods and content analysis of citing passages can lead to a "collective review" of a field (Small, 1986). Citation patterns can thus be interpreted as assimilations of earlier knowledge claims. Through citation of one anothers' papers, scientists communicate about and define the components of their evolving knowledge base.

AUTHOR'S NOTE: We are grateful to Everett Rogers for sharing his AIDS information with us, and encouraging us to write up our results, and also to Linnea Berg of the University of Southern California for redrawing all of our figures.

The main bibliometric method we employ is co-citation analysis, which involves the application of clustering and scaling methods to data on the number of times earlier papers are cited together by later papers (Garfield, 1979a, chap. 4). These methods have been described elsewhere (Small & Garfield, 1985) and will only be briefly outlined here. The databases used are the annual cumulations of the combined *Science Citation Index* and *Social Sciences Citation Index*.

Co-citation frequencies are determined for each pair of about 60,000 cited items meeting an annual citation threshold. The co-citation links are normalized and input to a single-link clustering routine. After the clusters of highly cited papers have been generated (about 8,000 for an annual run), each cluster is taken as a unit of analysis for a second clustering process. Co-citation counts between clusters are determined and input to a second clustering. This process of reclustering is repeated until the file converges to a single supercluster. For samples of about 60,000 core papers, this usually requires four iterations, denoted C1, C2, C3, and C4, going from the least to the most aggregated level.

The building of nested sets of clusters allows us to view science with varying degrees of resolution, from narrowly focused problem areas to entire disciplines. This is a cross-sectional representation of science, specific to a given year of data. To explore longitudinal changes, it is necessary to see how clusters change from year to year. To do this we create cluster strings, which are sequences of annual clusters that share common cited documents (Small & Greenlee, 1986). To obtain these patterns of continuity, we use a year-to-year linkage measure and another single-link clustering operation to extract the most significant lines of development over a period of years.

In our AIDS study we use an eight-year cluster string to examine the development of the field. To study the relationship among research areas in a given year, four levels of cluster maps have been created using the technique of multidimensional scaling. This algorithm uses a measure of association among objects as input, in our case, normalized co-citation links, and produces a spatial representation of those objects in a specified number of dimensions, usually set at two (Schiffman, Reynolds, & Young, 1981). These representations are referred to as "maps of science" because they depict the relationships among fields or specialties or, at the document level, between scientific ideas or methods. By way of validation, a number of journalistic accounts have been referenced that corroborate and provide background for some of our findings.

## AIDS String and Pre-1984 Developments

An orientation to the development of research on AIDS is provided by the C1 cluster string (Figures 10.1 and 10.2). For ease of display the string has been divided into two parts that only weakly interact: a viral AIDS string (Figure 10.1) and a clinical AIDS string (Figure 10.2). The first AIDS cluster emerged in 1982, one year after the initial papers describing the clinical manifestations of the new disease were published by several investigators (see Figure 10.2). In 1983 the field expands dramatically and begins a process of "twigging," that is, the splitting off and proliferation of research areas that develop in parallel.

An initially separate line of development concerned with cancer viruses, the so-called human T-cell leukemia and lymphoma viruses (HTLV), at first proceeds independently (see Figure 10.1). But from 1983 to 1984 a weak but significant interaction between the clinical line and this virology line occurs when three core documents jump from the clinical to the viral string. This is indicated by dashed lines on Figures 10.1 and 10.2, which connect the viral string with the clinical string.

In subsequent years there are no further direct interactions between the viral and clinical lines of development, although, as we will see later on the maps, they were nevertheless in close intellectual proximity. In 1985 there is a significant splitting of the clinical cluster (Figure 10.2), components of which continue on their own developmental lines, with further smaller-scale splits and merges along the way. However, throughout most of the period, there have been only these two major lines of development in AIDS research.

The splitting that affects the clinical effort in 1985 does not occur for the viral line until 1987. Until then the viral AIDS work is remarkably concentrated in a single large cluster. In 1988 the twigging of the viral line continues, and in addition there is the merger of previously unconnected lines of work with the viral clusters. This illustrates how a line of research can change by linking

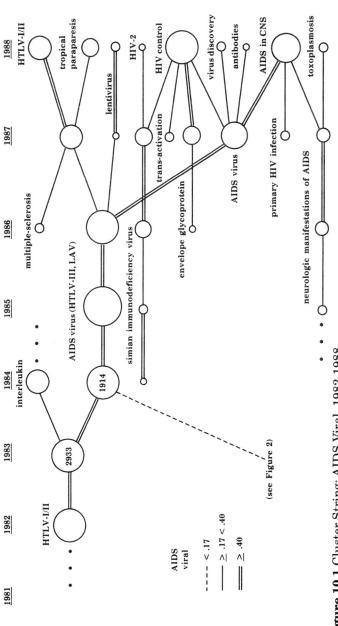

**Figure 10.1** Cluster String: AIDS Viral, 1982-1988

NOTE: The clusters for each year are indicated by circles. The circles are scaled in size (area) to reflect the number of core papers they contain. A link between clusters indicates that core papers are shared. The strength of a link is indicated by a dashed, solid, or double line. A dotted line means the string can be extended backward or forward in time.

169

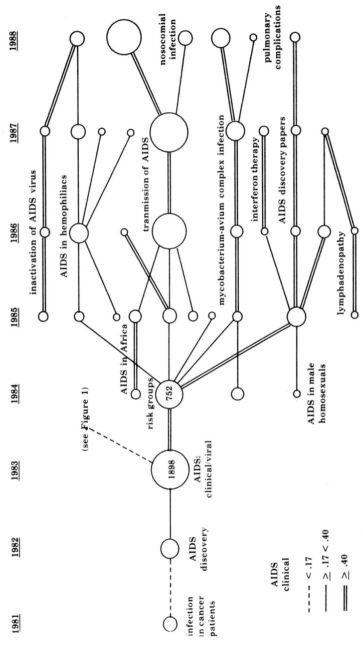

**Figure 10.2** Cluster String: AIDS Clinical, 1981-1988

NOTE: See note to Figure 10.1 for explanation.

TABLE 10.1
Growth in Number of AIDS Clusters

|                          | 1982 | 1983 | 1984 | 1985 | 1986 | 1987 | 1988 |
|--------------------------|------|------|------|------|------|------|------|
| Number of Clusters       | 1    | 8    | 20   | 36   | 48   | 60   | 80   |
| Number of Core Documents | 14   | 80   | 147  | 215  | 253  | 453  | 669  |

up with another preexisting line, thus in effect rewriting their own histories.

The proliferation of AIDS research is summarized in a different way in Table 10.1, which gives the number of clusters from 1982 to 1988 that deal in some way with AIDS. These sets were compiled by performing a key word search on the approximately 8,000 C1 cluster names each year, searching for the acronyms AIDS and HIV or their word equivalents. The growth of the field in terms of clusters and core documents agrees well with a more traditional article count for AIDS carried out using Medline (Self, Filardo, & Lancaster, 1989). We will show later on how this explosion of research has changed the status of AIDS from a single research specialty in 1982 to nearly a discipline in its own right by 1987.

Many of the clusters counted in Table 10.1 are small and are not captured by the AIDS string or by our higher-level maps. These may correspond to research dead ends or to unpopular hypotheses that do not become incorporated into the mainstream of biomedical science. The role of these small AIDS areas is a topic for further research. Other clusters counted in Table 10.1 are among the largest in the entire SCI/SSCI file and are the main object of the present investigation. These represent the current consensus of the medical establishment on what causes AIDS, how it is transmitted, and how it should be treated.

The first cluster on AIDS in 1982 is weakly tied, by a single continuing core document, to a 1981 cluster on infections experienced by cancer patients (Figure 10.2). The continuing document was on the incidence of pneumocystis-carinii pneumonia in the United States, one of the opportunistic infections that later became closely associated with AIDS. The 1981 cluster, although not concerned with AIDS, dealt with the problems that arise when the immune system is suppressed by cancer therapy.

The 1982 cluster is the first true AIDS cluster and contains in its core many of the papers that were the first to recognize what has become the clinical syndrome of AIDS. These include the Gottlieb et al. paper (1981) from the UCLA School of Medicine, the Masur et al. paper (1981) from the Cornell Medical College in New York City, and the Siegel et al. paper (1981) from Mt. Sinai Medical Center in New York, all of which were published in a single December issue of the *New England Journal of Medicine*. In addition there is the Hymes et al. paper (1981) in *Lancet*, published three months earlier, from the New York University Medical Center. These papers describe outbreaks of a severe "acquired immunodeficiency" in the male homosexual populations of New York and Los Angeles. Of the 14 papers in the 1982 cluster, 7 deal with Kaposi's sarcoma and 3 with pneumocystis-carinii pneumonia, which were known to be manifestations of an impaired immune system.

At this time there was considerable speculation about the possible cause of the immune suppression. One paper in the 1982 cluster on amyl nitrite, a vasodilator drug used by homosexuals to enhance sexual experience, suggested that use of the substance might alter T-lymphocytes. Explanation by an infectious agent was more common, but there was no consensus on what the agent was. Cytomegalovirus (CMV) was one candidate, and five of the papers in the 1982 cluster dealt with this virus. Herpes virus was also suspect and figured in four of the papers.

In 1983 the clinical cluster exploded to 52 papers (Figure 10.3). One notable feature of the cluster is the number of papers that are actually letters, editorials, and other short communications. This reflects the feeling of urgency about the problem but the lack of solid results on which to proceed. Even a news item in *Science* (Marx, 1982), simply reporting the state of affairs, warrants frequent citation. Part of this sense of desperation may have resulted from AIDS being identified in other groups in addition to the male homosexual population (Altman, 1986, chap. 3).

Some of these risk groups begin to emerge as regions on the co-citation map. The original 1981 discovery papers, concerned mainly with the homosexual population, form the densest region around Gottlieb et al.'s (1981) paper on the right. Above this group is a less densely linked region on the incidence of Kaposi's sarcoma, a theme carried over from the previous year's cluster. Below this group, however, is a region of papers on hemophiliacs' risk of AIDS, later found to be due to exposure to contaminated, blood-derived clotting

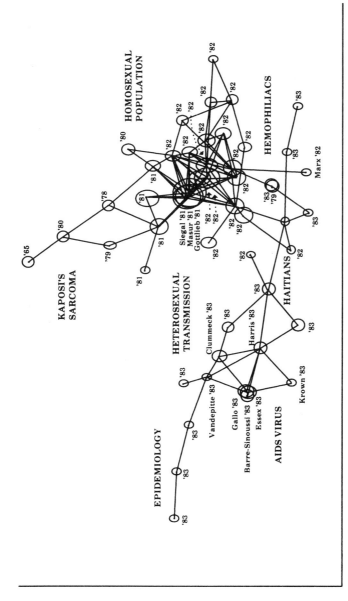

**Figure 10.3.** AIDS, 1983 C1 Map

NOTE: Circles represent highly cited papers, and lines are strong co-citation links between them. The size of the circle is proportional to the citation frequency of the paper, and the length of the line, the frequency of co-citation. (Complete bibliographic information available from the authors.)

factor. To the left of this region are papers on AIDS in the Haitian population and the possibility of heterosexual transmission.

As we move to the left on the map, the topic changes from the clinical description of AIDS to the possible origin and cause of the disease. There are papers on AIDS in Africa and even the suggestion that the agent is a variant of an African swine fever virus. But the most notable entrants into the cluster are a set of three papers, all published in the same issue of *Science* in May 1983, suggesting that the cause might be a human retrovirus (Kulstad, 1986). These include the now-celebrated papers by Gallo at the National Institutes of Health (NIH) and Montagnier (Barre-Sinoussi, Chermann, & Montagnier, 1987; Barre-Sinoussi et al., 1983) at the Pasteur Institute in Paris, which later became the focus of a priority dispute about which group was first to identify the AIDS virus. The third paper is by Essex et al. (1983) from Harvard and the Centers for Disease Control.

The three 1983 papers that embody the retrovirus hypothesis for AIDS are highly co-cited in 1983 and constitute a small region on the 1983 AIDS map that is otherwise almost entirely focused on the clinical manifestations of the disease. This position of the retroviral hypothesis papers is logical in that a causative agent for the disease was being sought, and antiviral treatments might have been effective. First we examine the nature of the co-citation links that bind the three retrovirus papers (Barre-Sinoussi et al., 1983; Essex et al., 1983; Gallo et al., 1983) to the clinical cluster.

The three papers at the lower left of the 1983 map are linked to four clinical papers, two of which were published in the *New England Journal of Medicine* and the two others in *Lancet*. Three of the four papers were concerned with aspects of the syndrome suggesting that a transmissible agent, probably a virus of some kind, was the causative agent. One paper pointed out the prevalence of AIDS in the female sexual partners of AIDS patients; another, AIDS in Black Africans. Because the retrovirus HTLV, discovered by Gallo and his group at the NIH, was known to be prevalent in certain regions of Africa, the connection with AIDS seemed plausible. The remaining paper reported on a partially successful treatment of Kaposi's sarcoma in AIDS patients using recombinant alpha-interferon. Because interferon is an antiviral agent, this partial success also pointed to the viral etiology. In short, the co-citation of the retroviral hypothesis papers in 1983 with these clinical papers was an expression of the need for a transmissible viral agent to explain what was known about the disease.

In 1984 we will find these three retroviral hypothesis papers in another branch of the cluster string. They will jump from the clinical string in 1983 to the virology string in 1984. To understand this development, however, we need to characterize the pre-AIDS virus cluster in 1983 (see Figure 10.1). The focus of this research was the so-called HTLV, or human T-cell leukemia and lymphoma virus family, which consisted of HTLV-I, responsible for adult T-cell leukemia, and HTLV-II, responsible for hairy-cell leukemia. The central figure in this work is Robert Gallo of the NIH. HTLV-I was discovered in 1980, and Gallo considered it to be the first human cancer virus and the first human retrovirus to have been isolated. Many of the core papers in the 1983 viral cluster were written by Gallo's group at the NIH. There were also several papers from researchers in Japan where adult T-cell leukemia was prevalent. Another contingent of papers in this cluster was concerned with interleukin-2, a promising antiviral agent also discovered by Gallo's group and originally called T-cell growth factor. This interleukin-2 work splits off from the HTLV cluster in 1984 as shown in Figure 10.1 and connects with other virology areas. There were, however, no papers in this 1983 HTLV cluster suggesting that the HTLV virus had anything to do with AIDS.

To see how the HTLV cluster relates to the cluster on AIDS in 1983, we can examine their relative positions on a higher-level map, namely, at the C2 level. Figure 10.4 shows the C2 cluster that contains both the HTLV cluster and the AIDS cluster. The C2 cluster covers various topics in immunology and immunotherapy such as monoclonal antibody therapy, cancer and the immune system, natural killer cells, interferon, lupus, and multiple sclerosis (MS). Later on, in 1985, HTLV will also be associated with MS (Marx, 1985), and in 1987 the HTLV and MS clusters will physically merge (see Figure 10.1). But in 1983 the HTLV cluster, labeled "human T-cell leukemia virus" on Figure 10.3, is linked to cancer immunology.

The AIDS cluster is more peripheral (on the lower left) and is flanked by two small AIDS-related clusters, on T-cell subsets and lymphadenopathy. It is also linked to lupus via a cluster on lymphocyte-T suppressor cells. However, the shortest path from AIDS to the

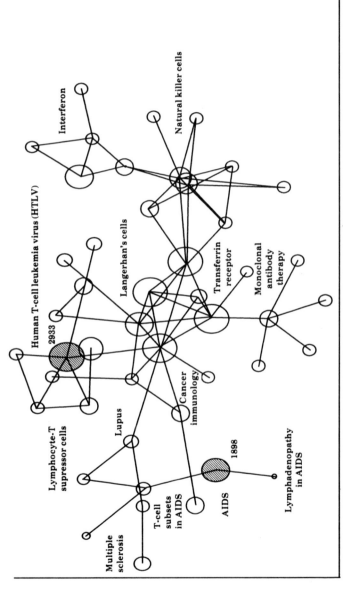

Interferon

Natural killer cells

Human T-cell leukemia virus (HTLV)

Langerhan's cells

Transferrin receptor

Monoclonal antibody therapy

2933

Lymphocyte-T supressor cells

Cancer immunology

Lupus

1898

Multiple sclerosis

T-cell subsets in AIDS

AIDS

Lymphadenopathy in AIDS

**Figure 10.4.** Immunology, 1983 C2 Map

NOTE: The previous C1 map of AIDS is a single circle (lower left, crosshatched) and is separated from the cluster concerned with the HTLV virus (upper center, crosshatched). Cluster numbers show relation to the AIDS string of Figure 10.1. (Detailed information available from the authors.)

HTLV cluster requires traversing five links on the map. We will see in the next year how these two topics become close neighbors.

If we broaden our view of science in 1983 by moving up to the C3 map containing this immunology C2 group, we would see immunology to be the second largest field in biomedicine and linked directly to the largest field, molecular genetics (Small & Garfield, 1985, figure 5). AIDS in 1983 is thus a subfield within immunology, although clearly not a large area in biomedical science and somewhat peripheral within immunology.

## AIDS in 1984

In 1984 AIDS emerges from its peripheral position within the immunology C2 cluster to become a C2 cluster in its own right (see Figure 10.5). AIDS is still closely linked to immunology, and the latter remains, as it was in 1983, the second largest biomedical field and directly linked to molecular genetics. AIDS has grown in terms of the number of research subspecialties and in autonomy but has retained its close tie with immunology.

We can specify more precisely the nature of the link between AIDS and the field of immunology by performing a content analysis of 1984 papers that cite core documents in both the AIDS and the immunology C2 clusters. It was found that co-citations to the two clusters were made both for methodological reasons—that is, immunological assays and tests were used in AIDS research—and for conceptual reasons—because AIDS relates to the wider problem of defects in immune response.

Next we examine the interior of the AIDS C2 cluster (Figure 10.6). There is a strongly linked central region, from which radiate several sparse branches. A majority of the clusters on this C2 map have a direct bearing on AIDS, while a few represent related topics such as Epstein-Barr virus, interferon, cytomegalovirus, organ transplantation (because of the drug suppression of the immune response), toxoplasmosis infection and so on. The related topics tend to be situated on the branches, while the areas specific to AIDS are more central. The central region is dominated by two large C1 clusters, one on virology and the other on clinical aspects of AIDS. The string Figures 10.1 and 10.2 show that these two clusters (numbers 1914 and 752) are on separate lines of development. They also correspond

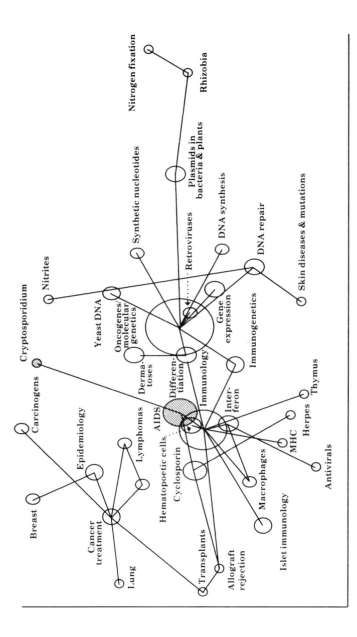

**Figure 10.5.** Genetics and Immunology, 1984 C3 Map

NOTE: AIDS emerges for the first time as a C2 cluster, still, however, with a direct link to immunology. (Detailed information available from the authors.)

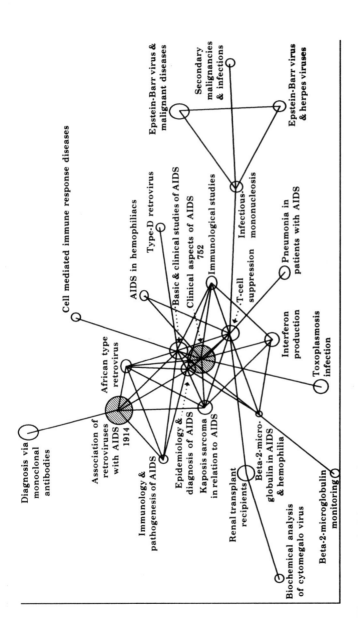

**Figure 10.6.** AIDS, 1984 C2 Map

NOTE: View of AIDS C2 cluster shown on previous C3 map for 1984. Work on the AIDS retrovirus (C1 cluster 1914) is now only one step removed from work on clinical aspects of the disease (C1 752). The two areas are indicated by crosshatching. (Detailed information available from the authors.)

179

to the same C1 clusters on the 1983 C2 map that were five steps removed from each other. In other words, HTLV virus research has moved to within one step of clinical AIDS.

We descend finally into the individual C1 clusters that show the pattern of document co-citations. The clinical AIDS cluster (Figure 10.7) is similar to the 1983 version in having regions devoted to various risk groups. But the number of such groups has increased as have the number of associated diseases. In the center of the map are the three principal clinical discovery papers from 1981 (Gottlieb et al.; Masur et al.; Siegel et al.). To the upper left is a region on the AIDS risk in hemophilia due to the contaminated clotting factor. To the lower left is a region concerned with AIDS in infants of infected mothers and women who are sex partners of AIDS-infected males. There are more papers on AIDS in the intravenous drug user population than in 1983, although they tend to be scattered on the map. The same is true of papers on AIDS in the Haitian population.

Most of the papers to the right of the center concern AIDS in the homosexual population and the various opportunistic infections due to suppressed immunity. These include Kaposi's sarcoma, pneumocystis-carinii pneumonia, myco-bacterium-avium intracellulare infection and thrombocytopenic purpura. To the upper right are papers on the characteristics of the immune defects in AIDS patients, such as the ratio of helper T-cells to suppressor T-cells (labeled lymphocyte-T subsets). An important set of three papers on the far right deals with the effects of AIDS on the brain and central nervous system, a newly discovered area of concern that will expand in later years.

Nowhere on this map, however, do we find papers describing the viral agent responsible for the disease. It turns out that the three papers proposing the retrovirus hypothesis that had appeared in the 1983 clinical AIDS cluster have jumped to an exclusively viral cluster in 1984, which is the large viral AIDS cluster shown on the previous C2 map (Figure 10.5), one step removed from the clinical cluster. This separation of viral from clinical research is indicative of major developments in the virology of AIDS that occurred in 1984.

Descending into the viral AIDS cluster (Figure 10.8), we see two very distinct regions separated by a single link. The densely linked right-hand lobe is a continuation of the HTLV-I/II work of the previous year and again features Gallo's NIH group and Japanese researchers. The more loosely linked region, on the left, is devoted

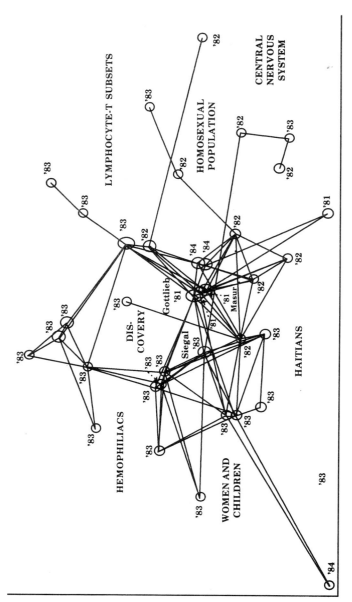

**Figure 10.7.** AIDS Clinical, 1984 Map

NOTE: View of clinical AIDS cluster shown on previous map (752). Shows three 1981 discovery papers surrounded by papers on various risk groups and disease manifestations. (Complete bibliographic information available from the authors.)

181

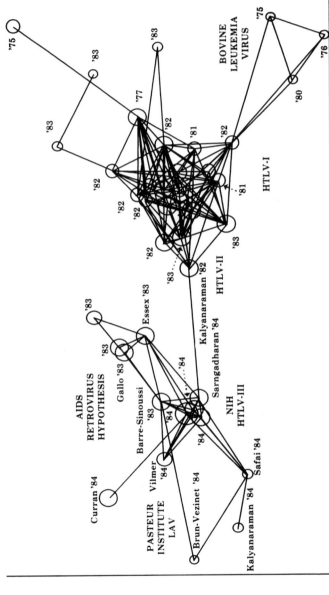

**Figure 10.8.** Association of Retroviruses with AIDS, 1984 C1 Map

NOTE: View of AIDS retrovirus cluster shown on figure 10.5 (1914). HTLV-I work appears on the right and AIDS virus (HTLV-II) work on the left, joined by a single link. Papers on the left are principally from Gallo's group at NIH and Montagnier's group at the Pasteur Institute in Paris.

to work on the AIDS virus, including the three 1983 retrovirus hypothesis papers from the NIH, the Pasteur Institute, and Harvard. These are grouped at the upper-right extremity of the left lobe, along with two additional 1983 papers from Harvard and the NIH. Below these and at the point of attachment to the right lobe are a tightly knit group of four papers all dated 1984. These papers are from Gallo's group and were published in the same May issue of *Science*. They represent Gallo's identification of a retrovirus that causes AIDS and the assertion that it is a member of the HTLV family, dubbed HTLV-III (Gallo, 1988).

AIDS researchers were not, however, unanimous about the designation HTLV-III and its membership in the HTLV family. The French group under Montagnier at the Pasteur Institute in particular, represented on the map by four papers arrayed in a semicircle around and to the left of the four Gallo 1984 papers, claimed that they had identified the AIDS virus the year before (Barre-Sinoussi et al., 1983) and denoted it LAV, for lymphadenopathy associated virus. The Pasteur Institute papers describe their further efforts at characterizing the LAV virus.

Another area of disagreement between the NIH and the Pasteur Institute under way was over the patent rights to the AIDS blood screening test (Norman, 1985). This marks the beginning of a long intellectual and patent dispute that would not be resolved until 1987, when Gallo and Montagnier published jointly the "official" chronology of AIDS research up to 1985 (Gallo & Montagnier, 1987).

The most striking feature of the AIDS virus cluster in 1984 is the single link that forms a bridge between the HTLV-I/II work on the right and the AIDS virus (HTLV-III or LAV) work on the left. To understand this link we performed a content analysis of the papers co-citing the two documents, namely, Kalyanaraman et al. (1982) on the HTLV I/II side and Sarngadharan et al. (1984) on the AIDS side. Sarngadharan et al. (1984) is one of the four papers by the Gallo group presenting HTLV-III as the AIDS virus. Kalyanaraman et al. (1982) is the paper by the Gallo group reporting the isolation of the HTLV-II retrovirus from a patient with hairy-cell leukemia.

Many of the co-citing papers are by the Gallo group as well and, examining the passages in which the two bridging papers are co-cited, we find that the new HTLV-III work is presented as a logical continuation or historical progression from the older HTLV-I/II work. Some co-citing passages are more technical and mention the similarity of the methods used in culturing the viruses and even the similarities in their structures. It is interesting that, in the corresponding AIDS virus cluster for 1985, one of the same documents (Kalyanaraman et al., 1982, on HTLV-II) plays an identical bridging role to HTLV-III work.

Without the insistence of Gallo in making the connection between his HTLV family and the new AIDS virus, it is unlikely that work on the AIDS virus would have separated from clinical AIDS work to form a separate virology cluster. We recall that the three AIDS retrovirus hypothesis papers jumped from the 1983 clinical cluster to this exclusively viral cluster in 1984. This is a clear instance of how the scientific interests and research program of a single laboratory can influence the collective patterns of specialization as manifest by the co-citation methodology.

But other factors, in addition to Gallo's intellectual dominance, were at work. In 1983 there was hope that antiviral agents such as interferon would be effective treatments for AIDS. When these treatments proved less effective than hoped, there was the need to retreat to basic biology to understand more about the virus and its possible points of vulnerability. Hence the separation of AIDS virology from clinical AIDS represents the need to focus and specialize on different aspects of the problem, that is, to divide and conquer.

The question of priority for the discovery of the AIDS virus between Gallo and Montagnier can be examined by an analysis of the citations to their 1983 papers, each of which postulated a retrovirus as the causative agent. By examining papers that cited either the Gallo et al. or the Barre-Sinoussi et al. (1983) papers, and the passages in which they are co-cited, we can learn whether their contributions were perceived as equivalent or different. Their equivalence is indicated when the reference to both papers is given at the same point in the text. Moravcsik calls such references "redundant" (Moravcsik & Murugesan, 1976). If the references are not redundant, they will occur at different points in the text, and the citing passages will differ in some regard.

In 1983 the Barre-Sinoussi et al. paper was cited fewer times than the Gallo paper (27 versus 38), and every time the Pasteur Institute paper was cited, the NIH paper was cited as well. In addition, the co-citing contexts for the two papers were 70% redundant, that is, attached to the same location in the texts and not differentiated in any way. In 1984 the French paper was cited more often than the

TABLE 10.2
Citations to Early Papers on the AIDS Retrovirus

| Paper | 1983 | 1984 | 1985 | 1986 | 1987 | 1988 | Total |
|---|---|---|---|---|---|---|---|
| Gallo et al. (*Science, 220*, p. 865, 1983) | 38 | 102 | 98 | 58 | 34 | 29 | 359 |
| Barre-Sinoussi et al. (*Science, 220*, p. 868, 1983) | 27 | 147 | 366 | 416 | 399 | 398 | 1753 |
| Gallo et al, (*Science, 224*, p. 500, 1984) | — | 116 | 410 | 384 | 341 | 284 | 1535 |

U.S. paper (147 versus 102), and only 45% of the times that the Barre-Sinoussi et al. paper was cited was the Gallo paper cited as well. Also in 1984, when both were cited, redundancy was lower, namely, 50%. Hence in 1983 their contributions were more often perceived as equivalent, but in 1984, authors began to differentiate between them. In 1983 about one-quarter of the contexts mentioned other viruses as possible causes of AIDS (herpes, CMV, Epstein-Barr, and so on) in addition to a retrovirus. In 1984 focus had narrowed to a retrovirus (only 1 of 14 contexts examined mentioned other viruses). A possible reason for the ascendancy of the French work is that the authors had more strongly asserted the uniqueness of the virus, while Gallo et al. claimed it was just another member of the HTLV family.

Although Montagnier's group appears to have received priority for discovery of the AIDS virus, Gallo's group has received credit for confirming that the virus actually caused AIDS. This is indicated by the number of citations received by Gallo's (1984) paper, which is comparable to the number received by the (1983) Pasteur Institute paper (see Table 10.2).

## Developments After 1984

As indicated by the string diagram of Figure 10.1, the development of the viral line was contained within a single main C1 cluster until 1987 when a splitting off of areas occurred. By contrast the development of the clinical study of AIDS (Figure 10.2) has been marked by considerable twigging of research lines. This was the fate of the 1984 clinical AIDS cluster, which in 1985 fragmented into several parts, the two main parts being AIDS in the male homosexual population and AIDS in women, children, and the heterosexual population. The larger of these 1985 clusters on the homosexual population contained the three principal clinical discovery papers from 1981, which dealt primarily with homosexual males with the disease. However, only 4 of the 14 papers in the cluster were new (that is, had not appeared in the 1984 clinical cluster) and none of the papers was published in 1984 or 1985. Similarly, the smaller clinical cluster on women and children with AIDS contained only two new papers out of a total of nine, and six of the nine had been published as early as 1983.

Although relatively little new to report was happening on the clinical line, some very significant developments were occurring on the viral line. The structure of the viral cluster for 1985 preserved the essential division between HTLV-I/II, on one side, and the AIDS virus, or HTLV-III, on the other, with a single bridge connecting them, but the AIDS side was greatly expanded. Of the 56 papers in the 1985 viral cluster, 27 are new, and most of the new papers appear on the AIDS side of the map (19 new on the AIDS side and 8 new on the HTLV-I/II side). Some of the new groupings of papers are as follows: identification of the molecular receptor for the AIDS virus, the complete nucleotide sequencing of the AIDS virus, the sequence homology between the AIDS virus and a slow virus called lentivirus, neurological manifestations of AIDS, and AIDS antibody screening tests. Many of these topics will continue as major regions through 1987.

If 1985 was a breakthrough year for work on the AIDS virus, 1986 was the year for a significant shift in clinical topics. On the cluster string diagram (Figure 10.2) we see three lines merging to form the clinical cluster in 1986: the 1985 cluster on AIDS in women and children, a previously separate cluster on AIDS in Africa, and a small cluster on the AIDS virus in saliva and semen. It is interesting that all of these topics relate to epidemiology and the transmission of the disease and not to clinical treatment. A possible reason for this is that most treatments had not proved successful, and the clinical emphasis shifted to the ways in which the disease was transmitted in the hope that prevention would solve the problem. The major regions on the 1986 cluster map are maternal transmission of AIDS to infants, heterosexual transmission, the AIDS virus in bodily secretions, the absence of transmission by casual contact,

AIDS in Africa, and health care workers' risk of AIDS. Interest in these topics would intensify in 1987.

By contrast the viral AIDS cluster in 1986 reveals no new topics from the previous year and a decrease in the density of links among the topical regions. The latter include distinct, but weakly linked, groups of papers on the HTLV-I/II viruses, the HTLV-III/LAV discovery papers, the molecular receptor for the AIDS virus, the nucleotide sequence and genetic expression of the AIDS virus, and neurological manifestations of AIDS. A small group of three papers located between the sequencing and neurological regions is concerned with the structural similarities of the AIDS virus to lentivirus. This region represents a growing contingent of researchers, first visible on the 1985 map, who did not believe the virus was a member of Gallo's HTLV family but that the virus was a member of the lentivirus family. This was also consistent with the new findings of neurologic involvement of the AIDS virus, similar to the action of visna virus, a member of the lentivirus family, in sheep (Barnes, 1986). The segmentation of virus work into various subtopics weakly linked to one another presages the splitting of the viral cluster that occurs in 1987.

The main clinical cluster in 1987, as in 1986, is concerned with the transmission of the disease, not its treatment. The cluster is a continuation and intensification of earlier themes, with some elaborations. An example of the latter is the appending of a group of papers on the transmission of Creutzfeldt-Jakob disease, caused by another slow virus that attacks the brain. Apparently AIDS researchers began to see similarities in the modes of transmission of various viruses. Linkage to the AIDS work is via a paper on the transmission of rabies by corneal transplantation. Generally this cluster is not concerned with how to treat AIDS but how to prevent AIDS from being spread.

Other branches of the clinical AIDS line, still significantly smaller than the transmission cluster, were continuing to focus on treatment problems, such as the mycobacterium-avium intracellulare infection cluster shown on Figure 10.2, one of the many opportunistic infections to which AIDS victims are prone. Work also continued on the protection of the hemophiliac population from contaminated clotting factor, and, as shown on the string, interferon-alpha therapy continued to be tested. Nevertheless, the primary focus of the clinical effort at this time was prevention.

On the viral front in 1987 a significant breakup of the main viral cluster occurs, splitting off work on HTLV-I/II into a separate cluster. At the same time a small MS cluster merges with the HTLV-I/II cluster. What remains in the larger AIDS virus cluster are three main topical regions: an HTLV-III/LAV discovery paper group, studies of the receptor for the AIDS virus, and a significantly expanded set of papers on neurological manifestations of AIDS, including isolation of the virus from various parts of the central nervous system (Barnes, 1987). Also splitting off from the main cluster are papers on the homologies with lentivirus. This splitting off of areas may represent a specialization of interests. However, it also marks a breakdown of the hegemony of Gallo's paradigm regarding the HTLV nature of the AIDS virus. From then on the term *HIV* (human immunodeficiency virus) replaces *HTLV-III* as the dominant way to refer to the AIDS virus.

In 1988 the clinical sideline mainly shows the continuation of prior themes, with relatively little splitting or merging and in some cases the termination of research lines. The largest clinical cluster, on AIDS transmission, splits off a nosocomial, or health care related, transmission cluster. Remaining in the large transmission cluster are document subgroups we have seen before: AIDS in Africa, modes of transmission, and AIDS in infants and children. The last named receives perhaps the greatest attention in 1988 with recognition of the "fetal AIDS syndrome." Another clinical line of research not contained in the large transmission cluster that continues strongly into 1988 are the mycobacteria infections that affect AIDS patients, for example, the myco-bacterium-avium complex, but with new emphasis placed on tuberculosis. The resurgence of this disease is related to the spread of AIDS. Finally, the termination of the interferon and lymphadenopathy lines and some of the lines on AIDS in hemophiliacs shows an overall diminution of effort on the clinical front.

Although clinical AIDS developments in 1988 are subdued, changes on the AIDS virus front are dramatic. There is a continuation of the splitting of the AIDS virus cluster that began in 1987, but at the same time a merging with other 1987 clusters and a resulting growth in size of the main clusters. The largest of these is labeled "HIV control" on Figure 10.1, which consists of three major document subgroups: new variants of the AIDS virus from Africa (e.g., HIV-2) including the simian AIDS virus, study of the

AIDS virus envelope glycoprotein (gp120) and its receptor (CD4) on human lymphocytes, and the regulation of viral replication of AIDS including the phenomenon of transactivation. These topics represent a convergence of separate lines of research that were previously unconnected to the main line of AIDS virus research. This merging of separate lines represents a synthesis of knowledge on the origin of the virus and its control at the molecular level. It suggests the possibility of strategies for controlling the virus by interfering with its replication or by preventing its attachment to human cells. The recent report of a vaccine for simian AIDS relates to this cluster and holds out the hope that a vaccine for human AIDS is feasible (Bolognesi, 1989). Thus the merger of research on human and simian AIDS that this cluster represents may signal an important step toward more effective therapies.

The second large cluster to split off from the 1987 AIDS virus cluster in 1988 concerns the virus in the central nervous system and the related AIDS dementia complex. It is a continuation of earlier work but the 1988 cluster represents a consolidation of this work, also bringing in a previously unconnected line on neurological manifestations of AIDS. A new finding is how early in the course of the disease the central nervous system can become involved. A related topic is the incidence of toxoplasmosis, an AIDS-related opportunistic infection by a parasite that can invade the nervous system. A small toxoplasmosis cluster also splits off from the 1987 neurologic cluster.

Other developments on the viral front in 1988 are the further splitting of the HTLV-I/II group to yield a separate tropical paraparesis cluster, and a continuation of the lentivirus cluster, suggesting that no dramatic breakthrough has been made relating this virus family to AIDS. Unlike the clinical developments, the viral front did not show the termination of any of its research lines, indicating greater vitality in the latter areas.

## Higher-Level Maps: 1985-1987

The C2 level is one step higher in aggregation than the C1 level we have just described. The C2 clusters consist of C1 clusters just as the C1 clusters consist of core documents. When viewed from this broader perspective, we see AIDS in the context of closely related specialty areas. On these maps the largest clinical and viral AIDS clusters described above are only one step removed from each other, as was the case in 1984. In each year from 1985 to 1988 they were the largest areas on the C2 maps for AIDS and formed the core of a densely linked central network, from which radiated two or more arms several links long.

This same spindly arm structure is seen in its nascent form in the 1984 C2 map. The subject areas represented by these arms varied from year to year but dealt with topics of clear relevance to AIDS. Also each year the density of the central core of AIDS clusters increased while retaining the spindly arm structure.

In 1985 the C2 map contained about 20 C1 clusters in its central core, among them the large viral and clinical clusters described above. One of the two long arms extending from the core was on the topic of CMV infections and other infections brought about by an immune system suppressed by cancer therapy or by antirejection drugs following organ transplants. The other arm dealt with interferon production as a diagnostic tool in immune diseases.

In 1986 the central core of AIDS clusters on the C2 map increased in number and density of linkage, to include about 30 C1 clusters. Three long arms extend from this core: one on interferon again, one on thrombocytopenia purpura, and a third on listeria-monocytogenes infections. In 1987 the central core grows to about 40 C1 clusters that are very tightly linked. Its two extended arms are on blood transfusions and CMV infections, particularly with reference to ocular complications. In 1988 the central core is again about 40 clusters but with three arms: mycobacterium-avium complex infection, CMV infections, and inhibition of viral gene expression. The last name arm is attached to a cluster dealing with the anti-AIDS virus drug AZT, which acts to inhibit virus replication.

The significance of this consistent C2 structure year to year is not clear, although we might hypothesize that it is characteristic of a field that is growing rapidly and rather chaotically. This would account for the dense central regions of each C2. The existence of the extended arms, whose topics change from year to year with some repetitions, such as with CMV infection and interferon production, may reflect a following out of implications that grow rapidly from the body of AIDS research but that ultimately lead away from the main object of investigation, much as an individual's thinking can become sidetracked while working on a difficult problem.

Moving up yet another level from C2 to C3, we reach the point where most of the discipline of biomedicine is visible on a single map. In 1985 and 1986, as in 1984 and 1983, AIDS is just another medium-sized domain in a continent of biomedical research including fields such as immunology, molecular genetics, cancer, and heart disease. From 1984 through 1986 AIDS is consistently attached to the larger field, immunology, which in turn is attached to the largest biomedical area, molecular genetics. The position of AIDS is, however, peripheral within the structure of biomedical fields, which might be expected of any disease area that applies basic biomedical principles. It might be argued that, given the gravity of the AIDS problem, the funding committed to it, and the importance of the basic biology involved, AIDS should be more centrally located in biomedicine. Nevertheless, it is likely to remain peripheral and somewhat isolated from the main biomedical fields for the same reason that its victims are distanced from the rest of society.

In 1987 AIDS does assume a new position and visibility in the structure of science. Prior to 1987 AIDS was contained within the large biomedical C3 cluster. In 1987, however, the increased volume of research and publication and its continued separation from other areas elevated it from its position within biomedicine to the status of a C3 cluster in its own right. It is directly attached to the large biomedical C3 but somewhat removed from the numerous smaller biological and medical domains that appear on the map. In 1987, extending from the AIDS C3 cluster and away from other areas, is an arm of smaller C3s, which, by analogy to the C2 maps, form a kind of trail of implications at the macro scale.

Within the 1987 AIDS C3 itself, we find a small number of related C2 clusters with the unifying theme of infectious diseases. AIDS is the focus of the large, central C2 of this group, which we have described above, and other AIDS clusters mix with the surrounding C2s, making it the main topic of the C3 cluster. AIDS thereby assumes the role of the dominant infectious disease in 1987.

The situation for AIDS in 1988 is very similar to 1987. AIDS continues to hold the status of a C3 region in its own right, attached to the large central biomedical region but unconnected to any other C3 regions. However, in 1988 the AIDS C3 consists of fewer C2 regions on related infectious diseases, thus increasing its isolation from other areas.

## Conclusions

The evolution of AIDS as a research field is still going on. One indicator of its growth is its progression through the cluster-level hierarchy. We first detected AIDS in 1982 as a single cluster of 14 papers. In 1984 AIDS covered multiple clusters and assumed the status of a C2 area. By 1987 the field had grown to such an extent that multiple C2 groups aggregated to form a macro cluster at C3. In 1988 this growth seemed to slow. In any event it seems unlikely that the field can continue to grow much further without seriously encroaching on resources of other fields. But as long as the disease remains unchecked and incurable, the effort is likely to remain at 1987 and 1988 levels.

The character of the research has also changed from clinical description to a preoccupation with halting transmission, as it became clear that a cure was not in the offing. The separation of viral from clinical research stemmed both from the specialized nature of virology and also from the personal dominance of Gallo and his insistence on an HTLV connection. The viral area itself changed as the HTLV connection weakened, and the focus shifted to how the virus affects the brain and its closer relationship to the lentivirus family. In 1988 there is a major shift in the viral area, which has the appearance of a new synthesis of knowledge on the molecular control mechanisms of the virus as well as on new results with animal models of the disease. In cluster terms this is represented as a simultaneous split in the prior AIDS virus cluster and a merger into a new viral cluster of previously unconnected lines of viral research, such as the simian AIDS work. In the new 1988 viral cluster we see the beginnings of work on the design and efficacy of antiviral drugs, such as AZT, and vaccines for AIDS.

The development of AIDS research as revealed by co-citation clusters raises a number of questions regarding the development of scientific fields in general. First, what is the significance of the merging and splitting patterns in the course of development? In a previous study of a research field over time (Small & Greenlee, 1986), we found a kind of pulsation of the field, alternating between small, fragmented areas and large, inclusive ones. Although AIDS shows a more continuous growth pattern, there are significant alternations between fragmentation and connectedness. We hypothesize that merging or increasing connectedness mark periods of synthesis or consolidation, while splitting or weakening of connections mark periods of creativity or innovation, when researchers are working more in isolation. When areas merge, these new pieces of knowledge wrought by creative individuals or small groups are integrated into a collective and consensual whole by the wider community of AIDS researchers. Each synthesis prepares the way for the next wave of fragmentary innovation, and vice versa.

Implicit in this developmental model is that co-citation links at the document level express relations between knowledge claims and can be viewed as syntheses of knowledge, that is, a bringing together of different ideas. Links change over time to express new kinds of understanding. An example is the jump of the three AIDS retrovirus papers from the clinical cluster, where they expressed the need for a viral agent, to the HTLV cluster, where they connected to the prior body of HTLV work. Another example is the forging of new links between simian and human AIDS in 1988. Hence changes in bibliometric structure can correspond to changes in scientific knowledge and understanding.

For predicting or forecasting changes, however, clusters at higher levels of aggregation may be most useful. At higher levels, co-citation links between areas also express syntheses of broader topics. The links are of a more general and stable nature, for example, the relation between AIDS and immunology. But higher-level links can also change dramatically, as did the relation between the HTLV-I/II work and clinical AIDS. In one year they were separated by four intervening clusters, and the next year they were directly linked on the map, reflecting a new understanding of the viral etiology of AIDS. We might also note that in 1983 the MS cluster is a few steps away from AIDS. In 1987 the string shows a merging of HTLV-I and MS, and this connection is now the focus of renewed interest (Drake, 1989).

Can cluster proximity on higher-level maps forecast a merger and synthesis of areas later on (Small & Garfield, 1989)? Or as Swanson seeks, using different methods, can maps be used to suggest hypotheses that scientists could fruitfully explore in the laboratory? Bibliometrics has not claimed that its methods could offer any special insights into scientific knowledge, past or future. Perhaps it is time to address the question of how the tools of bibliometrics could be put to the service of advancing scientific knowledge in actual practice. This is the task now before the field.

KATHERINE W. McCAIN

# 11. Mapping Authors in Intellectual Space: Population Genetics in the 1980s

Multidimensional scaling and clustering analysis of the co-citation patterns of 58 authors are used to explore the intellectual structure of population genetics and related specialties. In two dimensions, author clusters are arranged along a horizontal continuum reflecting a range of research specializations from highly molecular-oriented research to that focusing on the analysis of organisms with each other and their environment. The vertical dimension separates theoretical (formal) approaches from research that is primarily experimental or observational in nature. Author placement and cluster assignment may also reflect institutional affiliations and national research efforts. Co-cited author mapping, with the author as the unit of analysis, is likely to complement studies of informal communication networks.

Articles published in scholarly journals are a major formal channel of communication in the social and natural sciences. They serve,

AUTHOR'S NOTE: I am extremely grateful to the many population geneticists who were so generous with their time. I thank Richard Lewontin, Museum of Comparative Zoology, Harvard University; Warren Ewens and Harry Harris, University of Pennsylvania; Ron Burton, University of Houston (currently); Bonnie Bowen, (then) Villanova University; and Fred Schnee, Temple University, for granting extensive personal interviews. Michael Clegg, University of California, Riverside, and Philip Hedrick, Pennsylvania State University, participated in lengthy telephone conversations. I owe a particularly large debt to Bill Marks, Villanova University, and Marty Kreitman, Princeton University, for their willingness to discuss the project in all its phases and allow me to try out my ideas on them. The study is much the better for their friendly criticism and useful suggestions. I hasten to add that any errors of fact or interpretation are absolutely my own. This project was supported in part by a Faculty Development Minigrant from Drexel University and in part by the College of Information Studies. An abbreviated version of this chapter appeared in *Communication Research*, 16, 667-681.

among other functions, as a public archival record of individual scientific research activities (Garvey, 1989; Subramanyam, 1981; Ziman, 1968). Journal articles report research results, and announce the creation of experimental materials and research products and their viability for authors' use (McCain, 1989).

In bibliometric studies, the citations (references) in journal articles are analyzed as unobtrusive tokens of citing authors' use of this previously published information (Smith, 1981; White & McCain, 1989). Here, the choice of works to be cited in a scholarly paper is assumed to reflect the organization of a scientific community and its knowledge base, as perceived by the citing authors, and the value placed by the community (and the author) on previous contributions. Simple counts—of publications by authors and institutions as well as of citations of documents, authors, and journals—are a common approach to identifying the core literatures, central institutions, and major contributions in a field.

In contrast to document co-citation studies, co-cited *author* studies use frequently cited and co-cited authors' names as the unit of analysis (see the chapters by White and by Small & Greenlee in this volume). Here, the author's name represents an *oeuvre*—one or more single or coauthored (of which he or she is the first author) documents. Two authors are co-cited when at least one document in each author's oeuvre occurs in the same reference list. Elements of intellectual structure are likely to be at a higher level of generality than those observed in document clusters and maps: broad research schools of thought that guide or constrain scholarly activity, and overall trends or dimensions in scholars' approach toward research. Changes in co-cited author maps are less common than in the mapped document clusters and represent major shifts in research activity and scholarly orientation within the field, on the part of either the cited or the citing authors (McCain, 1984, 1985, 1986a).

Most previous co-cited author studies have explored various research areas in the social sciences (Bayer, Smart, & McLaughlin, 1984; Hopkins, 1984; McCain, 1983, 1984, 1985, 1986b; White, 1983; White & Griffith, 1981a, 1981b, 1982). This research showed that, although author clusters can represent a variety of field-specific social, geographic, temporal, and intellectual associations, authors and clusters are consistently arranged along two intellectual dimensions. One dimension is subject related and represents authors' choice of research topics; the other reflects the relative incorporation of formal approaches and quantitative analysis in their published research. Similarly, in a co-cited author mapping of *Drosophila* genetics, the genetics of fruit flies (McCain, 1985, 1986a, 1986b), the subject-based dimension represented a continuum of research interests across *Drosophila* genetics. The "formal" axis was illustrated by author cluster groups representing two distinctly different methodological approaches to research—population genetics and experimental analysis of gene structure, function, and expression in individual organisms.

The present study and White's essay in this volume are complementary. White presents a general overview of co-citation studies, with emphasis on the rationale, research goals, and major findings of co-cited author studies to date. In contrast, this chapter reports the results of a co-cited author analysis of population genetics and related areas, including details of data gathering, manipulation, and analysis and a discussion of the resulting maps and clusters.

## The Present Study

As the earlier study of *Drosophila* genetics suggested, population genetics research takes a primarily formal and mathematical approach to a variety of biological and genetic questions. Population genetics deals with the breeding structure and genetic composition of populations (Wallace, 1981). Research in population genetics is grounded in theory—formal mathematical and statistical modeling of the dynamic processes underlying changes in the genetic structure of populations over time. Theory both draws from and directs the analysis of genetic variation in populations obtained through observation and experiment, increasingly at the molecular level (Hedrick, 1985; Merrill, 1981). Quantitative genetics differs from population genetics (strictly speaking) in that the former is concerned with the inheritance of quantitative continuous traits (such as height, weight, resistance to pesticides) affected by a number of genes that are cumulative in their effect (Crow, 1986). By contrast, population genetics' focus tends to be on models or analysis of relatively clear-cut qualitative traits generally attributed to variation in single genes or small groups of genes, such as the variants in the enzyme alcohol dehydrogenase in the fruit fly and human ABO blood types. Finally, research in population and quantitative genetics is central to our understanding of the mechanisms underlying the evolutionary process. Field and laboratory studies, as well as theoretical modeling, have shown how natural selection and random variation produce gene frequency changes in populations—that is, evolutionary changes resulting in the development of new species.

Questions addressed in this study come both from previous observations and from the subject literature. They include the following:

(1) Texts such as Crow's *Basic Concepts in Population, Quantitative, and Evolutionary Genetics* (1986) stress the intellectual connections between these three areas. To what extent are population genetics, quantitative genetics, and evolutionary theory perceived as interrelated by researchers publishing in the 1980s?

(2) How are subject-based and formal/nonformal dimensions expressed in disciplines with a strong *overall* theoretical/mathematical orientation?

(3) Hedrick (1985) describes three major approaches to population genetics research: theoretical, experimental, and empirical work. (The last represents studies of *observed* genetic variation in naturally occurring populations.) To what extent are these distinctions visible in the co-citation networks that reflect citing authors' *perceptions* of others' work and their *use* of published research?

(4) A 1983 workshop on population genetics, sponsored by the National Institutes of Health, identified a number of recent changes in population genetics research (Anonymous, 1983). Research was characterized as shifting away from "the dominance of electrophoresis" and the "bitter debates" focusing on the presence and importance of neutral genetic variation (genetic changes not subject to natural selection). The increasing complexity (and decreasing biological relevance) of theoretical population genetics was noted, as was a "recent resurgence of interest in theoretical quantitative genetics." The impact of experimental research at the molecular level, particularly that using recombinant DNA techniques to study the genetics of human diseases, was emphasized. Future research directions included a call for collaboration between molecular and population geneticists and an "exploration of the interface of ecology and genetics." To what extent are any of these trends visible in the co-cited author mapping of literatures spanning the time in which these characterizations were made?

# Methods

The following section includes brief discussions of several major points in the process of data gathering, manipulation, and analysis, with accompanying illustration. A much more detailed account of procedures for author co-citation analysis, including a technical bibliography listing useful texts and software can be found in McCain (1990). The techniques of co-cited author retrieval are discussed in detail by White (1986). The reader is referred to these articles for more extensive treatment.

## Author Selection

Co-cited author mapping uses a set of authors' names, representing a varied range of research activities in a given field, to define that field, that is, the scholarly universe being explored and mapped. Researchers may start with a predetermined list of authors. Hopkins (1984), for instance, examined co-citation patterns within two "coherent groups" in sociology using authors listed in Mullins's (1973) study. On the other hand, if the researcher's goal is an overall examination of the intellectual structure of some area of scholarship, as in this study, it is critical to establish a diversified list of authors, possibly from a variety of sources. These may include published materials (reviews, texts, monographs), consultation with researchers in the area studied, personal knowledge, lists (membership directories, conference attendance lists, awards lists), or authors publishing in a particular set of journals (this last exemplified in the work of Penan, 1989).

For this study, the author set was assembled using a combination of print sources and knowledgeable informants. In this way, the current diversity of research specializations and organisms studied could be included as well as a historical overview of research development. The list began with seven of the eight population geneticists from the study of *Drosophila* genetics (McCain, 1985, 1986a, 1986b) and several prominent evolutionary theorists. Current texts, monographs, and review articles encompassing some major portions of the study scope were scanned for frequently cited authors. Several population geneticists critiqued these lists and provided names of both prominent scholars who had been missed and younger, less visible researchers whose work was gaining prominence.

TABLE 11.1
Co-Cited Author List for Population, Quantitative, and Evolutionary Genetics

| | | |
|---|---|---|
| R. W. Allard | R. A. Fisher | J. Maynard Smith |
| W. W. Anderson | W. M. Fitch | E. Mayr |
| C. F. Aquadro | J. Gillespie | N. Morton |
| J. C. Avise | M. Goodman | T. Mukai |
| F. J. Ayala | J. B. S. Haldane | T. Nagylaki |
| W. F. Bodmer | W. D. Hamilton | M. Nei |
| H. L. Carson | H. Harris | J. V. Neel |
| L. L. Cavalli-Sforza | D. L. Hartl | T. Ohta |
| R. Chakraborty | P. W. Hedrick | P. A. Parsons |
| B. Charlesworth | S. Karlin | A. Robertson |
| M. T. Clegg | M. Kimura | J. Roughgarden |
| J. Coyne | M. Kreitman | R. K. Selander |
| J. F. Crow | C. H. Langley | E. B. Spiess |
| T. H. Dobzhansky | R. Lande | G. L. Stebbins |
| L. Ehrman | D. A. Levin | J. M. Thoday |
| W. J. Ewens | R. C. Lewontin | M. Turelli |
| D. S. Falconer | W-H. Li | B. Wallace |
| M. W. Feldman | T. Maruyama | M. J. D. White |
| J. Felsenstein | K. Mather | A. C. Wilson |
| | | S. Wright |

The final author set is shown in Table 11.1. It includes research spanning the three major topics of the title; several "generations" of scholars, from the "founders" of theoretical population genetics (Wright, Haldane, Fisher), and later major figures in the various fields (e.g., Dobzhansky, Lewontin, Crow, Nei, Falconer, Thoday, Allard, Stebbins) to very recent authors (Kreitman and Aquadro); research focusing on a variety of organisms; and research in all three of Hedrick's (1985) categories.

## Data Collection

Each author's name represents a (partial) cited body of work—that work of which he or she is the first author. As illustrated in Figure 11.1, all authors' names were searched online, via DIALOG, in SCISEARCH File 87 (1981-1983) and File 34 (1984-February 1987).[1]

## Data Compilation and Analysis

Co-citation frequency counts for all author pairs were summed over the two files and assembled in a square matrix, with rows and columns labeled by cited authors' names. The values in the diagonal cells were treated as "missing data."[2]

Not all authors searched will have substantial citation or co-citation frequencies. Authors who consistently publish as coauthors, in the second or a subsequent position, will not be visible in the retrievals based on these contributions (see McCain, 1988, for a discussion of co-cited author retrieval in a highly collaborative specialty). Other authors may have entered the field relatively recently and, although well known among the research community, may not have built up a substantial citation history. Certain authors may even communicate the majority of their research results via informal channels and never publish in the research literature. The authors retained for analysis in this study had a mean co-citation rate above five (for six years of SCISEARCH data).[3]

As shown in Figure 11.2, this raw data matrix was converted to a matrix of proximity values—Pearson product-moment correlations among the various author pairs—using the FACTOR procedure in SPSSX (a program having a "pairwise deletion" option for missing data). Each correlation between two authors represents the similarity in co-citation pattern of the two across all the other authors in the set, with the exception of the two being compared. The use of the correlation coefficient has two advantages: It is a measure of *overall* similarity of use of the works of two authors (rather than simple pair co-citation frequency) and it also reduces the effects of difference in "scale" of citation and co-citation (Kerlinger, 1973).

In the matrix, the correlations function as "inverse distances"—the more similar two authors are, the higher their positive correlation, and the more closely they would be linked by clustering and placed by mapping.

The internal structure of this correlation matrix was explored using cluster analysis[4] (SPSSX CLUSTER: Ward's method and Complete Linkage approaches) to identify groups of authors with high intercorrelations, and multidimensional scaling (SPSSX ALSCAL) to display the overall relationships among authors in a two-dimensional map. As a rule, the two clustering methods produce slightly different set of clusters from the same correlation matrix. By comparing the results of the two, it is possible to identify boundary-spanning authors—those with strong links to more than one definable author aggregation.

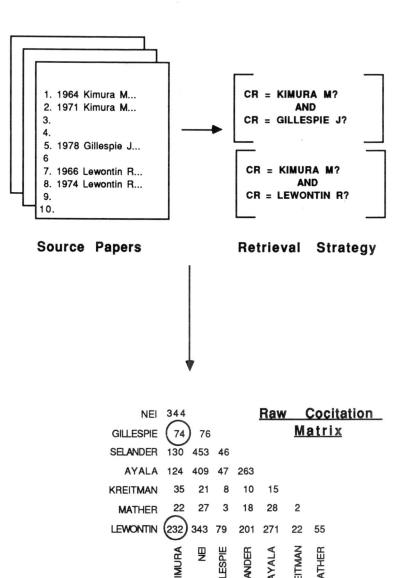

**Figure 11.1.** Population, Quantitative, and Evolutionary Genetics, 1981-1986—I

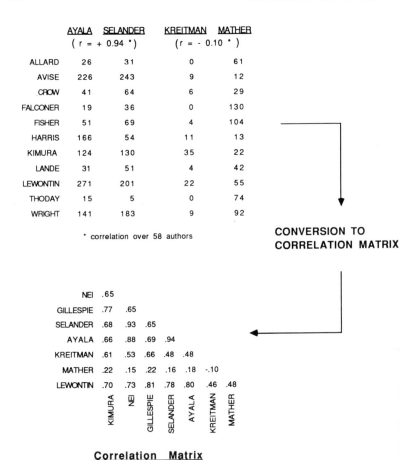

| | AYALA | SELANDER | KREITMAN | MATHER |
|---|---|---|---|---|
| | (r = + 0.94 *) | | (r = - 0.10 * ) | |
| ALLARD | 26 | 31 | 0 | 61 |
| AVISE | 226 | 243 | 9 | 12 |
| CROW | 41 | 64 | 6 | 29 |
| FALCONER | 19 | 36 | 0 | 130 |
| FISHER | 51 | 69 | 4 | 104 |
| HARRIS | 166 | 54 | 11 | 13 |
| KIMURA | 124 | 130 | 35 | 22 |
| LANDE | 31 | 51 | 4 | 42 |
| LEWONTIN | 271 | 201 | 22 | 55 |
| THODAY | 15 | 5 | 0 | 74 |
| WRIGHT | 141 | 183 | 9 | 92 |

* correlation over 58 authors

**CONVERSION TO CORRELATION MATRIX**

| | KIMURA | NEI | GILLESPIE | SELANDER | AYALA | KREITMAN | MATHER |
|---|---|---|---|---|---|---|---|
| NEI | .65 | | | | | | |
| GILLESPIE | .77 | .65 | | | | | |
| SELANDER | .68 | .93 | .65 | | | | |
| AYALA | .66 | .88 | .69 | .94 | | | |
| KREITMAN | .61 | .53 | .66 | .48 | .48 | | |
| MATHER | .22 | .15 | .22 | .16 | .18 | -.10 | |
| LEWONTIN | .70 | .73 | .81 | .78 | .80 | .46 | .48 |

**Correlation Matrix**

**Figure 11.2.** Population, Quantitative, and Evolutionary Genetics, 1981-1986—II

## Interpretation

Information to interpret and qualitatively validate the results of the clustering and mapping came from two sources: (a) the context and content of citations to the authors' work in texts and reviews and (b) extended personal interviews (eight) and telephone interviews (two) with population geneticists representing various research venues covered in the study.

# Results

Figure 11.3 shows a cluster-enhanced two-dimensional map of population, quantitative, and evolutionary genetics, based on the citing literature from 1981 through 1986.[5] The axes of the map, as output by the MDS program, are shown as dotted lines.

The relative positions of authors reflect their perceived similarity as represented by co-citation in the citing literature and as measured by the correlation between citation profiles. The more similar two authors are perceived to be, the closer they will be placed in the map. Authors with many links to others will be placed near the center of the map, whereas authors whose work is not seen as related are likely to be placed at some distance. In Figure 11.3, each author's position is indicated by his or her mean co-citation rate with the 57 other authors in the map. This mean co-citation rate serves as a rough measure of prominence or visibility; accordingly, mean rates over 45 are circled for emphasis. A low rate can reflect the recency of an author's contributions (Kreitman's first major paper was published in 1983), resulting in a small bulk of citations and co-citations. Alternatively, it may represent a generally lower frequency of co-citation across the field or an author's intellectual connections to only one portion of the field.

Summary co-citation statistics for this set of 58 authors are shown in Table 11.2. The number of papers co-citing two authors (oeuvres) varied from 0 (the connection was never made in the citing literature) to 453 (the number of articles co-citing works by Nei and Selander). On the average, a given pair of authors were co-cited in 32 papers published from 1981 through 1986. The Connectivity Ratio (percentage of unique pairings made) can be used as an indication of the degree of intellectual linkage or "connectedness" across a co-cited author set. At the time these data were collected from the Institute for Scientific Information (ISI) files, 98% of the possible unique author connections had been made in at least one citing paper, with only 38 pairs of authors never co-cited.[6] Almost twice as many pairings were made only once in the six years of citing literature. These single pairings tended to be made between relatively "distant" authors (e.g., Ehrman and Wilson, Fitch and Allard, Feldman and Aquadro). Approximately half of these single co-citations were made in review articles, with Lewontin's (1985a) review of population genetics contributing eight single pairings. The

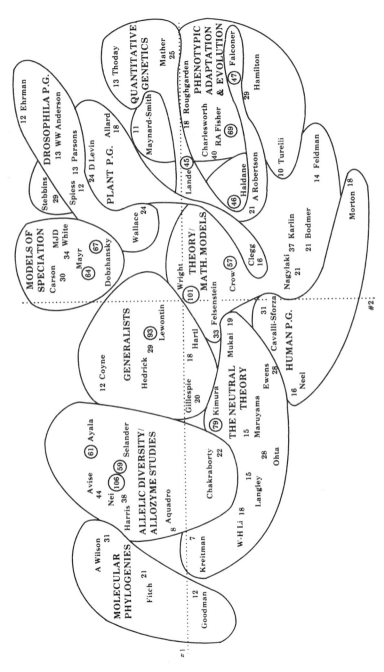

**Figure 11.3.** Population, Quantitative, and Evolutionary Genetics, 1981-1986—III

204

TABLE 11.2
Summary Statistics

| | |
|---|---|
| Mean co-citation rate (over 57 authors) | 32 |
| Range of raw co-citation counts | 0-453 (Nei & Selander) |
| Range of mean co-citation rates | 7-106 (Kreitman—low; Nei—high) |
| Number of unique author pairings never made | 38 (connectivity ratio - 98%) |
| pairings made only once · | 75 |

other half represent intellectual connections made in the research literature.

The two clustering programs (Complete Linkage and Ward's method) produced almost identical results (Table 11.3); the few authors differing in cluster assignment are highlighted in italic type. For simplicity, only the Ward's method clusters (11 cluster level) are shown on the map. Cluster labels are impressionistic reflections of the intellectual links among the authors and their contributions, developed from information gathered in interviews and analysis of citation context in texts and reviews.

The arrangement of clusters along the horizontal axis appears to reflect the source of the information used to answer evolutionary questions, from clusters representing highly molecular-oriented research to studies of variation, selection, and speciation via the analysis of interactions of organisms with each other and with their environment.

At the far left, the Molecular Phylogenies cluster includes three authors linked by research on the evolution of proteins, the idea of a "molecular clock," and the construction of evolutionary histories based on these data and assumptions. Molecular *evolution* was described in interviews as a large and important field that was peripheral and poorly connected to population genetics per se. There are links between the two, however, including the use, by evolutionary classification theorists, of Nei's (Allozymes cluster) measure of genetic distance to create phylogenetic trees based on molecular data. Also, the concept of a molecular clock assumes a constant rate of mutation, a prediction incorporated in the Neutral Theory. Nei's recent monograph on molecular population genetics (Nei, 1987) was used as a source for authors' names.

TABLE 11.3

Population, Quantitative, and Evolutionary Genetics: 1981-1986—Co-Cited Author Clusters

| *Complete Linkage* | *Ward's Method* |
|---|---|
| Molecular phyiogenies:<br>  Goodman, Fitch, Wilson | Molecular phylogenies:<br>  Goodman, Fitch, Wilson |
| Allelic Diversity/Allozyme studies:<br>  Aquadro, Chakraborty, Nei<br>  Ayala, Avise, Selander, Harris | Allelic Diversity/Allozyme studies:<br>  Aquadro, Chakraborty, Nei<br>  Ayala, Avise, Selander, Harris |
| Generalists:<br>  Coyne, Hedrick, Lewontin<br>  Gillespie, Hartl, *Mukai* | Generalists:<br>  Coyne, Hedrick, Lewontin<br>  Gillespie, Hartl |
| The Neutral Theory:<br>  Kreitman, Langley, W. Li<br>  Ohta, Maruyama, Kimura | The Neutral Theory:<br>  Kreitman, Langley, W. Li<br>  Ohta, Maruyama, Kimura<br>  *Mukai, Ewens* |
| Human population genetics:<br>  Neel, Morton, Cavalli-Sforza | Human population genetics:<br>  Neel, Morton, Cavalli-Sforza |
| Theory/mathematical models:<br>  Nagylaki, Bodmer, Karlin, Feldman<br>  Crow, Haldane, Felsenstein, Wright<br>  *Ewens, Turelli, Roughgarden* | Theory/mathematical models:<br>  Nagylaki, Bodmer, Karlin, Feldman<br>  Crow, Haldane, Felsenstein, Wright |
| Plant population genetics:<br>  Allard, Clegg | Plant population genetics:<br>  Allard, Clegg, *Stebbins, D. Levin* |
| Quantitative genetics:<br>  Lande, Robertson, Falconer<br>  Mather, Thoday | Quantitative genetics:<br>  Lande, Robertson, Falconer<br>  Mather, Thoday |
| *Drosophila* population genetics:<br>  Spiess, Parsons, Ehrman<br>  Anderson, Wallace | *Drosophila* population genetics:<br>  Spiess, Parsons, Ehrman<br>  Anderson, Wallace |
| Models of speciation:<br>  White, Mayr, Dobzhansky, Carson<br>  *Stebbins, D. Levin* | Models of speciation:<br>  White, Mayr, Dobzhansky, Carson |
| Phenotypic adaptation & evolution:<br>  Maynard-Smith, Hamilton, Fisher | Phenotypic adaptation & evolution:<br>  Maynard-Smith, Hamilton, Fisher,<br>  Charlesworth<br>  *Turelli, Roughgarden* |

Much of the research represented in the Generalists and Allelic Diversity/Allozyme Studies (Allozymes) clusters has been concerned with measuring the amount of genetic variation present in populations. Work in the Allozymes cluster focuses on this question, using gel electrophoresis and newer genetic engineering techniques to study the structure and frequencies of gene coding for different versions of the same enzymes (Allozymes). Nei is the major theorist associated with statistical analyses and interpretation of these data, with Ayala and Selander the most prominent "applied" researchers. Research of authors in the Generalists cluster is more diverse. For instance, Lewontin's oeuvre includes highly cited theoretical work (multilocus theory) and experimental contributions as well as at least one major technical innovation.[7] His influence on population genetics derives both through his own work and that of his graduate students and postdoctoral associates (including Hedrick and Coyne in this cluster and Kreitman in the one below).

The Neutral Theory cluster represents a debate centering on the evolutionary role of much of the genetic variation observed in populations—whether the bulk of genetic variation is maintained by Darwinian natural selection or whether this variation is selectively "neutral." In the latter case, changes in frequency of different alleles from one generation to the next represent random fluctuation (genetic drift, or the "Sewall Wright effect"). The arguments are most commonly presented as mathematical models, with data provided largely by Allozyme and Generalist researchers. This cluster includes theoretical population geneticists (Kimura, Ohta, Maruyama, Li, and Ewens) and authors (Kreitman, Langley, and Mukai) whose experimental and observational findings are discussed in the literature in the context of this debate.

The lower-central section of the map includes two related clusters. Three authors (Neel, Cavalli-Sforza, and Morton) represent Human Population Geneticists. Neel has studied genetic variation and mutation rates in groups such as the Yanomama Indians of South America. Cavalli-Sforza has published extensively on human population genetics and evolution and has coauthored with both Feldman and Bodmer (Theory/Mathematical Models). Morton, a student of Crow, is most frequently cited for mathematical modeling of human population structure and human genetic diseases.

The Theory/Mathematical Models (Theory) cluster includes Wright and J. B. S. Haldane, two of the three founders of theoretical population genetics (the third is R. A. Fisher). Wright is the most prominent author in this group (as well as the most central), having been an active contributor to theoretical population genetics for over 50 years. Crow is primarily known as an important "second-generation" theorist in the tradition of Sewall Wright and as a proponent of the Neutral Theory (along with his students, Kimura and Ohta). Other authors are recognized and cited for contributions in multilocus theory—mathematical models of selection and evolution that consider systems of two or more genes. Many, particularly those in the lower "lobe" of the cluster (e.g., Karlin and Feldman), tend to be described as "hard-core theorists," primarily trained as mathematicians, who latterly became interested in population genetics questions. Their work was characterized as highly formal, intensely mathematical, and difficult for many researchers to approach. The Human Population Genetics and Theory clusters are linked through authors such as Bodmer, Karlin, and Feldman, whose work includes statistical analysis and mathematical modeling in human population genetics (as does the *current* work of Ewens, in the Neutral Theory cluster).

Models of Speciation includes an "older generation" of authors whose work has addressed the roles of various types of isolation in the development of new species. Their "theoretical" contributions are basically descriptive rather than highly mathematical. Dobzhansky and Mayr are the dominant figures. Dobzhansky, a student of T. H. Morgan, established *Drosophila* population genetics. His students in this map include Anderson, Ehrman, Spiess, and Wallace in the adjoining cluster, and Lewontin and Ayala on the left-hand side. Mayr is generally considered an evolutionary biologist, an interpreter of evolutionary genetics, and a critic of mathematical genetics. His presence in this map reflects the influence of his writings (especially *Animal Species and Evolution*, 1963) and his intellectual position as a strong proponent of geographic isolation (allopatry) as a requirement for species formation.

The five authors in the adjoining cluster represent experimental and observational work concentrating on *Drosophila*. Parsons, an Australian, is an ecological geneticist with a strong interest in various aspects of the genetic basis of environmental adaptations in *Drosophila*. He has coauthored (second author) a text in general behavioral genetics with Ehrman. Parsons, Ehrman, and Spiess have all written on aspects of the mating behavior of *Drosophila*.

The Plant Population Genetics cluster consists of two subgroups with divergent orientations. In overviews of the historical development of evolutionary theory, Stebbins is often characterized as the "botanical" counterpart of Dobzhansky, Mayr, and others, who were early exponents of the modern "Evolutionary Synthesis" (see, e.g., the discussion in Futuyma, 1986, pp. 10-13). He is linked with D. A. Levin, whose work has also focused on genetic variation, isolation, and speciation in plants. The two are clustered with their "zoological" counterparts (in terms of interests) by the Complete Linkage clustering and with the other pair of plant population geneticists by Ward's method. The other subgroup, Allard and Clegg, are professor and student, respectively. Allard is an experimental plant population geneticist working primarily on breeding patterns within plant populations. Clegg's oeuvre, by contrast, has included work on both plants and *Drosophila*. His theoretical work on *Drosophila* appears to be the portion of his oeuvre that has had the greatest impact on the literature of the 1980s.

Quantitative Genetics links four "older-generation" British geneticists (Falconer, Mather, Thoday, and Robertson) with Lande, a major recent contributor, whose work brings quantitative genetics and population genetics together through his theoretical (mathematical) models of the evolution of quantitative traits. The marked distortion of this cluster in the map arises from secondary links between the quantitative genetics authors and those in other clusters. Thoday, for instance, worked almost exclusively on *Drosophila* and is located near other fly geneticists, while Robertson, a theoretician, is placed in the midst of (largely British) theorists.

Phenotypic Adaptation and Evolution includes various authors who have developed mathematical models of the relationship between phenotype and fitness—the evolution of various adaptive phenotypic traits and life history characteristics of populations. Four British theorists, Fisher, Hamilton, Maynard Smith, and Charlesworth, are grouped by both clustering programs. Roughgarden and Turelli, two U.S. researchers, form a separate subgroup. In the literature of the 1980s, Fisher's work appears to be particularly relevant to researchers interested in understanding selection mechanisms and evolution of social/behavioral traits affecting the interactions of organisms (Maynard Smith and Hamilton) and in models incorporating demographic variables such as age and geographic dispersion (Charlesworth and Roughgarden). Turelli, primarily identified as a theorist, has extended Roughgarden's work in modeling variable environments. This links him with Roughgarden in the 1980s literature and may account for their joint connection to the Theory cluster (as mathematical theorists) and to the Phenotypic Variation cluster (as modelers concerned with these issues).

## Interpretation of Map Axes

As noted earlier, research along the horizontal axis ranges from highly molecular-oriented research to authors studying variation, selection, and speciation via the analysis of interactions of organisms with each other and with their environment. The continuum appears to reflect the source of the information used to answer evolutionary questions. From left to right, authors' research includes theoretical modeling or experimental/observational analysis of genetic variation in populations and change over time at the level of

(1) nucleotide sequences or restriction sites in lengths of DNA molecules representing individual genes,

(2) amino acid sequences representing differences among proteins (coded for by individual genes),

(3) chromosome variation (e.g., inversions) within populations,

(4) differences in phenotypic expression of inherited characteristics deriving from single genes or many genes working in concert, and

(5) the genetic basis of organisms' interactions with each other and with the environment.

The vertical axis separates authors based on the *perceived* formal content of their oeuvre. This split is emphasized in Figure 11.4. Here, cluster boundaries are eliminated and authors' names and mean co-citation rates removed. Hedrick's three-part classification is used, with the term *observational* substituted for *empirical*. Authors' positions are indicated on the map by codes representing the perceived content of their oeuvres—theoretical (T), experimental (X), observational (O), or some combination of the three. Authors whose work is characterized by citation context and in interviews as primarily *theoretical* tend to be placed below the midline by the mapping program, with the mathematical population geneticists of the Theory/Mathematical Models cluster the farthest out. Authors whose major contributions are described as generally experimental or observational (e.g., research based on observations

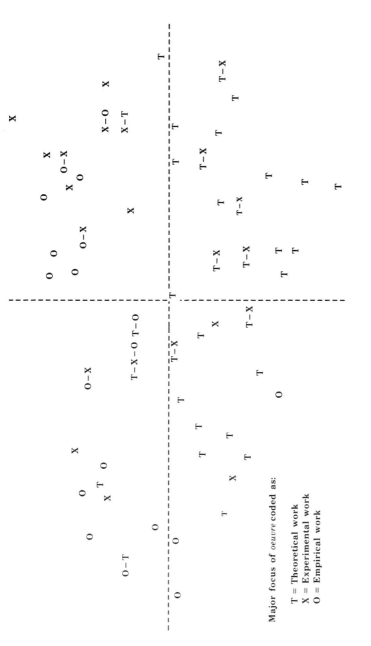

**Figure 11.4.** Population, Quantitative, and Evolutionary Genetics, 1981-1986—IV

of naturally occurring variation rather than the results of laboratory manipulation of breeding populations) are generally found above the midline—distributed across the upper half of the map. Authors perceived as combining "theory" and "experiment" are more common below the midline; those whose work includes both "observation" and "experiment" are found above.

## Discussion

Co-cited author studies provide one view of the organization of scholarly specialties—a view representing the consensus of a very large number of scholars concerning the representatives among important writers in the field. They are most usefully employed as one of a set of "multiple indicators," complementing and cross-validating analyses of data representing scholars' perceptions of the field, social relationships, and informal communication networks. (See, for example, Hargens, Mullins, & Hecht, 1980; Lievrouw, Rogers, Lowe, & Nadel, 1987; McCain, 1986b; Mullins, Hargens, Hecht, & Kick, 1987.) Taken together, bibliometric, sociometric, cognitive, and communication data provide the researcher with overlapping, incompletely congruent views of structure in a chosen research specialty. Although it is unlikely that *all* differences between analyses can be explained (and the researcher should not strain to account for all anomalous observations), an exploration of these differences can highlight the particular advantages of one approach vis-à-vis another.

In this study, for instance, the co-cited author clusters and the placement of authors in the two-dimensional map both appear to correspond well with characterizations of the author's work obtained in texts, reviews, and interviews. Authors tend to be associated with and placed near those others with whom they share common research interests (with the same or strongly opposing views) or with whom they have strong institutional, national, educational, and/or social ties. Those authors placed in different clusters by the two algorithms had clearly identifiable links to different bodies of research literature. In interviews, the various map features generally "made sense" to the geneticists in that they tended to see, based on their own knowledge, reasonable connections among the authors and their contributions.

One major exception was the Adaptation cluster. Here, although the aggregate association is made in text discussion (see, e.g., Futuyma, 1986, chap. 9), interviewed geneticists saw little coherence among the six clustered authors, although they were comfortable with selected subgroups based on nationality or specific research content of their oeuvres. This difference appears to reflect the orientation of most of the geneticists with whom in-person interviews were conducted. Most have roots in, and tend to do research in, areas represented on the left-hand side of the map. It may be that, although they are *aware* of the contributions of many of the Adaptation authors (certainly those of Fisher), they may not be very deeply involved with major portions of these authors' oeuvres. White (this volume) cites a similar instance in a comment of Derek Price on the map of information science authors (White & Griffith, 1981a): Price knew "everyone about halfway across and then no one." Similarly, one of the subjects (right side based) in the present study was very familiar with the authors and their contributions for half the map but was familiar with those on the other half only if they had written major texts. It seems evident that well-designed co-cited author studies can go beyond the knowledge and insights available from even the most knowledgeable, well-connected single researcher in the field. Were authors selected for mapping whose works were *really* not relevant to the field, it could be easily demonstrated by their lack of reasonable levels of co-citation, resulting in a marked isolation on the map and inability to cluster with other authors. That was certainly not the case in this multidisciplinary area.

## Mapping Research Activity

Co-cited author mapping is an analysis of past patterns of information generation and use, reflecting citing authors' perceptions of the nature and content of existing oeuvres. Because of the time required for research results to be transferred into the formal literature and to be cited, for the aggregation of citations to an authors' oeuvre, and for the cumulation of several years' citation data, co-cited author maps can provide a general historical view of the intellectual structure of a research area.

Thus the co-cited author map of population, quantitative, and evolutionary genetics covering the citing literature from 1981

through 1986 highlights *relatively* current research topics and
trends noted in the 1983 NIH population genetics workshop. The
"Neutralist-Selectionist" debate of the 1970s is still prominent, as
are "applied" studies of allelic diversity; the perceived importance
of newer molecular genetic approaches in these latter studies is
reflected in the relatively high mean co-citation rate to Kreitman's
(1983 and later) work (and likely the more recent contributions of
Aquadro and Avise as well): peripheral location of the "hard-core
mathematicians" in the Theory cluster supports the characterization of this work as "increasingly complex" and having "decreasing
biological relevance." Increasing interest in theoretical quantitative
genetics is demonstrated in Lande's high co-citation rate in the
Quantitative Genetics cluster. A subsequent mapping, based on data
for the late 1980s and early 1990s, could test the success of the calls
for research in "the interface between ecology and genetics" and for
collaboration between molecular and population genetics as well
as testing the impact of recombinant DNA techniques in studies of
the genetics of human diseases.[8]

## Mapping Science

Price (1979) speculated that the major features of science could be
demonstrated in two-dimensional maps. This study adds additional
support to his suggestion. Here, as in previous co-cited author maps,
authors and clusters are arranged along a subject dimension and a
"style of work" dimension. The horizontal continuum from molecular
questions to "biological" questions is a close parallel to that seen
in the *Drosophila* genetics map. Overall, the vertical dimension
reflects, in this relatively quantitative set of fields, an increasingly mathematical formalization of theory in authors' work. The
strong vertical partitioning of oeuvres perceived as "mathematical/
theoretical" versus "experimental" and "observational" in content is
similar to the sharp division between single-gene experimental and
*Drosophila* genetics and *Drosophila* population genetics. One noticeable departure from this distribution is the placement of Nei in the
upper-left quadrant, reflecting his strong ties (as a theorist) to the
experimental and observational research focusing on estimation of
genetic diversity.

In interviews, the most common distinction made by subjects in
describing the intellectual organization of population genetics was

that between "theory" and "applied" or "empirical" research. Theory generally meant mathematical modeling (more or less approachable by nonmathematicians), while applied research included *both* studies of variation in natural populations (in the laboratory and the field) as well as experimental studies of breeding populations in laboratory settings. This perceived dichotomy is also clearly demonstrated in the map, based on publishing authors' use of prior work. Hedrick's distinction between experimental and observational (empirical) work could be made by subjects when the explicit question was asked but generally was not offered spontaneously; neither are these two modes of research distinguished on the map.

## Summary

Co-cited author mapping shows the type of structure deriving from information transfer through formal communication channels and the use of this information in subsequent formal communication as well as the associated intellectual and citation links between mentors and students working in the same research tradition. The data are limited in the extent to which they can demonstrate networks of collaboration in research, for instance, between a "theorist" and an "applied" researcher, because each author's oeuvre represents first or sole-authored works only. Coauthorship patterns may be implied in many cases, if each author has a sufficiently large oeuvre, but are not directly visible.

Still, communication researchers should find much of value in co-cited author mapping. The co-citation data are easily gotten and amenable to analysis using a variety of well-established techniques to explore hidden patterns within large matrices. They are derived from a much larger body of literature than is likely to be manageable using subject bibliographies or core journal lists. They represent an aggregate consensus that is likely to influence, if not constrain, information use and communication patterns. Finally, using the *author* as the unit of analysis allows the researcher to study several complementary aspects of scholarly activity—the intellectual structure, based on links among bodies of published work; the cognitive structure, deriving from citing authors' perceptions of their field; and the interpersonal networks among the currently publishing mapped authors, including patterns of collaboration and coauthorship, social structure, and informal communication networks.

## Notes

1. The truncation symbol (?) generalizes the search request to all cited works by an author, of which he or she is the first or sole author.

2. Another alternative is to insert an artificial "scaled" value in the diagonal cell. See White and Griffith (1981a) for this approach and McCain (1990) for general discussion.

3. In general, researchers concerned with the possible instability of small co-citation counts have selected for further analysis only those authors meeting certain ad hoc criteria—for example, mean co-citation rates above nine (for ten years' SOCIAL SCISEARCH data) or above four (for five years' SCISEARCH data) and co-citation with at least one-third of the entire author set (McCain, 1985; Griffith, personal communication). Penan (1989) has experimented with proportional thresholds. All results have been satisfactory in terms of face validity and interpretability of the maps and clusters.

4. Both of these clustering programs have been used successfully in a number of co-cited author mapping studies, as has VARCLUS, a "top-down splitting algorithm" based on principal components analysis. One other popular algorithm, "K-means" clustering, does not produce interpretable results. See discussion in McCain (1990).

5. The stress measure is a criterion for determining the "best fit" between the original input matrix "distances" and the estimated distances in the chosen low-dimensional solution. The stress value reported and the proportion of variance explained (R-square in ALSCAL) are indicators of the overall "goodness of fit" of that point configuration. The configuration in this two-dimensional map accounts for 85% of the variance in the data; Stress 1 (the reported measure of distortion) = 0.17. These parameter values are similar to those for two-dimensional maps in *Drosophila* genetics. (See McCain, 1985, p. 57.)

6. By contrast, the *Drosophila* genetics authors had a Connectivity Ratio of between 86% and 87%, primarily due to the lack of connections made in the citing literature between population genetics and research on the "experimental genetics of individuals."

7. In the citing literature, the gel electrophoresis innovation is represented by two coauthored papers (Hubby & Lewontin, 1966; Lewontin & Hubby, 1966) as well as by Harris's solo contributions (Harris, 1966, 1969). Lewontin has asserted (1985b) that many citations to "Lewontin & Hubby" refer to material only in "Hubby & Lewontin," thus giving him undue credit for Hubby's intellectual contributions. He views this as a clear case of the "Matthew effect" (Merton, 1968).

8. The first of these may be represented, in part, by the Adaptation cluster; in the third case, I was unable to link researchers highlighted in Clegg and Epperson's (1985) review with those in the rest of the map.

HENK F. MOED
RENGER E. de BRUIN

# 12. International Scientific Cooperation and Awareness: Bibliometric Case Study of Agricultural Research Within the European Community

This chapter examines scientific integration among scientists from different countries. It focuses on changes in the past decade with respect to the extent to which scientists from different countries cooperate and are aware of one anothers' research activities. An attempt is made to obtain indications of these processes by analyzing the formal scientific literature. The chapter reports on a study performed for the Commission of the European Communities. A bibliometric method is applied to the research in the field of agriculture within member states of the European Community.

## General Framework

This chapter deals with the phenomenon of integration among scientists from different countries. "Integration" is conceived as the participation of scientists in communication networks on research questions, methods, and findings. It is characterized by scientific cooperation among scientists, participation in meetings, visiting, and awareness of research activities in other countries. In several studies this phenomenon is examined through an analysis of the formal scientific literature. Lomnitz, Rees, and Cameo (1987) studied the emergence of national as well as international groups with

AUTHOR'S NOTE: We acknowledge Dr. G. Lewison (Commission of the European Communities, Brussels, Belgium), Dr. A. F. J. van Raan (University of Leiden, the Netherlands), and Dr. H. Grupp (Fraunhofer Institut für Systemtechnik und Innovationsforschung, Karlsruhe, Federal Republic of Germany) for their contributions to the original design of this project.

217

common research interests crossing institutional or national boundaries. The interaction between scientists was measured through citations to other scientists' work and through coauthorship between scientists from different locations. Schott (1988) analyzes the global scientific network in terms of the influence of one country on another. He assumes that this influence can be indicated with reasonable validity by bibliographic references in articles published in the formal serial literature. Schott shows that the influence of one country on another depends partly on social, political, and cultural factors. Several of these factors also appear in a study by Frame and Carpenter (1979) on the use of international coauthorship, derived from journal articles, for the measurement of international scientific cooperation. It should be noted that not all forms of cooperation will result in coauthorship in the serial literature.

Recently, Lewison and Cunningham (1989) applied bibliometric data on international coauthorship to evaluate research programs of the Commission of the European Communities. Tijssen and Moed (1989) performed an analysis on the international orientation of Dutch scientific research within the natural and life sciences using specific data-analytical techniques (correspondence analysis).

As in the studies mentioned above, in this chapter we will examine the process of integration through a bibliometric analysis of the formal scientific literature. We assume that changes in the degree of integration over time will be reflected in the formal literature, although with a time lag of several years. There is usually a delay of one or two years between the time a paper is submitted to a journal and the time it is published. Moreover, there may be a considerable delay between the time scientists decide to work on a joint project and the time they write a paper reporting the results of their joint activities.

## Scope and Structure

Two aspects of integration will be assessed. The first is international scientific cooperation as reflected in coauthorship between scientists from different countries. The second aspect is awareness of research activities and findings, as reflected in reference lists of scientific articles. The question of whether citations measure influence is subject to intensive debate. Serious criticism is given by MacRoberts and MacRoberts (1986), who claim that only a small part of the real influence of a paper is contained in its references. Here we focus on awareness rather than on influence. Line and Sandison (1974) developed a model of the use of literature over time. They distinguish between "updating" and "basic" use of the scientific literature. Updating use is date dependent. It concentrates on recently published items and is the result of scanning the most recent journal issues of updates of current awareness systems/indexing services as well as suggestions from personal contacts. Basic use is considered to be date independent. Older papers may be as relevant as recent ones. It is usually restricted to a specific topic of interest that is new to the reader. In practice, the two types of use will overlap.

We focus on citations to recent papers. More specifically, we consider only citations to 0- to 4-year-old articles (e.g., an article published in 1985 and cited in 1988 is, according to the year of citation, 3 years old). In terms of the distinction made by Line and Sandison, we focus on the "updating" use of the formal literature. We assume that such citations reflect the author's perception of the cognitive and social background in which he or she locates his or her own research activities. The assumption that this type of citation indicates *influence* seems questionable. In our view, *awareness* is a more appropriate term.

Here we concentrate on agricultural research. Several authors have pointed out that this field differs from other disciplines within the natural and life sciences, such as biochemistry or physics (Arvanitis & Chatelin, 1988; Busch, 1980). These authors emphasize that agriculture has a strong applied mission orientation. As a consequence, the goals and structures of agricultural science were different from those of other types of natural or life science. Interaction with "users" of results is much stronger in this field than in many others. Moreover, agricultural research responds to the needs of local productive sectors. In agriculture, complex processes of knowledge transfer take place. Meijer, Nederhof, and van Raan (1990) studied such processes in the Netherlands. We focus on interactions between researchers with one another rather than on relations between researchers and the users of their results outside the scientific community.

We will concentrate on the applied bibliometric method. On the research results, we report only in broad terms. The chapter is structured as follows. In the second section, we outline the policy background of the study and the specific research questions. The third section deals with data collection and research methods. The adequacy of coverage of the database we created will be discussed in the fourth section. Section five contains the main results of our study. We draw conclusions in the final section.

## Policy Background and
## Purpose of the Study

The original purpose of our study was to perform a bibliometric analysis for an evaluation panel organized by the Commission of the European Communities to evaluate the commission's program on agricultural research (Moed, de Bruin, & Straathof, 1989). The commission has carried out three programs for agricultural research running from 1975 to 1978, from 1979 to 1983, and from 1984 to 1988. Each consists of common activities under which research projects in defined areas are supported through cost-shared contracts and coordinated activities, with the purpose of bringing scientists together through scientific meetings and short-term exchanges and missions (Lewison, 1989).

To establish the effects of the commission's coordinated activities, the panel asked whether there has been an increase in scientific cooperation between member states of the European Community (EC) during the last decade and whether researchers from EC member states have been more aware of research activities in other EC countries in recent years than they were in the past. On the basis of the considerations outlined in the preceding section, the panel's general questions were specified in bibliometric terms, resulting in three specific research questions:

(1) Has there been an increase in the proportion of scientific papers, in the field covered by the community's agricultural research program, that are coauthored by scientists from two or more member states during the last decade?

(2) If so, how does this compare with the proportion of papers coauthored by an EC scientist and one or more from a non-EC country?

(3) Do these papers by EC scientists now cite work by scientists from other EC member states more frequently (as a

proportion of the total number of citations), and, if so, how does this compare with their citations to non-EC authors during the same period?

The panel carried out interviews and requested special studies: a questionnaire and a bibliometric study. In this chapter we will deal with the bibliometric study. For an overview of the evaluation procedure as a whole, we refer to Lewison (1989). The conclusions of the panel are presented in its final report (O'Sullivan et al., 1989).

## Data Collection and Method

### Selection of the Database; Definition of the Field

We obtained bibliometric data from SCISEARCH, the online version of the *Science Citation Index* (*SCI*), published by the Institute for Scientific Information (ISI). In the fourth section, below, we discuss differences between SCISEARCH and the printed version of the *SCI* with respect to journal coverage.

Carpenter and Narin (1981) concluded that *SCI* coverage is excellent with respect to the core literature in the physical and biological sciences, at least for English-speaking countries. They do not give explicit statements on the field of agriculture as such. A study on an agricultural subfield (tropical soil sciences) was performed by Arvanitis and Chatelin (1988), who concluded that the *SCI* in the field of agriculture does not give adequate coverage of non-English-speaking countries, especially Third World countries. One of their findings was that French authors—at least in the subfield under study—published mainly French articles in journals from French-speaking countries that are not processed for the *SCI*. In the following sections, we will examine the adequacy of coverage of the SCISEARCH database and possible national biases in our data.

We created a dataset of articles in the field of agricultural research published by authors from EC member states. The field of agriculture was defined through a set of SCISEARCH journals whose titles contain significant word stems, such as *agr*, one in agriculture and dairy and animal science developed by Noma (1986).

TABLE 12.1
Number of EC Articles per Year

|                    |      |      | Years |      |
| ------------------ | ---- | ---- | ----- | ---- |
|                    | 1979 | 1982 | 1985  | 1988 |
| Number of articles | 2659 | 2506 | 2898  | 2631 |

NOTE: Total articles for all years listed: 10,694.

We judged discrepancies between the lists and adapted our dataset accordingly. From SCISEARCH we extracted data on articles published in the selected journals by authors from EC member states in the years 1979, 1982, 1985, and 1988.

Member states were considered to be the nine countries that were already members of the EC before 1979: Belgium, Denmark, the Federal Republic of Germany, France, the United Kingdom, Ireland, Italy, Luxembourg, and the Netherlands. As no articles from Luxembourg were identified, this country was not included. The "new" member states (Greece, Spain, and Portugal, entering the EC in 1981 and 1986) were not included either, as their inclusion might disturb a trend analysis for the period 1979-1988. However, we obtained results on the number of coauthorships and citations from the "old" and the "new" member states (Moed, de Bruin, & Straathof, 1989). The total number of articles published by the eight "old" EC member states is given in Table 12.1.

Table 12.1 shows that the number of articles per year varies between 2,500 and 2,900. No trend is visible in the data. The variations in the annual scores are largely due to changes in coverage of the database (*SCI*/SCISEARCH). Table 12.2 gives the number of articles published by each member state for each of the years 1979, 1982, 1985, and 1988. It should be noted that this table includes "double counting." For instance, an article by an Italian author and a French author is counted as one article for Italy and one for France.

Table 12.2 shows that large variations exist in the annual numbers for several countries. Changes in *SCI* coverage are an important factor here. For instance, the decrease in the number of articles from Ireland in 1988 is due to the removal of the *Irish Journal of Agricultural Research* from the *SCI* in that year. A somewhat surprising finding is the relatively low number of articles from France

TABLE 12.2
Number of Articles by Member States

| Country | 1979 | | 1982 | | 1985 | | 1988 | |
|---|---|---|---|---|---|---|---|---|
| | N | % | N | % | N | % | N | % |
| Belgium | 137 | 5.1 | 153 | 6.0 | 188 | 6.4 | 73 | 2.7 |
| Denmark | 76 | 2.8 | 65 | 2.6 | 73 | 2.5 | 70 | 2.6 |
| Federal Republic of Germany | 899 | 33.7 | 856 | 33.8 | 933 | 31.8 | 788 | 29.8 |
| France | 376 | 14.1 | 190 | 7.5 | 206 | 7.0 | 303 | 11.3 |
| United Kingdom | 877 | 32.9 | 972 | 38.4 | 1108 | 37.7 | 973 | 36.3 |
| Ireland | 49 | 1.8 | 56 | 2.2 | 63 | 2.1 | 29 | 1.1 |
| Italy | 91 | 3.4 | 87 | 3.4 | 106 | 3.6 | 145 | 5.4 |
| The Netherlands | 164 | 6.1 | 154 | 6.1 | 261 | 8.9 | 302 | 11.3 |
| Total | 2669 | 100.0 | 2533 | 100.0 | 2938 | 100.0 | 2683 | 100.0 |

as compared with the other large countries, Germany and the United Kingdom. This is partly due to the removal of the *Annales de Biologie Animale* after 1979. We discuss this point further in the fourth section of the chapter. The numbers of French, Dutch, and Italian papers in the publication dataset increase considerably in 1988, relative to the scores for both 1982 and 1985, while Germany and the United Kingdom do not show such an increase. One possible explanation is that, at the beginning of the 1980s, French scientists did not publish frequently in the international journals covered by the *SCI* but in national periodicals instead. During the course of the decade, they have published more frequently in the international journals covered by the *SCI*. A similar conclusion may be drawn with respect to Italy and the Netherlands.

## Analysis of Transnational Publications

A "transnational publication" is defined as a publication with authors from at least two different countries, as reflected in the corporate source field of SCISEARCH. We selected all transnational publications to which authors from EC member states have contributed. Next, we established which transnational articles were co-authored by scientists from two or more member states (EC-EC transnational papers) and which papers were by scientists from a member state and a non-EC country (EC/non-EC transnational

TABLE 12.3
Data on the Average Number of References per (citing) EC Paper

| Citations to | Number |
|---|---|
| All papers | 20.0 |
| 0- to 4-year-old papers | 6.5 |
| 0- to 4-year-old journal papers | 5.0 |
| 0- to 4-year-old papers published in SCISEARCH journals | 4.0 |
| 0- to 4-year-old papers published in our cited journal set | 2.0 |

papers). Only a few publications were coauthored by scientists from two member states as well as by authors from non-EC countries.

Transnational publications may be analyzed both from the perspective of individual EC member states and from the perspective of the EC as a whole. In this chapter, we will take the latter approach. Consequently, all articles from the various member states aggregated into one single publication set. Results at the level of the individual member states are given in Moed, de Bruin, and Straathof (1989).

## Analysis of Transnational Citations

A "transnational citation" is defined as a citation given in a publication by an author from one country to a paper that was authored by scientists from another country. We distinguish between citations to other EC member states (intra-EC transnational citations) and citations to countries outside the EC (extra-EC transnational citations). Therefore, the country of origin was determined for a large collection of cited papers by looking up these papers in SCISEARCH and by extracting information on the geographic location of all contributing authors. Data on the number of references involved are given in Table 12.3.

We considered only a part of all cited papers, applying three selection criteria. First, only cited papers between 0 and 4 years old were investigated. The main reason for doing so is outlined in the introductory section of this chapter. Table 12.3 shows that some 33% (6.5/20) of all citations were to papers between 0 and 4 years old. This percentage is known in the bibliometric literature as Price's Index. Second, we only considered cited papers published in journals processed for SCISEARCH. The reason for this is a technical one:

For cited papers not processed for SCISEARCH, it is extremely difficult to establish the country of origin. The percentage of citations to 0- to 4-year-old papers published in journals amounts to 77% of the total number of citations to 0- to 4-year-old papers. Citations to journals were operationalized as those indicating some starting page number of the cited item. Apparently, the authors of our EC articles—which are, of course, all journal papers—cite other journal papers rather frequently. Moreover, it appears that 80% of the cited journal articles are published in journals processed for SCISEARCH. It follows that the overall coverage by SCISEARCH of the literature cited in our EC articles is reasonably good. The third selection criterion holds that we investigated only cited papers published in a limited number of journals. A "cited" journal set was defined containing all journals in the EC publication dataset as well as all other frequently cited journals, except the general biochemical, general physiological, and multidisciplinary journals. The percentage of citations to our extended journal set is some 50% of the total number of citations to SCISEARCH journals. The average number of cited papers per citing article for which the country of origin was determined amounts to two. Because the total number of EC publications is about 2,500 per year (see Table 12.1) the total number of citations analyzed (per sighting year) amounts to 5,000.

We explored a fractional counting scheme. For example, a citation in an article coauthored by a French and a German scientist to a paper published by a French scientist was counted as "half" a transnational (intra-EC) citation and as "half" a national citation. Although such a counting scene seems to be plausible, the indicators based on transnational publications and citations become technically dependent one on another, in the sense that the number of transnational (citing) publications directly affects the number of transnational citations. To minimize this effect, all addresses of non-EC authors from our (citing) EC publication dataset were deleted. Non-EC addresses of cited papers were kept. Consequently, numbers of citations to countries outside the EC are not affected by EC/non-EC transnational (citing) publications. Still, numbers of citations to the home country (national citations) and to other EC countries (intra-EC citations) are influenced by transnational (citing) publications with authors from more than one member state. However, in the fourth section, below, we show that the percentage of EC-EC transnational publications (relative to the total number of

EC publications) appears to be rather low, a maximum of 2% in 1988. Consequently, the effect seems to be sufficiently small, because the number of national citations is affected by at most 1%.

## Technical Problems and Possible Biases of SCISEARCH

### SCISEARCH Versus *SCI*

Considerable differences exist between the journal coverage of the online database SCISEARCH and the printed edition of the *SCI*. SCISEARCH contains all journals processed for the *SCI* as well as journals not included in the *SCI* but processed for another product of ISI, the *Current Contents*. Large fluctuations exist in the number of such journals processed during the period 1979-1988. In 1985 the discrepancy between SCISEARCH and *SCI* is the larger for all years. Many articles published in the *Current Contents* non-*SCI* journals are not processed completely in SCISEARCH. Because only one address is extracted, even if the articles have more than one, these papers are unusable for an analysis of international coauthorship. Moreover, the reference lists are not processed, which makes this category easily identifiable. So, we selected only articles containing references.

However, it appears that some journals are not included in the *SCI* although the articles published in these are processed completely for SCISEARCH in some, but not in all, years involved in this analysis (particularly in 1985). In several of these journals, scientists from EC member states publish very frequently. The articles published in these journals were removed from our EC publication dataset because their inclusion might have disturbed our trend analysis.

For the analysis of transnational citations, we included all journals in our cited journal set, regardless of whether they were processed for the *SCI* or not. Consequently, by including journals processed for SCISEARCH but not for the *SCI*, many cited papers were included for which only one address was processed. We hypothesized that inclusion of such papers would not cause biases in this analysis because there is no reason to assume that cited papers from

EC member states would be advantaged (or disadvantaged) more than papers from non-EC countries. This hypothesis will be tested in the fifth section of this chapter.

## Possible National Biases of SCISEARCH/*SCI*

In Table 12.2 we showed data on the number of articles published by scientists from the various member states. The number of papers by French authors is roughly one-third of the number of papers from Germany or the United Kingdom and, in 1988, equals the number of Dutch papers. Most probably these outcomes do not adequately reflect differences in the size of the research activities within agriculture in these countries. We hypothesized that our dataset does not cover the output of each member state equally well and that it is subject to ISI selection criteria (e.g., a language bias) or to differences in national publication strategies. We observed in the beginning of this section that some important "national" journals are not included in our set (*national* not in terms of the country of publication, as operationalized by Arvanitis and Chatelin, but in the sense that the overwhelming majority of papers in a journal are published by scientists from one country only).

To test our hypothesis, we first collected publication data from AGRIS, another scientific literature database covering the field of agriculture. In contrast to the *SCI*, this database does contain "gray" literature. However, we did not succeed in obtaining reliable results. It appeared that only about 35% of all items in the database contained information on the country of origin of the publishing authors. The results we obtained diverged largely from the ones presented in Table 12.2 (for instance, the number of French papers was more than two times the number of papers from the United Kingdom) but there seems to be no reason to assume that these results are reliable.

A second attempt to test our hypothesis was to perform an additional analysis on the reference lists in our (citing) EC papers. We hypothesized that authors from countries of which the output is badly covered by SCISEARCH will cite relatively fewer articles published in SCISEARCH journals than authors from "well-covered" countries. Therefore, we determined, for the (citing) year 1988 and for each EC country separately, the percentage of citations to papers published in our cited journal set relative to the total number of

TABLE 12.4
Percentage of Citations to Cited Journal Set, Relative to Total Number of Citations
Given

| | | Cites in Set | |
| Country | Total Cites | N | % |
| --- | --- | --- | --- |
| Belgium | 510 | 156 | 30.6 |
| Denmark | 440 | 145 | 32.9 |
| Federal Republic of Germany | 4931 | 1417 | 28.7 |
| France | 1902 | 646 | 33.9 |
| United Kingdom | 5462 | 1834 | 33.6 |
| Ireland | 148 | 73 | 49.3 |
| Italy | 713 | 170 | 23.8 |
| The Netherlands | 1896 | 552 | 29.1 |

citations given (for citations to 0- to 4-year-old papers only). The
results are presented in Table 12.4.

Table 12.4 shows that Italy has the lowest percentage (23.8%).
Ireland has the highest percentage (49.3%), but the number of articles and citations involved is very low. The other countries have
between 29% and 34%. According to our hypothesis, SCISEARCH
coverage is worst for Italy, whereas France and the United Kingdom
are covered equally well. It should be emphasized that these
outcomes are based on references given in articles processed for
SCISEARCH. Combining these results with those concerning the
overall coverage of SCISEARCH (discussed in the "Data Collection
and Method" section above), we come to the conclusion that our EC
dataset seems to cover a rather dense and relatively closed formal
communication system, with English as the dominant language. The
role of the participating French, German, and Dutch scientists does
not seem to be very different from that of researchers from the
United Kingdom, at least in 1988. Italy shows a perhaps deviant
pattern. There is some evidence that the participation of French
and Dutch scientists in this system becomes stronger during the
period 1979-1988 (see the "Data Collection and Method" section).
However, the possible existence and importance of other formal
communication networks among scientists outside the network covered by SCISEARCH cannot be assessed on the basis of our data and
awaits future research.

TABLE 12.5
Number and Percentage of Transnational Publications (relative to the total number of publications)

|  | 1979 | | 1982 | | 1985 | | 1988 | |
|---|---|---|---|---|---|---|---|---|
|  | N | % | N | % | N | % | N | % |
| EC-EC | 17 | 0.6 | 20 | 0.8 | 33 | 1.0 | 48 | 1.8 |
| EC/non-EC | 122 | 4.6 | 125 | 5.0 | 198 | 6.8 | 288 | 10.9 |

TABLE 12.6
Share of EC-EC and EC/non-EC Coauthorships in Transnational Publications

|  | 1979 | | 1982 | | 1985 | | 1988 | |
|---|---|---|---|---|---|---|---|---|
|  | N | % | N | % | N | % | N | % |
| EC-EC | 17 | 12.2 | 20 | 13.8 | 33 | 14.3 | 48 | 14.3 |
| EC/non-EC | 122 | 87.8 | 125 | 86.2 | 198 | 85.7 | 288 | 85.7 |

# Results on Transnational
# Publications and Citations

We calculated the numbers and percentages of transnational publications to which authors from member states contributed, relative to the total number of articles published by all member states. The results are presented in Table 12.5.

From Table 12.5 we can see that both the absolute number and the percentage of transnational publications increase during the period 1979-1988. The same conclusion holds for EC-EC transnational publications. Consequently, there is an increase in the proportion of papers on agricultural research coauthored by scientists from two or more member states. To investigate how this compares with the proportion of papers coauthored by an EC scientist and one or more authors from countries outside the EC, the percentages of EC-EC and EC/non-EC transnational publications were calculated, relative to the total number of transnational publications. The results are presented in Table 12.6.

Table 12.6 shows a slight increase in the percentage of EC-EC transnational publications, from 12.2% in 1979 to 14.3% in 1985,

TABLE 12.7
Number of Percentage of National and Transnational Citations

|                              | 1979  | 1982  | 1985  | 1988  |
|------------------------------|-------|-------|-------|-------|
| Percentage of national cites | 50.5  | 51.7  | 49.0  | 48.2  |
| Percentage of intra-EC cites | 13.4  | 13.4  | 13.7  | 14.4  |
| Percentage of extra-EC cites | 36.1  | 35.0  | 37.2  | 37.5  |
| Total number of cites        | 4,119 | 5,049 | 5,140 | 4,926 |

TABLE 12.8
Percentage of Intra-EC and Extra-EC Citations, Relative to the Total Number of Transnational Citations

|                     | 1979 | | 1982 | | 1985 | | 1988 | |
|---------------------|------|------|------|------|------|------|------|------|
|                     | N    | %    | N    | %    | N    | %    | N    | %    |
| Intra-EC            | 552  | 27.0 | 675  | 27.6 | 702  | 26.9 | 708  | 27.7 |
| Extra-EC            | 1487 | 73.0 | 1765 | 72.4 | 1911 | 73.1 | 1846 | 72.3 |
| Total transnational | 2039 | 100.0| 2440 | 100.0| 2613 | 100.0| 2554 | 100.0|

while the percentage for 1988 is equal to the one for 1985. These results suggest that there is no clear positive trend during the period 1979-1988 in scientific cooperation between member states as compared with cooperation with third countries.

As outlined in the third section of this chapter we subdivided all citations in our EC articles to 0- to 4-year-old papers published in some specific set of journals into national and transnational citations. Moreover, we subdivided the transnational citations into intra-EC citations and extra-EC citations and applied a fractional counting scheme. In Table 12.7 we present the results for the EC as a whole.

The percentage of national citations may seem to be rather high (some 50%, according to Table 12.7). However, one should keep in mind that self-citations—citations by authors to their own work—are included in these data. Table 12.7 shows that there is a slight decrease in the percentage of national citations, while the shares of both intra-EC and extra-EC citations seem to increase. To compare intra-EC citations with extra-EC citations, we calculated the percentage of intra-EC citations relative to the total number of transnational citations. The results are given in Table 12.8.

From Table 12.8 we can see that there is no significant increase in the proportion of intra-EC citations, relative to the number of extra-EC citations, during the period 1979-1988.

To examine the effect of including all SCISEARCH papers, rather than just those processed for the printed *SCI*, we recalculated the citation-based indicators presented in Table 12.8 considering only citing and cited papers from our data, published in journals included in the "1981 fixed journal set" created by Noma (1986). This set contains all journals processed completely for the *SCI* in 1981. The results we obtained were similar to those presented in Table 12.8. In fact, focusing on the percentage of intra-EC citations, relative to the total number of transnational citations in our EC papers, we found the scores 25.3%, 27.1%, 26.4%, and 27.1% for the years 1979, 1982, 1985, and 1988, respectively.

Finally, in Table 12.9, we present some data on the countries outside the EC cited by EC scientists.

Table 12.9 gives a list of the non-EC countries receiving more than 100 citations from EC papers during the period 1979-1988. In addition, we present the numbers of citations to the countries that joined the EC after 1980 (Greece, Spain, and Portugal). The percentages are relative to the total number of citations to countries outside the EC. Table 12.9 shows an increase in citations from "old" EC to "new" EC papers. Two other European countries outside the EC (Sweden and Switzerland) show a considerable increase in citations from EC scientists as well. It is interesting to note that, although the United States is evidently the country cited most frequently, citations to U.S. papers decrease from 59.7% in 1979 to 50.4% in 1988. This particular outcome suggests that the "awareness" of EC scientists of agricultural research in the United States—compared with other countries outside the EC—has diminished during the last decade. It would be interesting to validate this outcome with other types of data and to analyze the possible causes underlying this phenomenon.

## Conclusions

In this chapter we examined scientific integration among scientists from different countries within the field of agriculture. We focused on changes in the past decade with respect to the extent to

TABLE 12.9
Number and Percentage of Citations to New EC Countries and to Non-EC Countries
Receiving More Than 100 Citations from EC Papers During 1979-1988

| Country | Total | | 1979 | | 1982 | | 1985 | | 1988 | |
|---|---|---|---|---|---|---|---|---|---|---|
| | N | % | N | % | N | % | N | % | N | % |
| United States | 3789 | 54.0 | 890 | 59.7 | 947 | 53.6 | 1022 | 53.4 | 930 | 50.4 |
| Canada | 760 | 10.8 | 160 | 10.7 | 167 | 9.5 | 234 | 12.2 | 199 | 10.8 |
| Australia | 631 | 9.0 | 105 | 7.0 | 158 | 8.9 | 192 | 10.0 | 176 | 9.5 |
| Japan | 252 | 3.6 | 46 | 3.1 | 72 | 4.0 | 68 | 3.6 | 66 | 3.6 |
| Sweden | 192 | 2.7 | 22 | 1.5 | 41 | 2.3 | 47 | 2.4 | 82 | 4.4 |
| New Zealand | 189 | 2.7 | 50 | 3.3 | 41 | 2.3 | 46 | 2.4 | 52 | 2.8 |
| Switzerland | 133 | 1.9 | 20 | 1.3 | 32 | 1.8 | 42 | 2.2 | 39 | 2.1 |
| German Democratic Republic | 126 | 1.8 | 19 | 1.2 | 42 | 2.4 | 40 | 2.1 | 25 | 1.4 |
| Israel | 117 | 1.7 | 29 | 1.9 | 27 | 1.5 | 30 | 1.5 | 31 | 1.7 |
| India | 113 | 1.6 | 15 | 0.9 | 47 | 2.7 | 25 | 1.3 | 26 | 1.4 |
| Austria | 85 | 1.2 | 13 | 0.8 | 25 | 1.4 | 27 | 1.4 | 20 | 1.1 |
| Norway | 65 | 0.9 | 10 | 0.7 | 20 | 1.1 | 13 | 0.7 | 22 | 1.2 |
| South Africa | 63 | 0.9 | 14 | 0.9 | 19 | 1.1 | 18 | 0.9 | 12 | 0.6 |
| Spain | 30 | 0.4 | 2 | 0.1 | 7 | 0.4 | 7 | 0.3 | 14 | 0.7 |
| Greece | 13 | 0.2 | 2 | 0.1 | 2 | 0.1 | 4 | 0.2 | 5 | 0.3 |
| Portugal | 5 | 0.1 | 1 | 0.1 | — | 0.0 | — | 0.0 | 4 | 0.2 |
| All other | 466 | 6.6 | 95 | 6.4 | 120 | 6.9 | 103 | 5.4 | 148 | 8.0 |

which scientists from different countries cooperate and are aware of each other's research activities. Indications of these aspects were obtained by analyzing the formal scientific literature covered by SCISEARCH.

We gave a detailed outline of the applied bibliometric methods and discussed several serious methodological problems. We concluded that our EC dataset seems to cover a rather dense and relatively closed formal communication system, with English as the dominant language. The role of the participating French, German, and Dutch scientists does not seem to differ strongly from that of British researchers, but Italy appears to show a deviant pattern. There is some evidence that the participation of French scientists became stronger during the period 1979-1988. Our conclusions are only valid with respect to this system. The possible existence and importance of other formal communication networks among scientists, outside the networks covered by SCISEARCH, cannot be assessed on the basis of our data and awaits future research.

Our analyses of transnational publications and citations provide consistent results. These suggest that agricultural research within the EC has become more internationally integrated during the period 1979-1988. However, in our analysis of SCISEARCH journals, we found no evidence that integration among member states of the EC has increased significantly more than integration among member states and countries outside the EC.

One must keep in mind that a time delay exists between the occurrence of some specific "event" in the scientific enterprise and the time that event becomes visible in the formal, scientific serial literature. As a consequence, bibliometric results derived from the specific literature from, say, 1988 do not reflect the state of scientific cooperation or awareness in 1988 but that of some years before. The EC has set up three research programs for agricultural research, running from 1975 to 1978, from 1979 to 1983, and from 1984 to 1988, respectively. On the basis of the results presented in this study, the possible effects of the latest program cannot be assessed completely, because these may (at least partly) become visible in the literature published after 1988.

As indicated in the second section of this chapter, the evaluation panel for which we performed the study combined the outcomes of the bibliometric study with more "qualitative" information obtained from interviews and questionnaires. The two types of studies were considered by the panel as complementary, providing more or less consistent results. For a detailed description of the evaluation procedure as a whole, and of the integration of the outcomes of the bibliometric analyses, interviews, and questionnaires, we refer to the panel's final report (O'Sullivan et al., 1989).

In our view, the methodology presented in this chapter has proven to be a useful tool in the evaluation of the effectiveness of (supra)national science policies. Moreover, it raises a number of interesting research questions on the study of communication among scientists. Apart from the questions we raise in our chapter (but cannot yet answer), we mention the question of how individual countries relate to one another in terms of cooperation and awareness as well as which factors influence the strength of the relations between these countries. As indicated in the literature, such factors may relate to the type of scientific area under study and the nature of its research; to various social, economic, political, and historical processes; or to the international standing or quality of a country's research activities. At present we are working on a paper focusing on historical factors. Insight into such factors is a necessary condition for improving the problems of scientific communication as well as for stating the possible effectiveness of (supra-)national science policies aimed at stimulating integration among scientists from different countries.

TERRENCE A. BROOKS

# 13. Core Journals of the Rapidly Changing Research Front of "Superconductivity"

This chapter reports an analysis of the journals contributing articles to the literature of superconductivity during the last 15 years. The analysis reveals that the literature of superconductivity has tripled in absolute size and has grown more intense over time as well. Core journals were identified by the minimum perfect Bradford partition methodology. Citing/cited core journal analysis reveals a communication pattern dominated by a pair of journals. Problems of bibliometric methodology such as literature definition, Bradfordian mechanics, and citation analysis are critiqued.

A material performs as a superconductor when it offers no resistance to a direct electrical current, a phenomenon historically witnessed at temperatures near absolute zero. The discovery of superconductors functioning at relatively higher temperatures has ignited an explosion of research in anticipation of the profound impact superconductivity will have on electronic technology and computer design.

Scientific journals form one of the major communication channels reporting research on superconductivity. At least two antithetical bibliometric models for the composition of the journal literature of a rapidly evolving scientific field can be advanced: (a) The journal literature would be tightly clustered around several core journals that dominate a well-ordered information channel, or (b) the literature would be scattered across many journals reflecting the worldwide interest in the subject and reflecting, as Price (1963) hypothesized, the introduction of new, specialist journals. In such a

AUTHOR'S NOTE: I wish to acknowledge the research aid of Deb Wiley of INSPEC/IEEE and Gail Crockett of the University of Washington. Inquiries concerning *The Bibliometrics Toolbox* should be directed to me.

case, scholarly journals in superconductivity would represent a widely dispersed information channel.

The bibliometric study of publication activity is anchored in the work of Bradford (1934). Bradford's multiplier is a measure of the intensity of the clustering of a literature. Its possible application in the analysis of the superconductivity literature would be in measuring the change in clustering intensity of the literature over time. The calculation of the multiplier has been in some dispute, however, with rival theories presented by Goffman and Warren (1969) and Egghe (1986). Both of these calculations have been shown to be method-bound by Brooks, who suggested alternative measures: the clustering index (in press-a) and the minimum perfect Bradford partition (in press-b).

Bradford's most enduring theoretical contribution was the notion that the core zone of a literature contains the most productive journals. The methodological problems of calculating the multiplier, however, have prevented a satisfactory demarcation of the exact limits of the core zone. Despite the intuitive appeal of the core zone—especially to librarians and information workers of all fields, whose daily experiences demonstrate that some journals are more favored than others—the idea of a core zone has been attacked (Rousseau, 1987) as having no basis in theory. Given the amount of methodological and theoretical tumult in the area of Bradfordity during the last 50 years, there is little wonder why it has not been widely applied.

## The Literature of Superconductivity

The literature of superconductivity, like other subject areas, is neither precisely located nor rigidly defined: It is an artificial bibliographical construct. It is composed of the journal articles that indexers, catalogers, and database-maintenance people have considered germane to the topic. A possible bibliographic device for capturing the literature of superconductivity is an online database such as INSPEC (Information Services for Physics, Electronics and Computing). Brooks (in press-a) demonstrated that database files share similar bibliometric characteristics with their corresponding comprehensive bibliographies. INSPEC is the largest English-language database in the fields of physics, electrical engineering, electronics, computers, control engineering, and information technology. It is possible that high-quality scholarly articles in English about the phenomenon of reduced resistance to electrical current could exist beyond the INSPEC database, but it is unlikely. It is true, however, that INSPEC does not represent the world's literature in all languages on the topic. Using INSPEC gives the literature of superconductivity a precise location, but it is, admittedly, a bibliographical convenience.

Although the dictionary definition of *superconductivity* may have remained constant during the last decade, the purview of the term in the INSPEC database has both expanded and contracted. *Superconductivity* has been the preferred term for a changing group of synonyms since 1973. Table 13.1 illustrates these changes in regard to the use of synonyms (that is, the "used for" terms). For example, until 1975 material about the Ginzberg-Landau theory would have been placed under "superconductivity." Following 1975 the Ginzberg-Landau theory material would have been placed under its own heading (as a "related term"), thus contracting the semantic domain of "superconductivity" in the database. One may speculate that such a semantic domain contraction would have reduced the variety of journals producing articles indexed under "superconductivity" and create a more intense literature clustering. Since 1983, however, *superconductivity* has been the preferred term for five other terms and has had a larger semantic domain. One may speculate that such a semantic expansion would have increased the variety of journals producing articles indexed under "superconductivity" and create a less intense literature clustering. The combined effect, however, of such changeable database pragmatics over the years is difficult to assess without resorting to empirical measures.

The concept "superconductivity" has also been suspended between broader terms such as *low-temperature phenomena* and narrower terms such as *dirty superconductors* in each edition of the INSPEC thesaurus. There are thousands of articles that have been indexed under such a broader or narrower term and not specifically tagged for "superconductivity." Thus, in studying the literature of "superconductivity," one is not analyzing every document in the INSPEC database that is associated with the phenomenon of low-temperature reduced resistance to electrical current. Instead, one is analyzing the arbitrary host of documents that has been indexed under "superconductivity" over the years.

TABLE 13.1
Excerpts from the INSPEC Thesauri for "Superconductivity"

| | *Superconductivity* |
|---|---|
| 1973, 1975 thesauri | UF Ginzberg-Landau theory |
| | Meissner effect |
| | RT BCS theory |
| | Josephson junctions |
| | superconducting devices |
| | superconducting materials |
| | superfluidity |
| | tunneling |
| | vortices |
| 1979, 1981 thesauri | UF Superconductors |
| | RT BCS theory |
| | electrical conductivity of solids |
| | Ginzburg-Landau theory |
| | magnetic field effects |
| | Peierls instability |
| | superconducting devices |
| | superconducting materials |
| | superfluidity |
| 1983, 1985, 1987 thesauri | UF equilibrium properties of superconductors |
| | non-equilibrium properties of superconductors |
| | nonequilibrium properties of superconductors |
| | superconductors |
| | transport properties of superconductors |
| | RT BCS theory |
| | electrical conductivity of solids |
| | Ginzburg-Landau theory |
| | magnetic field effects |
| | Peierls instability |
| | superconducting devices |
| | superconducting materials |
| | superfluidity |

NOTE: UF = used for; RT = related term.

## Data Collection

When the data were collected, the INSPEC back file covered 1969 through December 1987. A database search with the command "superconductivity.de." captured 4,248 documents. This set was qualified by removing reports and report sections, books and book chapters, and conference proceedings and papers. The raw dataset was thus reduced to 3,086 journal articles. The 15 annual sets of data were analyzed by the *Bibliometrics Toolbox*, a computer program that facilitates bibliometric calculations.

Journal title listings, even in a well-maintained database like INSPEC, contain many small inconsistencies, and some minor editing was necessary to combine entries such as "Fiz. Met. & Metalloved. (USSR)" and "Fiz. Met. and Metalloved. (USSR)." A decision was made not to combine journals that had split into several sections but to treat each section as a separate journal.

Cumulative annual profiles of the "superconductivity" literature are presented in Table 13.2. During the last 15 years, the absolute size of the literature has about tripled. A measure of the intensity of the clustering of a literature is the ratio of the productivity of the recurring journals to the number of the "singleton" journals. The premise behind this ratio is that a disperse literature is one composed of a great many journals that publish only one article and has a great number of singleton journals. An intensely clustered literature, on the other hand, is one composed of recurring journals that publish many articles and only a few singleton journals. In terms of Table 13.2, a recurring journal is one that contributed two or more articles to the literature of "superconductivity." The mean annual growth of the recurring journals was 7.5 journals during the 15-year period. A singleton journal contributed only one article to the literature. The number of singleton journals remained constant in 1979 and contracted in 1985. During the 15 years, the singleton journals grew at a mean annual rate of 5.36 journals. Although singleton journals have grown at a slower rate, the rates of growth are not statistically different ($t[16] = 1.28, p < 0.28$).

Brooks (in press-a) defined a clustering index (CI) as the recurring journal productivity divided by the minimum Bradford zone. The minimum Bradford zone follows Goffman and Warren's (1969) definition as being one more than half the number of singleton journals. Brooks (in press-a) observed weakly clustered author series with CIs in the range 0.39 to 0.66 and strongly clustered journal series with CIs in the range of 3.5 to 35.82.

The CIs in Table 13.2 illustrate that "superconductivity" is an intensely clustered literature. There has been a steady growth in the absolute number of articles in the literature but only a modest growth in the number of singleton journals. The modest growth in the number of singleton journals may be the result of either of two

TABLE 13.2
Cumulative Annual Profiles of the Literature of "Superconductivity"

| | Cumulative Recurring Journals | Cumulative Singleton Journals | Cumulative Article Totals | Clustering Index |
|---|---|---|---|---|
| 1973[a] | 94 | 112 | 1,146 | 18.14 |
| 1974 | 110 | 114 | 1,289 | 20.26 |
| 1975 | 112 | 124 | 1,390 | 20.10 |
| 1976 | 118 | 129 | 1,490 | 20.94 |
| 1977 | 130 | 141 | 1,612 | 20.72 |
| 1978 | 142 | 143 | 1,752 | 22.35 |
| 1979 | 150 | 143 | 1,914 | 24.60 |
| 1980 | 159 | 150 | 2,069 | 25.25 |
| 1981 | 168 | 159 | 2,235 | 25.95 |
| 1982 | 175 | 161 | 2,379 | 27.38 |
| 1983 | 181 | 167 | 2,525 | 28.07 |
| 1984 | 185 | 175 | 2,680 | 28.47 |
| 1985 | 193 | 170 | 2,818 | 30.79 |
| 1986 | 195 | 176 | 2,935 | 31.00 |
| 1987 | 199 | 188 | 3,086 | 30.51 |

a. Prior to and including 1973.

factors: (a) Even though there is a worldwide interest and specific work in the area of superconductivity, there has been a very modest growth in the number of journals that have treated "superconductivity" over the years, or (b) journals have migrated from the singleton to the recurring category. Given the explosion of interest in "superconductivity," the second alternative seems much more likely. The CI of "superconductivity" has been growing steadily with only two early plateaus in 1975 and 1977. The slight dip for the CI for 1987 may be the result of an incomplete database listing for the last month of raw data collection. Extraordinarily, "superconductivity" is a literature that has been growing more intense as it has been growing larger. The cumulative record of increasing clustering intensity indicates a well-ordered scholarly journal channel that is dominated by recurring journals. Even though superconductivity is a widely discussed phenomenon with general application, the scholarly journal channel of "superconductivity" in the INSPEC database is not characterized by numerous singleton journals but appears to be a well-ordered information channel clustering around a core set of primary journals.

## Core Journals of "Superconductivity"

Table 13.3 presents the cumulative ranks of the core journals of the literature of "superconductivity" during 15 years. Each year is a snapshot of the cumulative journal ranks as the literature has grown and changed. Table 13.3 presents the journals arranged according to their 1987 ranks. By reading the ranks from right to left, from 1987 back to earlier years, one can determine the change in the ranking of individual journals. It is evident that the six top-ranked journals have been very stable, sharing the ranks 1 through 6. Since 1983 these six journals have made up the core zone of the literature.

A Bradfordian analysis was done on each progressive annual cumulation. As Brooks (in press-b) illustrated, there is usually one minimum perfect Bradford partition (MPBP) for each literature sample. The MPBP method is an objective method of determining a Bradford core zone and is preferred to the methods of Goffman and Warren (1969) and Egghe (1986), methods that ultimately depend on the researcher's judgment of core size.

The MPBP is Bradfordian because there is an equal or nearly equal number of articles placed in each zone of the partition. Succeeding zones of a partition have an increasing number of journals. The MPBP creates "perfect" zones in a partition based on Pratt's (1977) index of concentration. Each possible partition is assessed as to the equality of article distribution. A Pratt index of zero, indicating an even partitioning, is used to select only the small number of perfect Bradfordian partitions. And in almost every partitioning, a few of the singleton journals are left out as remainders. The MPBP is the one partition that leaves the smallest remainder. The MPBP thus includes the largest possible percentage of the literature in a perfect Bradford partition.

Table 13.3 gives the limiting core rank and the associated number of Bradford zones for the MPBP of each year. The limiting core rank is the largest rank of a core journal. For example, in 1987 the limiting core rank is 6, so the journals ranked 1 to 6 make up the core zone. By contrast, in 1973 the limiting core rank is 7. Journals in the main body of Table 13.3 make ranks 1 to 5, and 7 for 1973. Two core journals for 1973 are missing. *JETP Letters* and *Zeitschrift für Physik* held ranks 7 and 6, respectively, in the core zone for 1973. They are listed at the bottom of Table 13.3 as core-zone dropouts.

TABLE 13.3
Cumulative Ranks of Core Journals for "Superconductivity"

| Journals | Years | | | | | | | | | | | | | | |
|---|---|---|---|---|---|---|---|---|---|---|---|---|---|---|---|
| | 1973[a] | 1974 | 1975 | 1976 | 1977 | 1978 | 1979 | 1980 | 1981 | 1982 | 1983 | 1984 | 1985 | 1986 | 1987 |
| Physical Review B (Solid State) | 1 | 1 | 1 | 1 | 1 | 1 | 1 | 1 | 1 | 1 | 1 | 1 | 1 | 1 | 1 |
| Solid State Communications | 3 | 3 | 3 | 3 | 3 | 3 | 3 | 3 | 4 | 2 | 2 | 3 | 2 | 2 | 2 |
| Physics Letters A | 2 | 2 | 2 | 2 | 2 | 2 | 2 | 2 | 2 | 3 | 3 | 2 | 3 | 3 | 3 |
| Journal of Low Temperature Physics | 7 | 6 | 6 | 6 | 6 | 5 | 7 | 7 | 5 | 5 | 5 | 4 | 4 | 4 | 4 |
| Zhurnal Eskperimentalnoi i Teoreticheskoi Fiziki | 4 | 4 | 4 | 4 | 4 | 4 | 4 | 4 | 3 | 4 | 4 | 5 | 5 | 5 | 5 |
| Physical Review Letters | 3 | 4 | 5 | 5 | 5 | 6 | 5 | 5 | 6 | 6 | 6 | 6 | 6 | 6 | 6 |
| Journal of Applied Physics | 11 | 11 | 12 | 11 | 10 | 9 | 8 | 6 | 7 | 7 | 7 | 7 | 7 | 7 | 7 |
| Cryogenics | 17 | 16 | 18 | 15 | 15 | 12 | 9 | 8 | 8 | 8 | 8 | 8 | 8 | 8 | 8 |
| Fizika Nizkikh Temperatur[b] | | | | 27 | 22 | 17 | 14 | 12 | 10 | 10 | 11 | 10 | 10 | 10 | 9 |
| Soviet Physics-Solid State | 13 | 11 | 13 | 10 | 9 | 9 | 7 | 10 | 8 | 8 | 9 | 9 | 9 | 10 | 10 |
| Progress of Theoretical Physics | 5 | 5 | 7 | 7 | 7 | 7 | 6 | 9 | 9 | 9 | 10 | 11 | 11 | 11 | 11 |
| Applied Physics Letters | 21 | 21 | 24 | 24 | 24 | 21 | 18 | 15 | 15 | 16 | 15 | 14 | 15 | 13 | 12 |
| Phsica Status Solidi B | 20 | 17 | 20 | 16 | 16 | 15 | 13 | 14 | 11 | 13 | 14 | 12 | 12 | 12 | 13 |
| | | | | | | | | | | | | | | | |
| Limiting core ranks | 7 | 9 | 11 | 5 | 11 | 11 | 11 | 13 | 11 | 11 | 6 | 6 | 6 | 6 | 6 |
| Bradford zones | 2 | 2 | 2 | 3 | 2 | 2 | 2 | 2 | 2 | 2 | 3 | 3 | 3 | 3 | 3 |
| | | | | | | | | | | | | | | | |
| Ranks of core dropouts | | | | | | | | | | | | | | | |
| JETP Letters | 7 | 8 | 9 | | 11 | 10 | 11 | 13 | | | | | | | |
| Physics Letters | | | 11 | | | | | | | | | | | | |
| Physical Review | | 9 | 10 | | | 11 | | | | | | | | | |
| Zeitschrift für Physik | 6 | 7 | 8 | | 8 | 8 | 10 | 11 | 10 | 11 | | | | | |
| Journal of Materials Science | | | | | | | 11 | 13 | | | | | | | |

a. Prior to and including 1973.
b. First appearance in database in 1976.

Neither of these journals remained in the core zone by 1982. The core-zone dropout journals have increasing ranks over time as they drift farther away from the core. One journal of the top 13 listed, *Progress of Theoretical Physics*, is also drifting away from the core zone at this time. During the 15 years of the study, its rank has doubled from 5 to 11. On the other hand, other journals (*Journal of Applied Physics, Cryogenics, Fizika Nizkikh Temperatur, Applied Physics Letters*, and *Physics Status Solidi B*) have been closing in on the core. One of them (*Fizika Nizkikh Temperatur*) is a new journal that is making a rapid descent in ranks toward the core.

## Communication Among the Core Journals

Table 13.4 presents the citing/cited journal relationships at the 3% minimum level of significance for the core journals from the 1986 edition of the *Science Citation Index*. For example, *Physical Review B* spent 22.4% of its 1986 citation activity in self-citation, 10.8% in citing *Physical Review Letters*, and 3.8% in citing *Solid State Communications*. *Physical Review B* cited many other journals in 1986, but each represented less than 3% of the total number of citations given.

The major pattern of citation communication among the core journals is to cite both *Physical Review B* and *Physical Review Letters*. Between the two of them, *Physical Review B* cites *Physical Review Letters* heavily. The explanation for this coupling is that these two journals are published by the same institutions and are designed as vehicles for early brief publication of new developments (the *Letters*) and for subsequent more substantial development (the *Review*). *Physical Review B* is the dominant journal of the core literature of "superconductivity."

The 3% level is an arbitrary level of significance. At this level there are hints of other relationships, such as *Physical Review B* citing *Solid State Communications*, and the *Journal of Low Temperature Physics* citing *Zhurmal Eskperimentalnoi i Teoreticheskoi Fiziki*. At a 5% minimum level, both of these relationships disappear, but so does the citing activity of the *Zhurmal* by *Physical Review B*.

There are several interesting patterns for journals not in the core. *Cryogenics* does not cite any journal other than itself beyond the 3% level, and *Physical Review*, a journal that fell from the core zone in

TABLE 13.4
Citing/Cited Journal Relationships

| Citing Journals | Cited Journals (by number) | | | | | |
|---|---|---|---|---|---|---|
| | 1 | 2 | 3 | 4 | 5 | 6 |
| (1) *Physical Review B* | 22.4 | 3.8 | * | * | * | 10.8 |
| (2) *Solid State Communications* | 15.4 | 8.6 | * | * | * | 7.6 |
| (3) *Physics Letters A* | 5.5 | * | 6.7 | * | * | 7.0 |
| (4) *Journal of Low Temperatures Physics* | 12.3 | * | * | 12.0 | 3.2 | 11.4 |
| (5) *Zhurmal Eskperimentalnoi i Teoreticheskoi Fiziki* | 4.4 | * | * | * | 15.8 | 5.4 |
| (6) *Physical Review Letters* | 8.2 | * | * | * | * | 18.6 |

*Less than 3%.

1978, was cited by the top three journals in 1987 in the following fashion: 3.9% from *Physical Review B*, 3.0% from *Solid State Communications*, and 3.2% from *Physical Letters A*.

The citation communication of the core journals of "superconductivity" illustrates some order, but it is order based on an arbitrary choice of the 3% or 5% criterion level. These data do not convincingly illustrate that citation frequency activity follows Bradfordian frequency analysis. A finer subject analysis would be needed to determine reasons for certain citation patterns, for example, the role played by *Physical Review*.

## Perspective on the Literature of "Superconductivity"

This study has attempted to study the scholarly journal channel reporting the developments concerning low-temperature reduced resistance to electrical current by analyzing the journal cohort producing articles indexed under "superconductivity" in the INSPEC database. Assuming that this artificial bibliographical construct does reflect the nature of the scientific journal activity in this field, it is then possible to conclude that the scholarly journal communication channel of "superconductivity" is a well-ordered one that is dominated by a pair of mutually supporting journals. This pair of journals is itself supported by a cohort of supplementary journals that cite the leading pair. Six journals have made up the core of the literature for the last five years.

The most surprising characteristic of the journal literature of "superconductivity" is that it has been growing more intense as it has been growing larger. It appears that, once a journal has published an article indexed under "superconductivity," the journal eventually publishes more of the same. Not found was a large host of journals that published only one article pertaining to "superconductivity." During the study period, there was only one new journal introduced that found a location near the core journals. Such a finding does not diminish Price's new-journal thesis. The lack of new journals may have been offset by the changing focus of established journals during the study period. A final analysis of the contents of such core journals may reveal that adjustments in the focus of the journal by the editors over time have in fact created a new journal, even though the name of the journal remains unchanged.

## Critique of the Bibliometric Methodology

Bibliometrics, as employed in this chapter, is an attempt to find corresponding regularities in two different bibliographic provinces: the publishing activity of scholarly journals in the field of "superconductivity" and the intellectual links among journals created by citations. Bradfordian analysis was used to calibrate the important journals of the publishing activity, and the *Science Citation Index* was used to chart the corresponding citation activity. There is no special reason why these two bibliographic provinces should correlate, given the peculiarities of both publishing and private citation behavior. In the present case of "superconductivity," however, they seem to do so. Such correspondences imply that the most voluminous journals in this literature are also the most prestigious. It is easy to imagine counterexamples: There are many voluminous journals that are not prestigious and many prestigious journals that are not voluminous. In the area of "superconductivity," however, this study found a few journals that both achieve heavy output and maintain high regard. These results characterize one possible pattern of the communication channel of a well-ordered, and rapidly changing, scientific field. It is dangerous to speculate beyond the present case as to the nature of the scholarly journal communication channel for other rapidly developing fields. They beg for their own analyses.

The bibliometric analysis in this chapter rests on several arbitrary foundations that must be addressed by future work.

## Literature Definition

Literatures are casually discussed as if they were well-defined beings located in well-known places. In fact, the literature of a rapidly developing field is in no special place and is usually hiding under a number of headings. One of the possible reasons that this has not hindered librarians and researchers is that work in a rapidly changing field obsolesces very quickly. It is likely that work indexed last year under a variant term is too old to matter. It is only in attempting a longitudinal bibliometric study that one runs into definitional problems, such as the scope of the database, the meaning of the thesauri terms, and changing journal names.

## Bradfordian Mechanics

Although the minimum perfect Bradford partition represents a conceptual advance in Bradfordian studies, it is still a mechanical process that produces arbitrary and hard-to-explain results. The flip-flop of limiting core ranks of Table 13.3 is an example of this mechanical result that defies explanation. Sometimes the limiting core rank is about 11, when two zones are created; and sometimes the limiting core rank is about 6, when three zones are created. This seems to be a serious methodological difficulty that must be explained theoretically. How, or why, do core zones expand or contract so violently from year to year?

The suggestion of limiting the number of zones to two or three or four, and so on, must be rejected immediately. Using a preset number of zones in a Bradfordian partition is exactly the arbitrariness in Bradford's own work that was challenged by both Goffman and Warren (1969) and Egghe (1986). The evolution of the Bradfordian methodology, which has resulted in the application of the MPBP, has produced, in this analysis of "superconductivity," the arbitrary results that one should expect of an arbitrary methodology. What is needed now is either a methodological advance to solve this problem or a theoretical advance to explain it. Although it is heartening to see how the citation activity at the 3%-5% level seems to agree with the Bradfordian analysis, this correspondence cannot provide the necessary theoretical explanation on which to rest Bradfordian analysis.

## Citation Analysis

Charting the citation activity among journals, and determining significant communication patterns, ultimately rests on the analyst's decision to use a certain criterion level. In the absence of a criterion level, there is no discernible pattern except that each journal cites a few other journals copiously and many journals sparingly (which is itself a classic Bradfordian pattern). Even the *Journal Citation Reports* of the *Science Citation Index* does not list every journal cited. Journals that are cited at approximately the 0.1% level and below are lumped together. Often this category includes hundreds of titles.

## Conclusion

Bibliometric measures can provide some useful perspectives on the scholarly communication channel of a rapidly developing field. The literature of "superconductivity" was found to be an intensely clustered journal cohort. At this time, exact procedures and techniques of bibliometrics have not been satisfactorily developed, despite the fact that in this study pleasingly congruent results were obtained from both Bradfordian and citation analyses. What is missing from this correlation is the explanatory insight that would draw journal core analysis and scholarly citation analysis into a conceptual whole.

SANDOR ZSINDELY
ANDRAS SCHUBERT

# 14. Editors-in-Chief of Medical Journals: Are They Experts, Authorities, Both, or Neither?

The professional status and influence of the editors-in-chief of 769 medical journals were studied using the methods of citation analysis. Two indexes were formed: (a) the Index of Editor Expertise (IEE)—the ratio of the editor-in-chief's mean citation rate per cited paper to that of his or her journal—and (b) the Index of Editor Authority (IEA)—the ratio of the editor-in-chief's percentage of in-journal citations to that of his or her journal. According to these indexes, the editors-in-chief are not necessarily experts but are authorities—at least in their own specialties.

"We collaborate. I'm an expert, but not an authority, and Dr. Gelbis is an authority, but not an expert." (Cartoon of Sidney Harris in *Current Contents*)

Beyond doubt, editors of scientific journals have utmost influence on the scientific communities of their respective subject fields. As "gatekeepers" of the communication flows, they are in a position to decide what the legitimate scientific questions are and what results may gain publicity in the primary formal information channel of science: the journal literature (Crane, 1967).

Various journals honor their editors with various titles: calling them members of editorial boards or advisory boards, associate editors, managing editors, and so on. In almost all cases, however, the *primus inter pares* is the editor-in-chief: a respected scientist or scholar, assuming, as it were, personal responsibility for the papers published in his or her journal. In one of our earlier studies (Zsindely, Schubert, & Braun, 1982a), an attempt was made to find correlations between the eminence of international chemistry journals and that of their editors (both measured by citation indicators). The main conclusion was that "the editorial bodies . . . are true gatekeepers and their professional status is positively correlated with the scientific quality of the international journals. The person of the Editor-in-Chief alone seems to have much less influence." Similar conclusions have been drawn in a more detailed study within the subfield of analytical chemistry (Braun & Bujdoso, 1983).

In this chapter, an attempt is made to be even more inquisitive about the professional status and influence of the editors-in-chief of 769 medical journals. By using the methods of citation analysis, answers are sought to the question of whether the editors-in-chief as authors have larger influence and/or authority than an average scientist in the respective subject field.

## Data Sources

Journals covered by the *Science Citation Index (SCI)* database are categorized into subject fields in each *SCI Annual Guide*; a related classification has been developed by Computer Horizons, Inc. (Narin, 1976). On the basis of these schemes, 769 journals in 28 medical subject fields were included in our study. The 894 editors-in-chief of these journals were identified from *Ulrich's International Periodical Directory* (1986, 1987, and 1988 editions on CD-ROM). Source data from the years 1981 to 1985 and citations to them in the same five-year period were used in our analysis. Journal citation indicators were produced by processing the magnetic tape version of the *SCI* database; citation data of the editors-in-chief's first-authored papers were searched manually from the printed volumes. Prior studies indicate that first-author citation counts are a reasonably good and reliable approximation of total citation count (Roy, Roy, & Johnson, 1983).

## Methods and Results

For each journal and editor-in-chief, the following data were collected:

— the number of cited publications (papers published between 1981 and 1985 and cited in the same period)

— the number of citations received between 1981 and 1985 by the above papers

— the percentage of in-journal citations, that is, the percentage share of the citations from the journal itself in all citations received (for the editors-in-chief, the percentage share of the citations from their own journals in all citations received by their papers published in their own journals)

From these data, two main indicators were formed:

— an Index of Editor Expertise (IEE): the ratio of the editor-in-chief's mean citation rate for cited paper to that of his or her journal

— an Index of Editor Authorities (IEA): the ratio of the editor-in-chief's percentage of in-journal citations to that of his or her journal

Both indexes have a value of 1.00 if there are no specific differences between the editor-in-chief and an average author. All editors-in-chief having at least one cited paper in the period in question (709 persons, 855 editorial chairs) were included in the determination of the Index of Editor Expertise (IEE); all editors-in-chief having at least one cited paper in their own journals in the period in question (353 persons, 435 editorial chairs) were included in the determination of the Index of Editor Authority (IEA). The overall average IEE value was 0.59; the overall average IEA value was 1.64. (The subset of editors considered in evaluating IEA had an average IEE of 0.61, i.e., no significant difference from the total set has been found.) The values of both indicators are presented at a subfield aggregate level in Tables 14.1 and 14.2, respectively.

Subfield differences among IEE and IEA indexes, although interesting to consider, are, in general, not statistically significant.

## Discussion

The main inference to be drawn from the data presented in Tables 14.1 and 14.2 is obvious. In all but 3 of the 28 subfields of medicine,

TABLE 14.1

Mean Citation Rate per Cited Paper and the Index of Editor Expertise

| Subfield | Number of Editors | Mean Citation Rate per Cited Paper | | IEE |
|---|---|---|---|---|
| | | Journals | Editors | |
| Allergy | 8 | 3.46 | 3.46 | 1.00 |
| Andrology | 5 | 3.02 | 2.57 | 0.85 |
| Anesthesiology | 8 | 3.53 | 3.33 | 0.94 |
| Cancer | 48 | 4.72 | 3.39 | 0.72* |
| Cardiovascular system | 46 | 5.30 | 2.72 | 0.51* |
| Dentistry and odontology | 21 | 2.86 | 2.00 | 0.70* |
| Dermatology and venereal diseases | 18 | 3.17 | 2.60 | 0.82 |
| Endocrinology and metabolism | 46 | 6.09 | 4.27 | 0.70* |
| Gastroenterology | 19 | 4.15 | 2.11 | 0.51* |
| General and internal medicine | 65 | 2.89 | 2.26 | 0.78 |
| Geriatrics and gerontology | 10 | 2.61 | 2.66 | 1.02 |
| Hematology | 32 | 5.81 | 3.10 | 0.53* |
| Immunology | 66 | 6.02 | 3.13 | 0.52* |
| Neurosciences | 106 | 5.47 | 3.13 | 0.57* |
| Obstetrics and gynecology | 27 | 3.56 | 2.10 | 0.59* |
| Ophthalmology | 15 | 3.53 | 2.20 | 0.62* |
| Orthopedics | 9 | 2.45 | 2.12 | 0.87 |
| Otorhinolaryngology | 9 | 2.61 | 1.87 | 0.71 |
| Pathology | 39 | 4.61 | 2.96 | 0.64* |
| Pediatrics | 31 | 2.92 | 2.59 | 0.89 |
| Psychiatry | 36 | 3.72 | 2.31 | 0.62* |
| Radiology and nuclear medicine | 40 | 3.64 | 1.90 | 0.52* |
| Research and experimental medicine | 28 | 3.77 | 3.02 | 0.80 |
| Respiratory system | 19 | 4.22 | 2.62 | 0.62* |
| Rheumatology | 13 | 2.68 | 2.78 | 1.04 |
| Surgery | 58 | 3.02 | 1.92 | 0.63* |
| Tropical medicine | 12 | 2.71 | 2.57 | 0.95 |
| Urology and nephrology | 21 | 2.81 | 2.78 | 0.99 |

NOTE: Asterisks denote a statistically significant deviation between the journal and the editor values at the 95% confidence level (using a simple $t$-test).

the editors-in-chief are, on average, less cited than their own journals; and in all but 6 subfields, the average percentage of in-journal citations is higher for the papers of the editors-in-chief than for those of a "GI" author. The answer to the question in this title of this article is thus clear: The editors-in-chief are not necessarily experts (in the sense of a higher-than-average citation rate) but, as a rule, authorities—at least in their own specialties.

TABLE 14.2
Percentage of In-Journal Citations and the Index of Editor Authority

| Subfield | Number of Editors | Percentage of In-Journal Citations | | IEA |
| | | Journals | Editors | |
| --- | --- | --- | --- | --- |
| Allergy | 5 | 20 | 29 | 1.44 |
| Andrology | 5 | 13 | 25 | 1.92 |
| Anesthesiology | 6 | 25 | 69 | 2.79* |
| Cancer | 21 | 14 | 14 | 1.00 |
| Cardiovascular system | 25 | 13 | 26 | 1.94* |
| Dentistry and odontology | 12 | 29 | 38 | 1.30 |
| Dermatology and venereal diseases | 14 | 25 | 32 | 1.27 |
| Endocrinology and metabolism | 20 | 14 | 12 | 0.84 |
| Gastroenterology | 9 | 10 | 26 | 2.56 |
| General and internal medicine | 35 | 21 | 50 | 2.33* |
| Geriatrics and gerontology | 5 | 20 | 52 | 2.52 |
| Hematology | 21 | 12 | 21 | 1.72* |
| Immunology | 30 | 15 | 23 | 1.58* |
| Neurosciences | 51 | 16 | 22 | 1.38 |
| Obstetrics and gynecology | 8 | 12 | 16 | 1.38 |
| Ophthalmology | 10 | 21 | 18 | 0.86 |
| Orthopedics | 4 | 11 | 7 | 0.63 |
| Otorhinolaryngology | 7 | 19 | 49 | 2.56 |
| Pathology | 18 | 13 | 26 | 1.94 |
| Pediatrics | 19 | 20 | 35 | 1.70 |
| Psychiatry | 17 | 17 | 30 | 1.77 |
| Radiology and nuclear medicine | 15 | 21 | 39 | 1.87* |
| Research and experimental medicine | 16 | 17 | 35 | 2.07 |
| Respiratory system | 10 | 15 | 13 | 0.92 |
| Rheumatology | 7 | 17 | 5 | 0.27 |
| Surgery | 29 | 18 | 23 | 1.29 |
| Tropical medicine | 6 | 23 | 39 | 1.67 |
| Urology and nephrology | 10 | 17 | 29 | 1.74 |

NOTE: Asterisks denote a statistically significant deviation between the journal and the editor values at the 95% confidence level (using a simple $t$-test).

The question now arises: If not their research eminence, what else might be the source of the authority of these scientists? An obvious explanation would be to relate present authority to past expertise, to assume that 1981-1985 is too recent a period to represent properly the real scientific performance of the editors-in-chief. To check this hypothesis, the citation rate of a subsample of 267 editors-in-chief (those having 6 to 15 cited papers in the 1981-1985 period) was also searched for the 1970-1974 period (1970-1974 citations to 1970-1974 papers). It is surprising that the average was only insignificantly higher in the earlier period, namely,

3.10 citations per cited paper in the 1970-1974 period

2.84 citations per paper in the 1981-1985 period

This difference does not account for the observed underperformance of the editors-in-chief in their citation levels.

We are inclined to interpret our results as evidence that editing a scientific journal requires qualities somewhat different from those of a prolific and highly cited author. Although most of the editors under study were active as publishing scientists and also received citations in the period in question, their influence seems to be shorter range—presumably more personal in nature—and their authority domains are more limited. We even suspect that the same qualities that make someone an eminent editor-in-chief (strong personal influence, ability to make quick, intuitive decisions, and so on) may prevent him or her from being a universally acknowledged, highly cited researcher. Of course, the most fortunate cases are those in which the two sets of qualities coincide, but this is the exception rather than the rule.

Again, our results lead us to stress that scientometric indicators, however useful they may be in assessing larger scientific communities (attempts to use "gatekeeper indicators" for countries and institutions were reported in Bakker & Righter, 1985; Righter, 1986; Zsindely, Schubert, & Braun, 1982b), easily fail in evaluating individuals. Or, rather, in our opinion, although eminence reflected in scientometric indicators can hardly be a failure, the lack of eminence in these indicators does not necessarily prevent anyone from being an extremely valuable and respected member of the scientific community: for example, an editor-in-chief of a scientific journal.

JAMES R. BENIGER

# 15. Identifying the Important Theorists of Communication: Use of Latent Measures to Test Manifest Assumptions in Scholarly Communication

Bibliometric analysis of the 1989 *International Encyclopedia of Communications*, a four-volume, 1,800-page work containing 569 articles by 465 authorities from 27 countries, is used to identify the most important theorists in communication. Manifest and latent measures of importance are distinguished; latent data are found to undermine conclusions based on manifest assumptions in scholarly communication. Using an ordinal (rank order) measure of importance comprising six separate, ordered, ranked counts, both manifest and latent, the top 120 theorists in communication are identified. They are listed both in rank order and chronologically with their years of birth and death, field of specialization, and nation in which their major work was formulated. These data are used to make inferences about the historical development of communication theory.

Who are the important theorists of communication? Despite centuries of theoretical work on various aspects of communication, the field itself still lacks even the loose consensus on important theory that characterizes most other academic disciplines. In a 1983 special issue of the *Journal of Communication* devoted to "critical issues and research tasks of the discipline," for example, 41 contributors from 10 countries advanced almost as many different views of their field's theoretical foundations (as reflected in the special issue's title, "Ferment in the Field"). "We must ask whether we have produced only *ingredients* of communication theory," Wilbur Schramm wrote in the introductory essay. "Are the pieces of a general theory of communication lying around us ready to be assembled? Or, for

254

some reason, is a central theory of communication beyond our capability at this time?" (Schramm, 1983, p. 14).

One reason for the lack of consensus on the field's central theoretical foundation may be that, despite centuries of work relevant to communication theory, the *concept* of communication has only recently surfaced in theoretical discourse. In the Encyclopedia Britannica's 54-volume *Great Books of the Western World* (Hutchins, 1952), for example, *communication* did not make the list of 102 terms used to organize 520 works from Homer to Freud. Nor did *communication* make Britannica's penultimate list of 115 terms, nor even the 88 additional ones ranked "among the most likely candidates for inclusion" (Adler, 1952, pp. 1223-1224). Only in the publication's 1,798-item "inventory of terms" does *communication* appear—24 times among 163,000 citations (related terms *information* and *control* do not appear at all; Beniger, 1986, p. 39).

Lack of consensus on a unifying body of theory may be responsible for the more general lack of focus on *any* central body of work within the field of communication. A comprehensive recent survey of American communication, the 946-page *Handbook of Communication Science* (Berger & Chaffee, 1987), for example, includes a 34-page author index containing 3,496 different names, an average of more than 3.96 unique author names per page of text! Despite the staggering number of authors cited, however, the *Handbook* contains not a single mention of many important theorists of communication: John Austin, Mikhail Bakhtin, Umberto Eco, Nelson Goodman, Martin Heidegger, Louis Hjelmslev, Edmund Husserl, Roman Jakobson, Claude Lévi-Strauss, Charles Morris, Charles Peirce, Vladimir Propp, Ferdinand de Saussure, John von Neumann, and Ludwig Wittgenstein, among others (Beniger, 1988, pp. 210-212).

Growing isolation of the communication field from theoretical and related work in other disciplines has been documented in several bibliometric studies. In research "to determine whether the communication sciences are becoming better integrated with other social sciences over time," Paisley (1984) analyzes core journals from 1950 to 1981 to find: "The answer to that question, according to the citation data, is no." This Paisley (1984, p. 28) attributes to what he calls *ethnocentrism*, "the social-cognitive rejection of persons, values, ideas, etc., simply because they originate outside the culture that judges them." For the period 1977-1981, Reeves and Borgman (1983) find communication researchers "less dependent on other social science journals in the conduct of their research." Using additional citation data through 1985, Rice, Borgman, and Reeves (1988) continue to find what they term "inbreeding" even within subfields ("cliques") such as those devoted to the separate studies of interpersonal and mass communication.

Insofar as inbreeding and ethnocentrism might be expected to result in a discipline's *convergence* on a central theoretical foundation, the field of communication has thus far managed to achieve the worst of both opposing tendencies: growing isolation from other disciplines, on one hand, along with a continuing lack of theoretical consensus, on the other. The remedy seems obvious though not easily achieved: If the various subfields of communication are to overcome their inbreeding, and the field as a whole to find its theoretical foundations, the potentially integrative theorists, theories, and theoretical works most central to communication must be identified and promoted (through undergraduate and graduate teaching, for example) by a broad range of credible scholars within the field itself.

Interest among communication scholars in achieving at least modest consensus on theory might be seen in their growing interest in the topic of this volume, bibliometric analysis of scholarly communication. As editor Christine Borgman notes, interest in scholarly communication has increased within the communication field, in part for reasons "exemplified by [its] continued introspection about [its] constituency and viability as [a] discipline." She cites as evidence of such continued introspection four communication sources published since 1983, including "Ferment in the Field" and the *Handbook of Communication Science*. As demonstrated by the examples of physics, chemistry, and medicine, she concludes, "A field's interest in its own scholarly communication is a sign of its maturity" (Borgman, this volume).

The problem remains to identify the most important theorists, theories, and theoretical works, as acknowledged by the broadest range of communication scholars, that might provide a central focus for the field. Until recently, such a consensus would have been difficult if not impossible to engineer. With the 1989 publication of the *International Encyclopedia of Communications*, however, communication might have at last found its theoretical core. Through bibliometric analysis of this unique source of scholarly communication about communication, a four-volume, 1,800-page work containing 569 articles on different subfields by 465 authorities from 27 countries, a broad, international, elite consensus on the theoretical foundations of the field might at last be identifiable.

Appearance of a major multiple-author secondary work has been shown to be a key stage in the development of other scientific disciplines (Mullins, 1973, chaps. 1, 2). For example, Nicholas Mullins finds the 29-author *Sociology Today* (Merton, Broom, & Cottrell, 1959) "the high point of the specialty stage" in the development of "standard American sociology" (Mullins, 1973, pp. 65-67). Whatever use bibliometric analysis of the *International Encyclopedia* might be to communication in finding its identity as a discipline, in other words, such analysis can also be expected to provide new insights into the development and structure of scholarly communication in this field.

## The Source

*The International Encyclopedia of Communications*, a project of the Annenberg School of Communications at the University of Pennsylvania, was published by Oxford University Press on April 6, 1989, under the guidance of editor-in-chief Eric Barnouw, professor emeritus of dramatic arts at Columbia University. Four other names appear on the title page: editorial board chair George Gerbner and associate editor Larry Gross, both professors at the Annenberg School, University of Pennsylvania; consulting editor Wilbur Schramm (since deceased), director emeritus of the Institute for Communications Research, Stanford University; and editorial director Tobia L. Worth, employed by the *Encyclopedia* itself.

The work consists of four volumes with 569 articles totaling exactly 1,800 pages (1,938 pages including the 87-page index, 17-page directory of contributors, 8-page topical guide, and other supporting material). According to the editors, the work represents 30 distinct topics, "each of which represents a major field of interest in the evolving communications discipline" (Barnouw, 1989, Vol. 4, p. 361). As suggested by 2 of the 30 topics, "theories of communication" and "theorists," the editors give explicit attention to areas useful to our analysis here. According to them, 27 separate articles, ranging from information theory and cybernetics to historiography and poetics, and from Marxist theories and structuralism to social cognition and cognitive consistency theory, cover the topic "theories of communication." They also designate 61 of the 134 people accorded individual entries in the *Encyclopedia* as "theorists" (Barnouw, 1989, Vol. 4, pp. 367-368).

Of the 465 contributors to the *Encyclopedia*, 356 (76.6%) work in the United States; the remaining 109 (23.4%) in 26 other countries. These include England (42; 9.0%), Canada (13; 2.8%), Israel (8; 1.7%), France (6; 1.3%), and Australia and Japan (each 4; 0.9%); the remaining 20 countries represent 32 contributors (6.9%). Europe (including the Soviet Union) accounts for 15 countries and 68 contributors (14.6%); the Third Word, 7 countries and 12 contributors (2.6%). A total of 388 contributors (83.4%) have university affiliations; the remaining 77 (16.6%) work in governmental, other nonprofit, and commercial sectors.

Of the 388 contributors with academic affiliations, 297 (76.5%) represent a total of 116 U.S. universities; the remaining 91 (23.5%) come from 58 foreign institutions (see Table 15.1). Of the 77 contributors with affiliations outside of academe, 59 (76.6%) work in the United States; the remaining 18 (23.4%) in 12 other countries. As can be seen in Table 15.1, academic contritutors to the *Encyclopedia* come predominantly from major centers of communication studies (the universities of Pennsylvania, Wisconsin, Illinois, Indiana, Texas, Michigan, Washington, and California at San Diego, plus Stanford, Temple, New York University, Rutgers, and the University of Southern California), other major U.S. universities (Columbia, City University of New York, Harvard, Chicago, Yale, and Duke), and important foreign universities (Oxford, Hebrew University, Cambridge, École des Hautes Études, and York University). As shown in Table 15.1, more than 42% of the contributors to the *Encyclopedia* and more than 43% of its articles come from the 27 most-represented U.S. and foreign universities.

In summary, the *International Encyclopedia of Communications* has several advantages for identifying the theoretical foundations of communication—through bibliometric analysis—not approximated in any other work published to date. Among these advantages:

- an unusually large number of contributors (465, compared with 29 for *Sociology Today*, 38 for the *Handbook of Communication Science*, and 41 for "Ferment in the Field");

TABLE 15.1
University Affiliations of Contributors to the International Encyclopedia of
Communications

| Rank | University | Contributors | Percentage | Articles | Percentage |
|---|---|---|---|---|---|
| 1 | University of Pennsylvania | 30 | 6.5 | 42 | 7.1 |
| 2 | Stanford University | 11 | 2.4 | 21 | 3.5 |
| 3 | University of Wisconsin | 10 | 2.2 | 12 | 2.0 |
| 4 | Temple University | 10 | 2.2 | 11 | 1.8 |
| 5 | Oxford University* | 8 | 1.7 | 13 | 2.8 |
| 6 | University of Southern California | 8 | 1.7 | 9 | 1.5 |
| 7 | University of Illinois | 8 | 1.7 | 8 | 1.3 |
| 8 | Columbia University | 7 | 1.5 | 20 | 3.4 |
| t9 | Indiana University | 7 | 1.5 | 8 | 1.3 |
| t9 | University of Texas | 7 | 1.5 | 8 | 1.3 |
| t11 | City University of New York | 7 | 1.5 | 7 | 1.2 |
| t11 | Harvard University | 7 | 1.5 | 7 | 1.2 |
| t11 | Hebrew University | 7 | 1.5 | 7 | 1.2 |
| t11 | University of Michigan | 7 | 1.5 | 7 | 1.2 |
| 15 | New York University | 6 | 1.3 | 12 | 2.0 |
| 16 | University of California, San Diego | 6 | 1.3 | 8 | 1.3 |
| 17 | Cambridge University | 6 | 1.3 | 6 | 1.0 |
| 18 | University of Washington | 5 | 1.1 | 7 | 1.2 |
| 19 | Rutgers University | 5 | 1.1 | 6 | 1.0 |
| t20 | University of Chicago | 5 | 1.1 | 5 | .8 |
| t20 | University of Massachusetts | 5 | 1.1 | 5 | .8 |
| t20 | Yale University | 5 | 1.1 | 5 | .8 |
| 23 | University of Houston | 4 | .9 | 6 | 1.0 |
| t24 | Duke University | 4 | .9 | 5 | .8 |
| t24 | University of California, Los Angeles | 4 | .9 | 5 | .8 |
| t26 | École des Hautes Études* | 4 | .9 | 4 | .7 |
| t26 | York University* | 4 | .9 | 4 | .7 |
| | Total | 197 | 42.4 | 258 | 43.4 |
| | Other U.S. universities (N = 94) | 129 | 27.7 | 160 | 26.9 |
| | Other foreign universities (N = 53) | 62 | 13.3 | 76 | 12.8 |
| | All other universities (N = 147) | 191 | 41.1 | 236 | 39.7 |
| | Nonuniversity U.S. | 59 | 12.7 | 77 | 12.9 |
| | Nonuniversity foreign | 18 | 3.9 | 24 | 4.0 |
| | Total nonuniversity | 77 | 16.6 | 101 | 17.0 |
| | Totals—all contributors | 465 | 100.0 | 595** | 100.0 |

*Foreign universities.
**Multiple-author articles counted multiple times (total 569 articles).

- global representation (contributors work in 27 countries on all continents, 23.4% outside of the United States);
- representation of a wide range of universities (116 U.S. and 58 foreign) with concentration in the major American centers of communication studies and other elite U.S. and foreign institutions (as seen in Table 15.1);
- interdisciplinary representation (only 19.6% of the contributors come from the field of communication narrowly defined; 22 other disciplines and professional specializations are represented by five or more contributors);
- substantial volume of text for bibliometric analysis (1,800 large-sized pages, compared with 359 standard pages in "Ferment in the Field" and 895 in the *Handbook of Communication Science*);
- unusually wide coverage of communication (569 separate articles) in 30 fields of interest ranging from the sciences (animal communication) to the social sciences (institutions, political communication) and from professional fields (advertising and public relations, journalism, education) to the humanities (arts, music, theater, literature); and
- explicit attention to theorists and theories of communication (two of thirty fields covered, including separate entries for 61 people designated as theorists and 27 other articles intended to cover aspects of communication theory).

## Importance: Latent Versus Manifest Measures

Given the unique features and relative advantages of the *Encyclopedia* as a source of data on communication, how might this work be used to determine the field's most important theorists and theories? Although all content analysis is unobtrusive measurement (Webb, Campbell, Schwartz, & Sechrest, 1966; Webb, Campbell, Schwartz, Sechrest, & Grove, 1981), a distinction parallel to the obtrusive-unobtrusive one might be drawn between data that directly result from the centralized decisions of the *Encyclopedia*'s editors, on one hand, and data aggregated from the independent decisions of all 465 contributors, on the other.

Because the former type of data derive from behavior (like editorial planning) that is "obtrusive" for the source of communication (the *Encyclopedia*'s editors) and obvious to its audience, these might be called *manifest* data. The latter type of data, by contrast, emerge only through activities of the analyst (like aggregation) that are "unobtrusive" to the communication source and transparent to virtually all of the audience; these might be called *latent* data. Manifest measures of a theorist's importance to the *Encyclopedia* might include, for example, whether the editors have selected him or her to be the subject of an individual article as well as the length of the entry. Latent measures of importance, by contrast, might include the number of authors or articles (some authors contributed more than one) that mention a theorist, the number of pages on which he or she is mentioned, the number of his or her works cited, or the number of times that these works are cited.

Because the strategy here is to exploit the aggregate expertise of the *Encyclopedia*'s 465 contributors rather than that of its few editors or its editorial board, we will emphasize latent measures of theorists' importance. Because it is impossible entirely to disentangle the influence of some editorial decisions on many latent measures, however, it will be useful to include manifest measures as secondary data. The goal, therefore, will be to combine both latent and manifest data in a single measure of importance but also to report here constituent measures for the use of those who might like to analyze the data in other ways.

Three readily quantifiable and objective latent measures of importance to a field (whether of a person, work, idea, or term) are suggested by the format of an encyclopedia: the number of entries, authors (including joint authorships), and pages of mention. These three counts stand in the relationship:

[mentions] ≥ pages ≥ entries ≥ authorships

This relationship obtains because every author (or authorship) must write at least one article, every article must occupy as least one page, and every page on which a theorist is mentioned must contain at least one mention.

Here we use the number of pages on which a theorist is mentioned rather than the count of mentions themselves not only because the former is more readily obtained (via the index) but also because pages of mention are likely to be more distributed over an entire encyclopedia than are mentions themselves (we are interested in importance to the entire field of communication rather than to any of its subfields). By the same reasoning, the number of entries that mention a theorist is more useful for our purposes than is the number of pages: Entries are also more likely to be distributed over the entire subject matter than are pages of mention. It is more important, for example, to be mentioned on one page in each of five articles (total: five pages) than on six or more pages in four or fewer articles.

Because contributors who write two or more articles might still be expected to write in a single area of expertise, the number of authors who mention a theorist might seem to be a more useful measure—given our interest in the entire field of communication— than are the number of entries of mention. Indeed, we will consider the number of authorships to be more useful for our purposes than is the number of pages. Unlike both authorships and pages, however, entries in an encyclopedia are purposively chosen and engineered to be mutually exclusive and exhaustive subsets of the entire field. Moreover, only 61 (13.1%) of the *Encyclopedia* contributors wrote two or more entries; 25 (5.4%) wrote three or more; and 5 (1.1%) wrote seven or more.

For these reasons, we will consider the number of entries that mention the theorist to be more useful for our purposes than is the number of authors (a decision that, incidentally, preserves the logic of citation counts, which are usually counts of articles rather than of authors or pages). It is more important to be mentioned in six or more articles by fewer than five authors, in other words, than in five articles by five authors.

To summarize the latent measure of importance used here, it is an ordinal (rank order) measure itself comprising three separate, ordered, ranked counts—of the number of entries, authors (including joint authorships), and pages, respectively:

Rank (importance) = ordered rank (entries, authors, pages)

Because the three constituent measures are not independent (constrained as they are by the relationship pages $\geq$ entries $\geq$ authorships), and indeed are highly correlated, their ordered ranking is preferable to any unweighted linear combination.

## Applying the Measure

With the 465 authors and 569 articles of the *International Encyclopedia of Communications* as the source of data on the field, we might
now reconsider the question that began this chapter: Who are the
important theorists of communication? Applying the latent measure
of importance developed in the previous section to the *Encyclopedia*,
we find a total of 261 persons (not only theorists) mentioned in at
least four entries (the arbitrary cutoff for discussion here); an additional 43 persons are mentioned in three entries, by three authors,
and on four or more pages. This means that persons mentioned in
three entries, by three authors, and on only three pages (the level
at which the hierarchy appears—by subjective standards—to degen-
erate into noise) would rank no higher than 305th in importance in
the *Encyclopedia* (actual rank depending on secondary manifest
measures as discussed below).

Those mentioned in 10 or more articles constitute the 25 most
important persons (see Table 15.2). Aristotle ranks first, with 37
articles, 36 authors, and 51 pages; followed by Plato (32, 31, 42);
Saussure (22, 21, 29); Shakespeare (16, 16, 19); and Chomsky (15,
15, 18). The 25 most often named persons include 18 theorists; fields
represented include philosophy (7), linguistics (4), literature and
politics (3 each), anthropology (2), and motion pictures, printing,
psychology, rhetoric, semiotics, and sociology (1 each).

Although the three constituent measures used in the latent ranks
in Table 15.2 are obviously highly correlated (recall that they are
constrained by the relationship pages ≥ entries ≥ authorships), the
overall ranking of importance would change somewhat if the con-
stituents were reordered. If the number of authors mentioning a
person had been considered the most important constituent measure, for example, Charles Peirce (mentioned by only nine authors)
would have dropped from 15th to 24th place. If, on the other hand,
the number of pages of mention had been considered most important, Peirce (cited on 18 pages) would have risen to 6th place.

Peirce's particular profile of measures (relatively more pages
than authors of mention) characterizes persons whose impact on a
field is relatively more specialized. The opposite profile, in which
the number of pages approximates or equals the number of authors,

TABLE 15.2
Most Often Named Persons, All Fields (named in ten or more articles)

| Rank | Name | Field | Articles | Authors | Pages | Biography |
|------|------|-------|----------|---------|-------|-----------|
| 1 | Aristotle* | Philosophy | 37 | 36 | 51 | Yes |
| 2 | Plato* | Philosophy | 32 | 31 | 42 | Yes |
| 3 | Saussure* | Linguistics | 22 | 21 | 29 | Yes |
| 4 | Shakespeare | Literature | 16 | 16 | 19 | No |
| 5 | Chomsky* | Linguistics | 15 | 15 | 18 | ** |
| 6 | Kant* | Philosophy | 15 | 15 | 17 | No |
| 7 | Barthes* | Semiotics | 14 | 13 | 17 | Yes |
| 8 | Hitler | Politics | 13 | 13 | 16 | No |
| 9 | Lenin | Politics | 13 | 13 | 14 | No |
| 10 | Freud* | Psychology | 13 | 12 | 17 | Yes |
| 11 | Jakobson* | Linguistics | 13 | 12 | 15 | Yes |
| 12 | Gutenberg | Printing | 12 | 12 | 17 | Yes |
| 13 | Bateson* | Anthropology | 12 | 10 | 16 | Yes |
| 14 | Sapir* | Linguistics | 12 | 10 | 13 | Yes |
| 15 | Peirce* | Philosophy | 12 | 9 | 18 | Yes |
| t16 | Lévi-Strauss* | Anthropology | 11 | 11 | 14 | Yes |
| t16 | Welles | Film | 11 | 11 | 14 | Yes |
| 18 | Rousseau* | Philosophy | 11 | 11 | 12 | No |
| 19 | Adorno* | Philosophy | 11 | 10 | 14 | Yes |
| 20 | F. Roosevelt | Politics | 11 | 10 | 12 | No |
| t21 | Goffman* | Sociology | 10 | 10 | 12 | Yes |
| t21 | S. Johnson | Literature | 10 | 10 | 12 | Yes |
| t23 | Augustine* | Philosophy | 10 | 10 | 11 | No |
| t23 | Milton* | Literature | 10 | 10 | 11 | Yes |
| 25 | Cicero* | Rhetoric | 10 | 9 | 13 | Yes |

*Classified as a communication theorist in this chapter.
**Not eligible for biographical entry (living; born after December 31. 1919).

characterizes persons of relatively more general impact. This relationship between authors and pages constitutes further reason to use the intermediate value—number of articles—as the first-order constituent measure; the possibility of derivative analysis (as illustrated by citation profiles) underscores the wisdom of including all constituent measures in reports of the data.

Table 15.2 also informs the question of manifest measures: 17 of the 25 most often named persons are the subjects of individual entries (hereafter called *biographies*) and hence have totals directly inflated—relative to those of other persons without biographies—by editorial decision alone. Of the eight persons without biographies, one (Noam Chomsky) was ineligible (the editors of the *Encyclopedia* arbitrarily established the birth date of December 31, 1919, for according *living* persons biographies; Barnouw, 1989, Vol. 1, p. xxiii). Of the other seven persons, four (Shakespeare, Hitler, Lenin, and Franklin Roosevelt) are not cited for their contributions to communication theory (although Lenin is a social theorist, he is mentioned in the *Encyclopedia* primarily as a political leader). Three other persons (Kant, Rousseau, and Augustine), however, are cited for theory relevant to communication.

These results indicate how latent data can undermine manifest assumptions. Even without controlling for citations from the 133 individual biographies, three theorists without biographies placed among the 25 persons most cited in the *Encyclopedia*. One (Kant) garnered more mentions than all but three persons *with* biographies. Even the least cited of the three without biographies (Augustine) ranked higher than all by 15 of the 134 persons with separate entries devoted to themselves (the two Lumiére brothers are covered in a single biography). The editors' decision that Kant, Rousseau, and Augustine are not important enough to communication to merit their own entries is belied by latent measurement: Inordinate numbers of contributors chosen by the editors cite Kant, Rousseau, and Augustine in the same publication—a fact not manifest to most of its readers.

Because the influence of manifest measures on latent measures cannot be isolated, however, the three counts—articles, authors, and pages—that *include* all mentions from biographies (i.e., the three data columns in Table 15.2) will be given the first three places in the new ordered rank measure. By including the direct influence of the biographies in the first-order constituent measurements in this way, we bring the resultant rankings of importance closest to those underlying the editors' decisions, thereby providing the strongest test for possible latent contradictions of these manifest assumptions. The same three counts (articles, authors, and pages), with citations from all biographical entries removed, will be used to compute a secondary ordered ranking, thereby yielding the six-count combined manifest-latent measure of importance used in all subsequent analyses here.

## Identifying the Most Important Theorists

The new six-count, ordered rank measure can be used to determine a more extensive ranking of theorists—beyond the top 18 already identified—based on the 1,800 pages of the *International Encyclopedia of Communications*. Of the total of 261 persons mentioned in at least four entries (the arbitrary cutoff used here), 120 can be classified as theorists. These are listed in the rank order determined by the new six-count measure in Table 15.3 (note that the first 18—Aristotle through Cicero—correspond to the 18 persons designated as theorists in Table 15.2).

Classification as theorist is based primarily on citation for scholarly writing rather than for fiction, drama, or journalism; for production of art, music, motion pictures, or inventions; or for leadership in politics or religion (the 9 fields of the 141 nontheorists). This general rule has only six exceptions: Three persons associated with film (Eisenstein, Bazin, and Morin), two famous literary figures (Dante and Milton), and one political leader (Gramsci) are included among the theorists of communication based on the preponderance of allusions to their more theoretical works (for example, Milton's *Areopagitica* and Gramsci's *Prison Notebooks*). Several other theorists also worked in one or more of the 9 "nontheoretical" fields (for example, Walter Lippmann in journalism).

Validity of the ranking of theorists might be seen by comparing it with the theorists selected for separate biographical entries in the *Encyclopedia*. Of the 61 biographies (among the total 133) described by the editors as those of "theorists" (Barnouw, 1989, Vol. 4, p. 368), 54 (88.5%) of the subjects are included among the 120 theorists most often cited as determined by the six-count measure used here (as indicated by asterisks in Table 15.3).

As would be expected, if the two indicators of theorists' importance were measuring similar phenomena, the two are related: The 54 doubly designated theorists include 22 of the top 30 (73.3%) in Table 15.3, 16 (53.3%) of the second quartile, and 8 (26.7%) of each of the third and fourth quartiles. For deciles (ten groups of 12 each), the counts—from top to bottom—are 10, 8, 9, 5, 6, 3, 4, 4, 0, and 5. This pattern suggests that the six-count ranking has greater validity for the top 96 places (four or more articles and authors and five or more pages) than for the next 24 (one reason not to extend the analysis lower into the overall ranking).

TABLE 15.3
Most Often Named Theorists of Communication (named in four or more articles)

| Theorist | | All Articles | | | Excluding Biographies | | | Overall |
| Rank | Name | Articles | Authors | Pages | Articles | Authors | Pages | Rank |
| --- | --- | --- | --- | --- | --- | --- | --- | --- |
| 1 | Aristotle* | 37 | 36 | 51 | 35 | 35 | 48 | 1 |
| 2 | Plato* | 32 | 31 | 42 | 30 | 30 | 38 | 2 |
| 3 | Saussure* | 22 | 21 | 29 | 19 | 18 | 25 | 3 |
| 4 | Chomsky | 15 | 15 | 18 | 12 | 12 | 15 | 5 |
| 5 | Kant | 15 | 15 | 17 | 14 | 14 | 16 | 6 |
| 6 | Barthes* | 14 | 13 | 17 | 13 | 13 | 15 | 7 |
| 7 | Freud* | 13 | 12 | 17 | 11 | 11 | 14 | 10 |
| 8 | Jakobson* | 13 | 12 | 15 | 11 | 10 | 13 | 11 |
| 9 | Bateson* | 12 | 10 | 16 | 9 | 8 | 12 | 13 |
| 10 | Sapir* | 12 | 10 | 13 | 9 | 9 | 9 | 14 |
| 11 | Peirce* | 12 | 9 | 18 | 8 | 7 | 13 | 15 |
| 12 | Lévi-Strauss* | 11 | 11 | 14 | 10 | 10 | 12 | 16 |
| 13 | Rousseau | 11 | 11 | 12 | 10 | 10 | 11 | 18 |
| 14 | Adorno* | 11 | 10 | 14 | 8 | 8 | 10 | 19 |
| 15 | Goffman* | 10 | 10 | 12 | 9 | 9 | 9 | 21 |
| 16 | Augustine | 10 | 10 | 11 | 9 | 9 | 10 | 23 |
| 17 | Milton* | 10 | 10 | 11 | 9 | 9 | 9 | 24 |
| 18 | Cicero | 10 | 9 | 13 | 9 | 9 | 13 | 25 |
| 19 | Lasswell* | 9 | 9 | 12 | 8 | 8 | 10 | t26 |
| 20 | I. A. Richards* | 9 | 9 | 10 | 7 | 7 | 8 | 29 |
| 21 | Foucault* | 9 | 8 | 10 | 8 | 8 | 8 | 32 |
| 22 | Whorf* | 9 | 8 | 10 | 7 | 7 | 7 | 33 |
| 23 | Lazarsfeld* | 9 | 7 | 12 | 6 | 6 | 8 | 34 |
| 24 | V. Turner | 8 | 8 | 9 | 8 | 8 | 9 | t35 |
| t25 | Bakhtin* | 8 | 8 | 9 | 7 | 7 | 7 | t38 |
| t25 | Weber* | 8 | 8 | 9 | 7 | 7 | 7 | t38 |
| 27 | Quintilian | 8 | 8 | 8 | 8 | 8 | 8 | t40 |
| 28 | F. Bacon | 8 | 8 | 8 | 7 | 7 | 7 | 42 |
| 29 | Marx* | 8 | 7 | 10 | 7 | 7 | 8 | 43 |
| 30 | M. Mead* | 8 | 6 | 10 | 5 | 5 | 5 | 44 |
| 31 | W. Weaver* | 8 | 6 | 10 | 4 | 4 | 4 | 45 |
| 32 | Shannon* | 8 | 5 | 14 | 3 | 2 | 7 | 48 |
| 33 | Durkheim* | 7 | 7 | 13 | 6 | 6 | 10 | 49 |
| 34 | Wittgenstein* | 7 | 7 | 9 | 6 | 6 | 7 | 52 |
| 35 | B. Russell | 7 | 7 | 9 | 3 | 3 | 4 | 53 |
| 36 | Locke* | 7 | 7 | 8 | 6 | 6 | 6 | 55 |
| 37 | K. Lewin* | 7 | 7 | 8 | 4 | 4 | 4 | 57 |
| t38 | Hegel | 7 | 7 | 7 | 7 | 7 | 7 | t58 |
| t38 | Leibniz | 7 | 7 | 7 | 7 | 7 | 7 | t58 |
| 40 | Horkheimer | 7 | 6 | 7 | 5 | 5 | 5 | 66 |
| 41 | Wiener* | 7 | 5 | 12 | 4 | 3 | 6 | 67 |
| t42 | Benjamin* | 6 | 6 | 9 | 5 | 5 | 6 | t69 |

(continued)

TABLE 15.3 Continued

| Theorist | | All Articles | | | Excluding Biographies | | | Overall |
|---|---|---|---|---|---|---|---|---|
| Rank | Name | Articles | Authors | Pages | Articles | Authors | Pages | Rank |
| t42 | Diderot | 6 | 6 | 9 | 5 | 5 | 6 | t69 |
| 44 | H. P. Grice | 6 | 6 | 8 | 6 | 6 | 8 | t72 |
| t45 | S. Eisenstein | 6 | 6 | 8 | 5 | 5 | 6 | t75 |
| t45 | W. Schramm* | 6 | 6 | 8 | 5 | 5 | 6 | t75 |
| 47 | W. James* | 6 | 6 | 8 | 4 | 4 | 4 | 77 |
| t48 | Derrida | 6 | 6 | 7 | 6 | 6 | 7 | t78 |
| t48 | G. Gerbner | 6 | 6 | 7 | 6 | 6 | 7 | t78 |
| t50 | Innis* | 6 | 6 | 7 | 5 | 5 | 5 | t84 |
| t50 | Piaget* | 6 | 6 | 7 | 5 | 5 | 5 | t84 |
| t52 | Hjelmslev | 6 | 6 | 6 | 6 | 6 | 6 | t87 |
| t52 | Lacan | 6 | 6 | 6 | 6 | 6 | 6 | t87 |
| t54 | Dante | 6 | 6 | 6 | 5 | 5 | 5 | t92 |
| t54 | McLuhan* | 6 | 6 | 6 | 5 | 5 | 5 | t92 |
| t54 | J. S. Mill | 6 | 6 | 6 | 5 | 5 | 5 | t92 |
| 57 | Darwin* | 6 | 5 | 12 | 5 | 5 | 9 | 97 |
| 58 | Habermas | 6 | 5 | 9 | 5 | 5 | 8 | 98 |
| 59 | G. H. Mead* | 6 | 5 | 9 | 3 | 3 | 4 | 99 |
| 60 | Gramsci* | 6 | 5 | 8 | 5 | 5 | 6 | 100 |
| 61 | Hovland* | 6 | 5 | 8 | 4 | 4 | 5 | 102 |
| 62 | Birdwhistell | 6 | 5 | 7 | 6 | 5 | 7 | 103 |
| 63 | Socrates | 6 | 5 | 7 | 4 | 4 | 5 | 104 |
| 64 | N. Goodman | 5 | 5 | 8 | 5 | 5 | 8 | 107 |
| 65 | Nietzsche | 5 | 5 | 8 | 4 | 4 | 7 | 108 |
| 66 | C. Morris* | 5 | 5 | 7 | 4 | 4 | 5 | t110 |
| t67 | P. Freire | 5 | 5 | 6 | 5 | 5 | 6 | t113 |
| t67 | W. von Humboldt | 5 | 5 | 6 | 5 | 5 | 6 | t113 |
| t69 | Althusser | 5 | 5 | 6 | 4 | 4 | 5 | t121 |
| t69 | E. Katz | 5 | 5 | 6 | 4 | 4 | 5 | t121 |
| 71 | J. Dewey* | 5 | 5 | 6 | 3 | 3 | 3 | t128 |
| t72 | N. Frye | 5 | 5 | 5 | 5 | 5 | 5 | t130 |
| t72 | J. Grimm | 5 | 5 | 5 | 5 | 5 | 5 | t130 |
| t72 | Labov | 5 | 5 | 5 | 5 | 5 | 5 | t130 |
| t72 | Seneca | 5 | 5 | 5 | 5 | 5 | 5 | t130 |
| t76 | A. Bazin | 5 | 5 | 5 | 4 | 4 | 4 | t143 |
| t76 | Hobbes | 5 | 5 | 5 | 4 | 4 | 4 | t143 |
| t78 | Descartes | 5 | 5 | 5 | 3 | 3 | 3 | t149 |
| t78 | T. M. Newcomb | 5 | 5 | 5 | 3 | 3 | 3 | t149 |
| t78 | Simmel* | 5 | 5 | 5 | 3 | 3 | 3 | t149 |
| 81 | Boas* | 5 | 4 | 8 | 2 | 2 | 4 | 154 |
| 82 | C. Osgood* | 5 | 4 | 7 | 3 | 3 | 4 | 155 |
| 83 | Engels | 5 | 4 | 6 | 4 | 4 | 5 | 157 |
| 84 | Jung* | 5 | 4 | 6 | 2 | 2 | 3 | t158 |

*(continued)*

TABLE 15.3  Continued

| Theorist | | All Articles | | | Excluding Biographies | | | Overall |
| Rank | Name | Articles | Authors | Pages | Articles | Authors | Pages | Rank |
|---|---|---|---|---|---|---|---|---|
| 85 | Vygotsky* | 5 | 4 | 5 | 2 | 2 | 2 | 162 |
| 86 | Gadamer | 4 | 4 | 10 | 4 | 4 | 10 | 165 |
| 87 | Heidegger | 4 | 4 | 7 | 4 | 4 | 7 | 166 |
| 88 | Propp | 4 | 4 | 6 | 4 | 4 | 6 | t168 |
| t89 | Arnheim | 4 | 4 | 5 | 4 | 4 | 5 | t178 |
| t89 | Condillac | 4 | 4 | 5 | 4 | 4 | 5 | t178 |
| t89 | D. Hymes | 4 | 4 | 5 | 4 | 4 | 5 | t178 |
| t92 | G. Allport | 4 | 4 | 5 | 3 | 3 | 4 | t188 |
| t92 | Lukács | 4 | 4 | 5 | 3 | 3 | 4 | t188 |
| t94 | W. Lippmann* | 4 | 4 | 5 | 3 | 3 | 3 | t192 |
| t94 | R. Park* | 4 | 4 | 5 | 3 | 3 | 3 | t192 |
| 96 | H. Cantril* | 4 | 4 | 5 | 2 | 2 | 2 | t197 |
| t97 | J. Austin | 4 | 4 | 4 | 4 | 4 | 4 | t199 |
| t97 | Bourdieu | 4 | 4 | 4 | 4 | 4 | 4 | t199 |
| t97 | Eco | 4 | 4 | 4 | 4 | 4 | 4 | t199 |
| t97 | C. Geertz | 4 | 4 | 4 | 4 | 4 | 4 | t199 |
| t97 | Genette | 4 | 4 | 4 | 4 | 4 | 4 | t199 |
| t97 | J. Goody | 4 | 4 | 4 | 4 | 4 | 4 | t199 |
| t97 | J. G. von Herder | 4 | 4 | 4 | 4 | 4 | 4 | t199 |
| t97 | Kristeva | 4 | 4 | 4 | 4 | 4 | 4 | t199 |
| t97 | E. Morin | 4 | 4 | 4 | 4 | 4 | 4 | t199 |
| t97 | Todorov | 4 | 4 | 4 | 4 | 4 | 4 | t199 |
| t97 | Vico | 4 | 4 | 4 | 4 | 4 | 4 | t199 |
| t108 | B. Berelson | 4 | 4 | 4 | 3 | 3 | 3 | t231 |
| t108 | Bergson | 4 | 4 | 4 | 3 | 3 | 3 | t231 |
| t108 | H. Herzog | 4 | 4 | 4 | 3 | 3 | 3 | t231 |
| t108 | T. Parsons | 4 | 4 | 4 | 3 | 3 | 3 | t231 |
| t108 | Pascal | 4 | 4 | 4 | 3 | 3 | 3 | t231 |
| 113 | L. Lowenthal* | 4 | 4 | 4 | 2 | 2 | 2 | t244 |
| 114 | Tinbergen | 4 | 3 | 7 | 4 | 3 | 7 | 249 |
| 115 | Von Neumann* | 4 | 3 | 6 | 2 | 2 | 3 | 251 |
| t116 | Cooley* | 4 | 3 | 5 | 1 | 1 | 1 | t253 |
| t116 | R. K. Merton* | 4 | 3 | 5 | 1 | 1 | 1 | t253 |
| 118 | Husserl | 4 | 3 | 4 | 4 | 3 | 4 | 257 |
| 119 | Marcuse | 4 | 3 | 4 | 3 | 3 | 3 | 258 |
| 120 | H. S. Sullivan* | 4 | 3 | 4 | 2 | 2 | 2 | t259 |

*Subject of individual biographical entry in the *International Encyclopedia of Communications*.

Of the 7 persons with individual entries in the *Encyclopedia* and designated by the editors as theorists who do not rank among the top 120 theorists, only 2—Aleksandr Luria and Jean-Gabriel de Tarde—rank among the 304 most often named persons. The six-count measures for the seven, ranked in order of importance: Tarde (3, 3, 4, 2, 2, 3), Luria (3, 3, 4, 2, 2, 2), Kenneth Burke (2, 2, 4, 1, 1, 2), Charles Babbage (2, 2, 3, 1, 1, 2), Alfred Schutz (2, 2, 3, 1, 1, 1), and Colin Cherry and Herbert H. Hyman (each 1, 1, 2, 0, 0, 0). In other words, Cherry and Hyman are not mentioned anywhere in the *Encyclopedia* except in the separate biographical entries devoted to them; Schutz, Babbage, and Burke are mentioned in only one other article.

This demonstrates how—via bibliometric analysis—latent measures might be used to test the decisions of editors as manifest in encyclopedias. If the editors had selected the 61 biographies (among the total 133) that they allocated to theorists based on the mentions of theorists in their own encyclopedia, they would have chosen the top 64 ranked in Table 15.3 (excluding three—Chomsky, Derrida, and Habermas—born after the editors' arbitrary cutoff date of December 31, 1919).

Of the 61 top theorists eligible, Aristotle through Nelson Goodman, the editors chose 39 (63.9%). Their 22 oversights, in rank order, include Kant, Rousseau, Augustine, Cicero, Victor Turner (born in 1920, but no longer alive at the time of decision), Quintilian, Francis Bacon, Bertrand Russell, Hegel, Leibniz, and Horkheimer (the entire list can be derived from Table 15.3). Conversely, of the other 22 theorists chosen by the editors, the most prominent deviations from the ranking based on mentions in the *Encyclopedia*, in inverse rank order, include Cherry and Hyman, Schutz, Babbage, Burke, Luria, and Tarde (as we have already seen) plus Harry Stack Sullivan, Robert K. Merton, Charles Horton Cooley, and John von Neumann (again the entire list can be derived from Table 15.3).

Of the 66 theorists listed in Table 15.3 *not* chosen for biographies, 14 were ineligible (they were born after the cutoff date and were still alive at the time of the editors' decisions). Of the 52 remaining, 22 ought to have been accorded their own biographies. Should the editors want to drop the cutoff date and consider all theorists, perhaps in a later edition of the *Encyclopedia*, the ones to add (in order of importance as measured here) would be Noam Chomsky, Jacques Derrida, Jürgen Habermas, Paulo Freire, Elihu Katz, William

Labov, Dell Hymes, Pierre Bourdieu, Umberto Eco, Clifford Geertz, Gérard Genette, Julia Kristeva, Edgar Morin, and Tzvetan Todorov.

Of the 120 leading theorists in Table 15.3, only five (Rudolf Arnheim, George Gerbner, Jack Goody, Elihu Katz, and Wilbur Schramm) contributed to the *Encyclopedia* (they wrote one article each except for Schramm, who contributed eleven). Because none of the five owes any part of his own six counts to self-citation, however, there is no need to control for self-citation in this particular ranking of theorists of communication. Although both Gerbner and Schramm appear on the *Encyclopedia*'s title page, and several other of the top 120 theorists (e.g., Birdwhistell, Hymes, and Labov) are associated with the University of Pennsylvania, such influences—if any—are difficult to measure and are not considered here.

## Periodization of Communication Theory

Bibliometric analysis thus far reveals the development of communication theory extending over some 2,400 years, from the teaching of Socrates in the fifth century B.C. to a spate of European theorists— Foucault, Derrida, Habermas, Bourdieu, Genette, Eco, Todorov, and Kristeva—born after 1925 and still active today. This history is illustrated by Table 15.4, a chronological listing of the 120 theorists divided into six historical periods, from the early theorists (pre-Enlightenment) to those of the twentieth century. Table 15.4 also gives, for each theorist, the years of birth and (where relevant) death, field of specialization, nation in which major theory was formulated, and rank among theorists.

At Table 15.4 shows, the development of communication theory— as reflected in its major theorists—has undergone several ups and downs during the past 25 centuries. The seven earliest theorists lived in ancient Greece and Rome during a period of less than 900 years. The next 1,100 years (430-1561), however, produced only a single theorist, Dante Alighieri. Clearly, the sixth through fifteenth centuries must be considered the Dark Ages of communication theory.

Developments since the Enlightenment are reflected in the counts of major theorists by century: Three were born in the sixteenth, five in the seventeenth, eight in the eighteenth, and 45 in the nineteenth century. For the latter 45 theorists, consider the

TABLE 15.4

Chronology of 120 Most Often Named Theorists of Communication

| Historical Period | Birth-Death | Name | Field | Nation | Rank |
|---|---|---|---|---|---|
| Early Theorists: | | | | | |
| | 469-399 | Socrates | Philosophy | Greece | 63 |
| | 428-347 | Plato | Philosophy | Greece | 2 |
| | 384-322 | Aristotle | Philosophy | Greece | 1 |
| | 106-43 | Cicero | Rhetoric | Rome | 18 |
| | 3-65 | Seneca | Philosophy | Rome | t72 |
| | 35-95 | Quintilian | Rhetoric | Rome | 27 |
| | 354-430 | Augustine | Theology | Rome | 16 |
| | 1265-1321 | Dante | Literature | Italy | t54 |
| Enlightenment and Eighteenth-Century Theorists: | | | | | |
| | 1561-1626 | F. Bacon | Philosophy | England | 28 |
| | 1588-1679 | Hobbes | Philosophy | England | t76 |
| | 1596-1650 | Descartes | Philosophy | France | t78 |
| | 1608-1674 | Milton | Literature | England | 17 |
| | 1623-1662 | Pascal | Philosophy | France | t108 |
| | 1632-1704 | Locke | Philosophy | England | 36 |
| | 1646-1716 | Leibniz | Philosophy | Germany | t38 |
| | 1668-1744 | Vico | Philosophy | Italy | t97 |
| | 1712-1778 | Rousseau | Philosophy | France | 13 |
| | 1713-1784 | Diderot | Philosophy | France | t42 |
| | 1715-1780 | Condillac | Philosophy | France | t89 |
| | 1724-1804 | Kant | Philosophy | Germany | 5 |
| | 1744-1803 | Herder | Philosophy | Germany | t97 |
| Nineteenth-Century Theorists: | | | | | |
| | 1767-1835 | W. von Humboldt | Philology | Germany | t67 |
| | 1770-1831 | Hegel | Philosophy | Germany | t38 |
| | 1785-1863 | J. Grimm | Philology | Germany | t72 |
| | 1806-1873 | J. S. Mill | Philosophy | England | t54 |
| | 1809-1882 | Darwin | Biology | England | 57 |
| | 1818-1883 | Marx | Philosophy | Germany | 29 |
| | 1820-1895 | Engels | Philosophy | Germany | 83 |
| | 1839-1914 | Peirce | Philosophy | U.S. | 11 |
| | 1842-1910 | W. James | Psychology | U.S. | 47 |
| | 1844-1900 | Nietzsche | Philosophy | Germany | 65 |

*(continued)*

counts by decade: Two were born before 1810; one each during the 1810s, 1820s, and 1830s; two during the 1840s; eight in the 1850s; four in the 1860s; two in the 1870s; five in the 1880s; and 19 in the 1890s. Of these latter 19 theorists, 15 were born between 1894 and

TABLE 15.4  Continued

| Historical Period | Birth-Death | Name | Field | Nation | Rank |
|---|---|---|---|---|---|
| Early Twentieth-Century Theorists: | | | | | |
| | 1856-1939 | Freud | Psychology | Austria | 7 |
| | 1857-1913 | Saussure | Linguistics | Switzerland | 3 |
| | 1858-1917 | Durkheim | Sociology | France | 33 |
| | 1858-1918 | Simmel | Sociology | Germany | t78 |
| | 1858-1942 | Boas | Anthropology | U.S. | 81 |
| | 1859-1938 | Husserl | Philosophy | Germany | 118 |
| | 1859-1941 | Bergson | Philosophy | France | t108 |
| | 1859-1952 | J. Dewey | Philosophy | U.S. | 71 |
| | 1863-1931 | G. H. Mead | Psychology | U.S. | 59 |
| | 1864-1920 | Weber | Sociology | Germany | t25 |
| | 1864-1929 | Cooley | Sociology | U.S. | t116 |
| | 1864-1944 | R. Park | Sociology | U.S. | t94 |
| | 1872-1970 | B. Russell | Philosophy | England | 35 |
| | 1875-1961 | Jung | Psychology | Switzerland | 84 |
| | 1884-1939 | Sapir | Linguistics | U.S. | 10 |
| | 1885-1971 | Lukács | Literature | Hungary | t92 |
| | 1889-1951 | Wittgenstein | Philosophy | England | 34 |
| | 1889-1974 | W. Lippmann | Literature | U.S. | t94 |
| | 1889-1976 | Heidegger | Philosophy | Germany | 87 |
| | 1890-1947 | K. Lewin | Psychology | U.S. | 37 |
| | 1891-1937 | Gramsci | Politics | Italy | 60 |
| | 1892-1940 | Benjamin | Literature | Germany | t42 |
| | 1892-1949 | H. S. Sullivan | Psychology | U.S. | 120 |
| | 1893-1979 | I. A. Richards | Literature | England | 20 |

*(continued)*

1899; 9 in the three years of 1894-1896. In other words, communication theory rebounded slowly from its ten-century Dark Ages, with only a gradual but steady increase in important theorists during the sixteenth through early nineteenth centuries. The latter half of the nineteenth century, however, especially the 1890s, produced the theorists for a revolutionary advance in communication theory not seen since ancient Greece and Rome.

As a general rule of thumb, we might add 40 years to a theorist's year of birth to estimate the beginning of his or her impact on the development of a field. Applying this rule to the discussion of Table 15.4, we can conclude that the modern renaissance in communication theory began between 1880 and 1900 with the first impact of early work by Peirce, James, Nietzsche, Freud, Saussure,

TABLE 15.4 Continued

| Historical Period | Birth-Death | Name | Field | Nation | Rank |
|---|---|---|---|---|---|
| Mid-Twentieth Century Theorists: | | | | | |
| | 1894-1952 | Innis | Economics | Canada | t50 |
| | 1894-1864 | Wiener | Mathematics | U.S. | 41 |
| | 1894-1978 | W. Weaver | Mathematics | U.S. | 31 |
| | 1895-1970 | Propp | Folklore | Soviet Union | 88 |
| | 1895-1973 | Horkheimer | Philosophy | Germany | 40 |
| | 1895-1975 | Bakhtin | Literature | Soviet Union | t25 |
| | 1896-1934 | Vygotsky | Psychology | Soviet Union | 85 |
| | 1896-1980 | Piaget | Psychology | Switzerland | t50 |
| | 1896-1982 | Jakobson | Linguistics | U.S. | 8 |
| | 1897-1941 | Whorf | Linguistics | U.S. | 22 |
| | 1897-1967 | G. Allport | Psychology | U.S. | t92 |
| | 1898-1948 | S. Eisenstein | Film | Soviet Union | t45 |
| | 1898-1979 | Marcuse | Philosophy | U.S. | 119 |
| | 1899-1965 | Hjelmslev | Linguistics | Denmark | t52 |
| | 1900- | Gadamer | Philosophy | Germany | 86 |
| | 1900- | L. Lowenthal | Sociology | U.S. | 113 |
| | 1901-1976 | Lazarsfeld | Sociology | U.S. | 23 |
| | 1901-1978 | M. Mead | Anthropology | U.S. | 30 |
| | 1901-1981 | Lacan | Psychology | France | t52 |
| | 1901- | C. Morris | Philosophy | U.S. | 66 |
| | 1902-1978 | Lasswell | Political Science | U.S. | 19 |
| | 1902-1979 | T. Parsons | Sociology | U.S. | t108 |
| | 1903-1957 | Von Neumann | Mathematics | U.S. | 115 |
| | 1903-1969 | Adorno | Philosophy | Germany | 14 |
| | 1903- | T. M. Newcomb | Psychology | U.S. | t78 |
| | 1904-1980 | Bateson | Anthropology | U.S. | 9 |
| | 1904- | Arnheim | Psychology | U.S. | t89 |
| | 1906-1969 | H. Cantril | Psychology | U.S. | 96 |
| | 1906- | N. Goodman | Philosophy | U.S. | 64 |
| | 1907-1987 | W. Schramm | Communication | U.S. | t45 |
| | 1907- | Tinbergen | Biology | England | 114 |
| | 1908- | Lévi-Strauss | Anthropology | France | 12 |
| | 1910- | H. Herzog | Psychology | Austria | t108 |
| | 1910- | R. K. Merton | Sociology | U.S. | t116 |
| | 1911-1960 | J. Austin | Philosophy | England | t97 |
| | 1911-1980 | McLuhan | Communication | Canada | t54 |
| | 1912-1961 | Hovland | Psychology | U.S. | 61 |
| | 1912- | B. Berelson | Sociology | U.S. | t108 |
| | 1912- | N. Frye | Literature | Canada | t72 |
| | 1913-1988 | H. P. Grice | Philosophy | England | 44 |
| | 1915-1980 | Barthes | Semiotics | France | 6 |
| | 1916- | C. Osgood | Psychology | U.S. | 82 |
| | 1916- | Shannon | Mathematics | U.S. | 32 |
| | 1918-1958 | B. Bazin | Film | France | t76 |

TABLE 15.4 Continued

| Historical Period | Birth-Death | Name | Field | Nation | Rank |
|---|---|---|---|---|---|
| Later Twentieth-Century Theorists | | | | | |
| | 1918- | Althusser | Philosophy | France | t69 |
| | 1918- | Birdwhistell | Anthropology | U.S. | 62 |
| | 1919- | G. Gerbner | Communication | U.S. | t48 |
| | 1919- | J. Goody | Anthropology | England | t97 |
| | 1920-1984 | V. Turner | Anthropology | U.S. | 24 |
| | 1921- | P. Freire | Education | Brazil | t67 |
| | 1921- | E. Morin | Film | France | t97 |
| | 1922-1982 | Goffman | Sociology | U.S. | 15 |
| | 1926-1984 | Foucault | Philosophy | France | 21 |
| | 1926- | C. Geertz | Anthropology | U.S. | t97 |
| | 1926- | E. Katz | Sociology | U.S. | t69 |
| | 1927- | D. Hymes | Anthropology | U.S. | t89 |
| | 1928- | Chomsky | Linguistics | U.S. | 4 |
| | 1928- | Labov | Linguistics | U.S. | t72 |
| | 1929- | Habermas | Sociology | Germany | 58 |
| | 1930- | Bourdieu | Philosophy | France | t97 |
| | 1930- | Derrida | Philosophy | France | t48 |
| | 1930- | Genette | Literature | France | t97 |
| | 1932- | Eco | Semiotics | Italy | t97 |
| | 1939- | Todorov | Linguistics | France | t97 |
| | 1941- | Kristeva | Literature | France | t97 |

Durkheim, Simmel, Boas, Husserl, Bergson, and Dewey. As might be expected, this corresponds precisely to the period of most rapid development of information, decision, and communication technology, a phenomenon that has been called the Control Revolution (Beniger, 1986). The most rapid addition of new theorists to the renaissance in communication came in the mid-1930s with the first major works by Propp, Horkheimer, Bakhtin, Vygotsky, Piaget, Jakobson, and Whorf, among others.

## Conclusion

Using bibliometric analysis, as we have seen, latent data can be made to undermine conclusions based on manifest assumptions in scholarly communication (here the editorial decisions about theorists to be accorded their own biographical entries in an encyclopedia). Such quantitative results might also overturn the hoary clichés of a discipline, for example, the claim by Bernard Berelson (1959) that communication had four founding fathers: Lewin, Lazarsfeld, Lasswell, and Hovland. This claim has been embellished several times by Schramm (1983, 1985) and repeated by a host of other communication researchers.

According to the data in Tables 15.3 and 15.4, however, no obvious special status can be accorded the Berelson Four: Chronologically, they appear near the middle of the progression of 120 theorists (between the 51st and 92nd positions) and published mostly after both the modern renaissance (1880-1900) and the period of most rapid addition of new work (the mid-1930s) discussed above. In importance, they rank only somewhat above the middle, between 19 (Lasswell) and 61 (Hovland). The four do not constitute a tight cohort—40 other theorists were born during the same span (1890-1912), including 20 who rank above one or more of the Berelson Four; four (Jakobson, Bateson, Lévi-Strauss, and Adorno) rank above all four. The cohort includes 20 other Americans (Berelson and Schramm among them), of which 13 (65%) were accorded biographical entries in the *International Encyclopedia of Communications*. The Berelson Four do not constitute the earliest empirical researchers among the 120, not even from the United States, nor are they the first from the field of communication (that might be said—for the same cohort—of Schramm and McLuhan; the Berelson Four worked in psychology, sociology, and political science). So what, we might well ask, did these four "founders" found?

Bibliometric analysis also casts new light on communication as reflected in its major professional organization, the International Communication Association (ICA). Of the 42 presidents of the ICA to date, *not one* ranks among the 120 top theorists, and only five (11.19%) are mentioned even one time in the *Encyclopedia*. By contrast, of the 81 presidents of the American Sociological Association, for example, 6 rank among the top 120 communication theorists (Cooley, Park, Lazarsfeld, Parsons, Merton, and Goffman); 17 (21.0%) are mentioned in the *Encyclopedia*. Clearly, the ICA has not reflected leadership in its field—whether in theory or elsewhere—as well as have other academic associations.

Perhaps bibliometric analysis of the *International Encyclopedia of Communications* can help the field of communication find its foundations as a discipline. This would seem to require, as necessary though hardly sufficient, the identification and promotion of the potentially integrative theorists, theories, and theoretical works most central to the field. Even short of this, however, bibliometric analysis of latent measures to test manifest assumptions promises to provide new insights into the development and structure of scholarly communication throughout the other academic disciplines.

# PART IV

# Conclusions

WILLIAM PAISLEY

# 16. The Future of Bibliometrics

There are two reasons for the rapid growth of bibliometric studies in the past three decades. The first is the number and accessibility of electronic databases, from which samples of bibliometric data can be drawn easily and affordably. The second is the development of conceptual frameworks in which bibliometric data are indicative of communication processes, such as the clustering of concepts in written communication, or of social processes, such as the evolution of scientific specialties. Despite a long history of bibliometric research focusing on text characteristics in literature (the original bibliometric, or "book measurements"), most bibliometric studies of the past three decades have focused on scientific communication—also for two reasons. The first was the scientific skew of electronic databases until the 1980s. The second was a concern that scientific communication was inefficient and was impeding scientific progress. This concern persists, as described in several chapters in the present volume, but bibliometric research has found additional applications that reflect the extraordinary expansion of electronic databases beyond scientific communication. New conceptual frameworks are forged and new relationships with other research methods are revealed as bibliometric methods adapt to these new applications.

Three generations or phases of bibliometric research can be identified, the third lying principally in the future. The first two were marked respectively by text-based measures and citation-based measures. The third will be marked by complementary use of both approaches, combined with an increased use of supplementary measures from nonbibliometric sources.

---

AUTHOR'S NOTE: After this chapter was completed, information on Talmudic bibliometricians came to me from Albert Joy, Bailey/Howe Library, University of Vermont. He explained that the Hebrew word for "scribe" is "sofer," which also means "to count." The scribes who copied the Talmud knew many of its statistical characteristics, which they used in part to verify the accuracy of each copy. More information about the "Soferim" can be found in the *Encyclopedia of Judaism* and the *Encyclopaedia Judaica*.

## First-Generation Bibliometric Research

Diligent historians of science may someday tell us who the first bibliometricians were. By some accounts they may have been Talmudic scholars in the Middle Ages whose concern for error in the much-copied texts led them to analyze textual characteristics as a means of verifying the copies. Certainly by the last quarter of the nineteenth century, statistical analysis of text was competently conducted and reported in studies of authorship (for example, of Shakespeare's plays; Mendenhall, 1887). The bibliometric hallmark of such research is that it focuses on characteristics of the text rather than on the meaning of the text.

Later studies of text characteristics include Zipf (1935) and Yule (1944), both of whom continue to be cited in information science and literary studies. With the simultaneous appearance of information theory and computer-analyzable text, it was of interest to test information theory propositions in text samples (for example, Paisley, 1966). The computer also rekindled interest in authorship characteristics. Mosteller and Wallace (1963) demonstrated the combined power of computer analysis and Bayesian statistics by attributing the disputed *Federalist Papers* to Madison rather than Hamilton with median odds of more than 3 million to 1. Paisley (1964) developed the principle of "minor encoding habits" that such studies had discovered.

The text-based genre of bibliometric research now finds many applications in communication and information science. Examples in studies of scholarly communication include (a) using the occurrence of particular concepts, such as "information theory," in materials as tracers of the influence of one researcher or group of researchers on other researchers; (b) using high-frequency concepts to profile the concerns of a field of research; and (c) using longitudinal shifts in concept clusters to characterize the succession of theoretical paradigms in fields of research. Paisley (1986) applied the second of these approaches to concepts appearing in 1,800 article titles in six journals, representing three communication and information science subfields as well as sociology, social psychology, and public opinion research. The rank ordered, high-frequency concepts were almost definitional statements for each field:

*Journal of the American Society for Information Science*—information, science, system, retrieval, searching;

*Communication Monographs*—communication, rhetoric, effect, group, analysis;

*Communication Research*—communication, media, television, effect, information;

*American Sociological Review*—social, structure, theory, effect, model;

*Journal of Personality and Social Psychology*—social, self, effect, behavior, attribution; and

*Public Opinion Quarterly*—polling, opinion, public, survey, media.

## Second-Generation Bibliometric Research

A different set of bibliometric measures began to receive attention in the 1940s. The reference list is a humble appendage to a scholarly paper, but citations reveal much about the information environments and intellectual networks in which scholars work. Whereas later citation studies focused on intellectual networks, the first studies (such as Fussler, 1949; Kessler & Heart, 1962; Patterson, 1945) focused on the information environments of physicists and chemists. For example, in what proportion did the scientists cite journal articles, books, unpublished reports, conference papers, and personal communications? Journal articles received more than 75% of the citations in these studies, a fact that may have discouraged later replications.

In the 1980s citation studies began to focus almost exclusively on journal-to-journal and author-to-author linkages, both of which can be used to define intellectual networks. In the case of journals, direct cross-citation measures can be used. In the case of authors, cross-citations are valid only if the authors are contemporaries, and, therefore, co-citation measures were developed (see White's chapter, this volume).

Linkage studies became the most common form of bibliometric research for at least three reasons. First, there was concern in several countries that high national investments in research were being undermined by poor scientific communication. It seemed that the transfer of knowledge among scientists and from scientists to technologists could be inferred from citation measures and that gaps or inefficiencies in the transfer could be detected.

Second, information scientists and others conducting research on science were impressed by similar conclusions reached by Kuhn (1962) and Price (1963): Scientists communicate with relatively small numbers of colleagues who constitute a scientific community and whose information and opinions guide their research. The composition and dynamics of scientific communities were of interest to both researchers and policymakers. It seemed that citation measures could be used to define the communities.

Third, and without doubt the most important in some respects, electronic databases of citations became available. Some citation studies were completed from hand counts in the articles, such as Dahling (1962) and Parker, Paisley, and Garrett (1967). They were soon outnumbered by studies using citation indexes or computer databases of other types, such as Kessler (1963) and Garfield, Sher, and Torpie (1964). The ensuing chronology of U.S. citation studies using electronic databases is well covered in the Editor's Introduction to this volume and in the chapter by White, with valuable perceptions provided in other chapters on citation studies in other countries. When the history of citation-based bibliometric research is written, much of the energy and enabling technology for these studies will be credited to the producer of the major citation indexes, the Institute for Scientific Information (ISI) in Philadelphia.

## Third-Generation Bibliometric Research

The continuing popularity of citation-based bibliometric research is evident in the composition of this volume, but the next major shift in emphasis is evident in some studies of the late 1980s. Just as citation studies multiplied rapidly after the ISI citation indexes became available online, the increasing amount of text available online and on optical disc are causing researchers to return to some of the questions of first-generation bibliometric research focusing on the text rather than on the reference list.

The justification for this focus is simply that a scholar makes his or her statement in the text, not in the reference list. The concepts and methods that scholars cite in the text can be used to place them in intellectual networks and in the historical development of their fields. Text-based studies will not only answer uniquely text-related questions but also help to resolve ambiguities in citation-based studies (and vice versa).

Examples of recent text-based bibliometric studies include the Paisley (1986) study of concepts in article titles discussed above. Earlier, Rice (1984) reported on the number of articles and reports concerned with new media in four online databases: *ERIC*, *Sociological Abstracts*, *Management Contents*, and *Magazine Index*. A rapid increase in new media coverage in the databases was interpreted as an indicator of the topic's growing importance. In Paisley (1989b), the online Magazine Index was used to chart the coverage received by social issues in magazines during more than two decades. This was called the "magazine barometer of attention" and reported coverage of 38 social issues such as abortion and discrimination over time in the file of 2 million articles.

During the ongoing transition from bibliographic records alone to bibliographic records plus full text online, the methodology of a study such as Paisley (1989b) had to be eclectic. In brief, searches of titles, descriptors, and full text (when available and searchable) are designed to err on the side of false positives—retrieved records that are not relevant—rather than false negatives—relevant records that are not retrieved. The researcher then screens the retrieved records and makes final judgments of relevance.

These studies made no reference to bibliometrics, because it was easy to pass them off as content analyses (which, however, differ from bibliometric studies in important ways that will be discussed below), but a similar study focusing on press coverage of the presidential candidates in the 1988 election was published under the title "The Bibliometrics of Politics" (Miller & Stebenne, 1988).

Miller and Stebenne (1988, p. 24) say that bibliometrics is "the science of word counting, a technique that can be applied to campaign and political coverage. Computerized press databases reveal the number of times that key words, phrases, and proper names have appeared in news stories."

By focusing on "key words, phrases, and proper names" in the stories rather than on the inferred meaning of the stories, Miller and Stebenne took a position on the bibliometric side of the boundary between bibliometric research and content analysis.

## Defining Bibliometric Research for
## Future Applications

In the future, a large proportion of all text that now appears in books, journals, magazines, and newspapers will be contained in electronic databases. In fact, the electronic databases will contain more than the published record, because there will be unpublished data collected just for the databases. This vast collection of electronic information is the future domain of bibliometric research. Both text-based and citation-based studies will flourish. The ease with which data can be gathered, analyzed, and updated will probably create a new genre of ongoing research reports, a composite of bibliometric Gallup polls and bibliometric economic indicators summaries. In industrialized societies that relentlessly report indicators, both the scholarly and the public communication systems will have their indicators too. The library community already collects many statistics on books, journals, journal articles, and bibliographic records that can be incorporated into future bibliometric indicator reports.

Today, however, bibliometric research is only exemplified, rather than defined, by the studies that have been conducted. Its opportunistic nature and range of appropriate applications have not been discussed adequately, and there has been little exploration of its relationships with other methods such as content analysis, indicators research, and sociometric research or meta-methods such as unobtrusive measures.

## The Opportunistic Nature of
## Research Methods

All research methods are not created equal, but all are equally created. Research methods are procedures designed to exploit opportunities for measurement. The opportunistic nature of research methods is evident not only in the parallel growth of bibliometric research and electronic databases but also in the use of written questionnaires with literate populations, experiments performed with available and compliant college students, observations of employees conducted with management approval, and the like. Direct methods of data collection such as interviews and questionnaires depend on the cooperation of respondents, while indirect methods such as bibliometric measures depend on the amount and type of information that was compiled for other purposes. In both cases the opportunities for data collection, although rich, are quite circumscribed.

Therefore, bibliometric research, which relies on particular sources of data (the printed page or the electronic database), already has a place in the spectrum of research methods. Like other methods, its place is bounded by its measurement opportunities.

There is a converse to opportunistic data gathering. If important data elements would not otherwise be available (for example, from a particular database or from respondents under a particular agreement of cooperation), researchers can seek to change the data gathering procedures. In the case of bibliometric research, if new data elements would enable valuable analyses to be performed, then it may be possible to add them to the electronic databases. Most managers of electronic databases are only now becoming aware of the research uses of their information. They may agree to include additional data elements for research because researchers are paying customers too.

## Misapplications of Bibliometric Research

Bibliometric methods are misapplied when their measurement limitations are ignored. For example, bibliometric methods do not directly reflect the quality of research in cited articles or the eminence of cited researchers. Periodic efforts by federal agencies to use citation counts for this purpose are misapplications of the method. There are too many ways in which ranks are raised or lowered by peculiarities in the citation sample or the publishing style of the researcher(s) under study. Beniger's analysis (this volume) goes as far as it can toward a multimeasure correction of some of these problems.

Reliability and validity are the criteria that a research method is being used appropriately. Bibliometric studies have relatively high reliability because of the well-maintained databases from which data are drawn, but databases change over time both because of internal management practices and because of external changes, for example, in journal titles.

More often, an application is disqualified by validity questions raised by the definition of an indicator as a social system variable. When bibliometric measures are used to describe the publication system itself (for example, the most studied topics or most cited journals in a field), they generally have high validity. When bibliometric measures are used to describe the social system that produced the publications (for example, eminence of researchers based on number of citations), they become surrogates for social variables and their validity is questionable. Independent corroborating measures are desirable even in bibliometric studies of the publication system, but they are essential in bibliometric studies of the social system.

## Bibliometric Research and Content Analysis

Content analysis has even more possible definitions than bibliometric research because it is so fundamental to the process of extracting meaning from data. It is used extensively to analyze what the mass media are telling us but also to reduce questionnaire responses to coded categories. It is used by historians on texts thousands of years old but also by rhetoricians on contemporary speeches. It is used to analyze the hesitations and slips of verbal behavior in the psychiatric interview but also to analyze posture, movement, and facial expression in the patient's nonverbal behavior.

According to the best-known definition of content analysis (Berelson, 1952, p. 18), it is "a research technique for the objective, systematic, and quantitative description of the manifest content of communication." In fact, however, content analysis is divided into quantitative and qualitative approaches, whose practitioners may never agree with the importance of counting occurrences versus the significance of the unusual expression, placement, or timing of the singular occurrence. It is also divided on the legitimacy of "reading between the lines" or adding latent content to the manifest content.

However, at the center of these diverse approaches and uses of content analysis is the goal of inferring meaning. What values does the communicator express? What are the communicator's intentions? What does the communicator want the audience to believe?

This is the view of content analysis that was shared by its early developers and practitioners: Lippmann, Lasswell, Berelson, Pool,

Osgood, and others. They applied it to propaganda analyses in the 1920s, studies of news bias in the 1930s, wartime studies of effective persuasive messages in the 1940s, the beginnings of empirical research on popular culture in the 1950s, and so on.

Therefore, the distinction between bibliometric research and content analysis does not focus on the materials that are studied, because scholarly articles can be content-analyzed and mass media can be the subjects of bibliometric study, or on the indicators that are chosen, because the same concepts may be chosen for both methods. Instead, the distinction focuses on the purpose of the study, whether to infer meaning via content analysis or to describe characteristics of the text via bibliometric research.

It is interesting that this distinction between bibliometric research and content analysis, like a border drawn in the middle of a settlement, creates some displaced studies. Two important types of public communication studies that have long been called content analyses now fall on the bibliometric side of the border, because they are not concerned with meaning but only with characteristics of the text.

One type of study, news flow analysis, traces the links in the communication network from the origins of news stories to their audiences, with particular concern for changes that occur in the texts at each relay point. The other type of study, coverage analysis, measures the attention a story or issue receives in one or more media over time.

As it happens, each of these methods has an analogue in bibliometric research applied to scholarly communication, and each has decades of applications that may suggest guidelines for improved bibliometric research.

News flow is harder to study than coverage because it includes behind-the-scenes decisions and events that occur as the story is researched, written, selected, edited, and relayed along the network. The time dimension in news flow analysis is that of a particular type of story moving through informal and formal channels toward publication. In coverage analysis, the time dimension is that of successive waves of stories that are analyzed only when they reach public media.

With many electronic media indexes available, the analysis of coverage has become easier and more complete. The analysis of news flow still requires probing behind the scenes.

Coverage analysis may have begun with the Lippmann and Merz (1920) study of coverage of the Russian Revolution in *The New York Times* between 1917 and 1920. Equivalent landmarks in news flow analysis were White's "gatekeeper" study (1950) and Cutlip's (1954) analysis of news story selection from a wire service.

Coverage analyses focus not only on news and issues but also on channel coverage characteristics such as the number of violent incidents per hour on telvision monitored over many years (Gerbner & Gross, 1976). Such studies are essentially violence-coverage analyses.

Representative titles of news flow and coverage analyses illustrate the range of applications:

"Multivariate analysis of news flow on a conversation issue" (Witt, 1972)

"Flow of news between Canada and the United States" (Sparkes, 1978)

"Analysis of television coverage of the Vietnam War" (Patterson, 1984)

"Magazine coverage of the mentally handicapped" (Bonnstetter, 1986)

News flow and coverage analyses have been described in some detail because they parallel in mass communication research two roles that bibliometric studies play in research on scholarly communication. One scientific journal's coverage of another is the basis for inferring impact of the cited journal on the citing journal. Reciprocal coverage is the unit of analysis for showing imbalances, such as the one-way flow of references between communication and psychology journals (Paisley, 1984). It is also the unit of analysis for journal cluster analysis (Rice, Borgman, & Reeves, 1988).

Scholarly communication flow is studied in two contexts: (a) the channels used by researchers to disseminate findings at each stage in a research project from early presentations and reports to final publication (Garvey & Griffith, 1965) and (b) the progress of an idea from its origins in one field to the distant fields that it influences (Dahling, 1962; Paisley, 1984). Both of these topics are more readily studied than news flow in mass media, because even informal scientific presentations and reports are frequently captured in databases.

There is some danger that the coming windfall of electronic information will take bibliometric research back to what McCormack (1982) calls "Lasswellian positivism"—that is, assuming that quantitative analyses have theoretical significance merely because of their scope or the importance of the texts (however, this is an unfair characterization of Lasswell's work). Content analysis has become more sophisticated than that, but the sophistication found in theory-based hands-on coding does not yet transfer well to the computer's algorithmic methods of analysis.

## Bibliometric Research and Indicators Research

Two decades ago the social indicators movement was given official status as a joint enterprise of social scientists and federal statistical agencies in Cohen's *Toward a Social Report* (1968). Federal data collection responsibilities were growing because of the evaluation requirements of Great Society programs. At the same time social scientists were being "priced out of the market" in survey fieldwork for any purpose other than evaluations and community experiments sponsored by the government. It was evident that federal agencies had the data but social scientists had the expertise and theoretical frameworks with which to analyze them.

However, indicators collected by federal statistical agencies are not the same as variables derived from social science theories. Indicators are administrative in their purposes and definitions. They overlap with theoretical variables at the level of demography and certain behaviors, such as the utilization of services (e.g., health care). Indicators offer little insight into intentions or effects, which are often key variables in theoretically grounded studies. Typically, indicators have high reliability and external validity, while their internal validity related to causation or dependency is difficult to assess.

Whereas the great majority of all surveys and experiments conducted by social researchers are cross-sectional or synchronic with respect to time, indicators are inherently longitudinal or diachronic. Almost as much as the availability of large samples of reliably collected data, the opportunity to analyze the effects of time won researchers over to indicators research.

The methodological concepts of multiple operationism and convergent validity were widely adopted in social science during the early period of social indicators research, together with statistical models that are well suited to indicators, such as the interrupted time series, regression-discontinuity analysis, and meta-analysis. The challenge to researchers was to remedy the questionable validity of indicators through the resourceful use of supplementary measures and appropriate statistical models.

Federal administrations since the 1960s have not been consistent stewards of the indicators databases, but vastly more indicators data have been collected than have been adequately analyzed.

Bibliometric studies focusing on indicators in electronic databases now present the same opportunities and problems that social scientists encountered when they began to work with social indicators. As before, it is possible to analyze many thousands of cases. Also as before, the internal validity of the findings must be buttressed with other measures and statistical analyses.

## Bibliometric Research and
## Sociometric Research

Sociometric research is based on interpersonal choices made in response to particular instruction, such as naming colleagues according to frequency of contact (unprompted choice) or assigning numeric "liking" values to a list of names (prompted choice). At the data collection stage, there is no correspondence between citation-based bibliometric research and sociometric research. However, both research methods produce matrices containing distributions of numbers linking persons (also journals in the case of bibliometric research) to each other. The distributions are usually skewed, and choices are not symmetical (A cites B more often than B cites A), resulting in a square rather than a triangular initial matrix. The challenge is to discover the underlying structure of these numbers and to represent the derived clusters validly (see Rice's chapter, this volume, for a discussion of analysis models).

As is true of content analysis and indicators research, the relevance of sociometric research to bibliometric research is often acknowledged but never fully examined. Sociometric research has benefited from 50 years of continuing development since its introduction by Moreno in the 1930s. Burt (1988) exemplifies current sociometric research that should be of value to bibliometric researchers.

## Bibliometric Research and Unobtrusive Measures

Unobtrusive measures are not a method but a meta-method, an approach to data collection that may take many different forms. As first proposed by Webb, Campbell, Schwartz, and Sechrest (1966, p. 2), unobtrusive measures are alternatives to the overused interview and questionnaire; they are "measures that do not require the cooperation of a respondent and do not themselves contaminate the response." The authors (1966, p. 1) emphasize "the necessity for multiple operationism, a collection of methods combined to avoid sharing the same weaknesses." They discuss two categories of weaknesses: lack of internal validity—or uncertainty in explaining the causes of the observed difference in the sample itself—and lack of external validity—or uncertainty in generalizing the observed difference to other samples.

Bibliometric measures qualify as unobtrusive measures: They do not influence the events being measured. However, bibliometric researchers seldom heed the call for multiple operationism to control threats to internal and external validity. For example, the validity criticisms raised by MacRoberts and MacRoberts (1989) have not been translated into one or more other methods that can be used to validate citation findings. In the present volume, only McCain uses bibliometric and nonbibliometric measures jointly.

## Strengthening Bibliometric Methods

These brief comparisons of bibliometric research with content analysis, indicators research, sociometric research, and unobtrusive measures have not sought to reflect unfavorably on bibliometric methods, whose weaknesses are no greater than those of other methods, only different. Each of the other methods also has different strengths that may have applications in bibliometric research.

For example, content analysis has procedures for drawing stratified samples that are minimally influenced by cycles in the media under study. The problem of drawing 1,000 representative newspaper pages or 100 representative television hours had to be solved with the knowledge that these media are subject to content cycles within each issue or broadcast day. Furthermore, days, weeks, and months of a year's sample differ systematically rather than randomly. Similar cycles occur in the journal literature, so that a composite-year sample should be drawn with the same care as a composite-week sample in a newspaper content analysis.

Indicators research reminds us that bibliometric research will probably progress through three phases with respect to time-based measures. Cross-sectional studies with no time dimension (for example, Price's pioneering study of French N-ray research, 1965) are succeeded, often upon replication, with equivalent data at two or more points in time. However, these are still discrete studies whose findings can be compared across time, not true time-based measures. In the third stage, data are collected at each available time interval, such as each quarter over many years, enabling the use of more powerful statistical models such as the interrupted time series.

Because of its great age and because of the difficult statistical problems posed by its nonnormal and nonsymmetrical data, sociometric research has reached a high level of analysis sophistication. Some bibliometric researchers (for example, Rice, this volume) are conversant with sociometric analysis models. On the whole, however, bibliometric studies use older and simpler analysis models than those used in sociometric studies, extending backward from multidimensional scaling to factor analysis (for example, Paisley, in press).

Bibliometric research can borrow two strengths from the unobtrusive measures movement. The first is a watchful eye for supplementary measures wherever they may be available. Studies of emerging research specialties should also include noncitation measures such as (a) researchers funded under relevant federal grant programs, to be found in the electronic FEDRIP database; (b) copresenters of relevant papers, and presenters within the same relevant sessions at conferences; or (c) unpublished dissertations written by students working under the researchers identified by the other methods.

Unobtrusive measures also provide strong examples of the statistical procedures used to incorporate multiple measures, particularly convergent-discriminant validation (Campbell & Fiske, 1959). Multiple measures are tested in the "convergent-discriminant matrix." If they pass that test, they can be scaled together in an improved composite measure.

## Further Elements of a Model of Bibliometric Research

In the Editor's Introduction to this volume, Borgman began to specify the variables and research questions that bibliometric research brings to the study of scholarly communication. The resulting matrix of three variables by four research questions was adequate to classify all of the theoretical and empirical chapters in this volume. To encompass not only the bibliometric research of previous decades but also the bibliometric research of the coming decade, Borgman's matrix should be extended in two ways. First, additional variables and research questions, if any, should be proposed. Second, additional dimensions of the matrix should be proposed if they provide insight into the methodological choices and trade-offs of bibliometric research.

## Variables

The three variables of producers, artifacts, and concepts are well defined by Borgman. Producers are the originators of information at any level of authors, research teams, institutions, fields, or countries. There are, of course, other principles and levels of aggregation—women or men, authors of different ages, and other geographical units (such as the European Community in the chapter by Moed and de Bruin, this volume)—whether or not electronic databases presently contain such information.

Artifacts are the information products themselves—books, journal articles, encyclopedia articles (see Beniger's analysis, this volume), conference presentations, and so on. Bibliometric research applied to public communication also focuses on news stories, magazine articles, speech transcripts, broadcast transcripts, and so on.

Concepts are what the imformation product embodies. It may not be immediately obvious that concepts include not only words or themes in the text but also citations and presentation details such as the inclusion of the statistical tables. Each decision of the author to include a word, theme, citation, or presentation detail is a concept for analysis.

All bibliometric research is performed on the artifacts, in which the producers, the artifacts themselves, or the concepts may be the variables under study. Artifacts, sampling frames, and units of analysis are distinct. For example, the journal article may be the artifact; a five-year collection of articles from selected journals may be the sampling frame; and the citation may be the unit of analysis.

There is no evident need to modify this list of variables. However, future bibliometric research will probably cause the list to be extended.

## Research Questions

The questions asked in bibliometric research are more contextual than the variables studied, which are uniform across scholarly versus public communication analyses because of the consistent properties of text and the conventions of electronic databases.

The first research question raised by Borgman concerns the composition of a social network or, in the context of her discussion, a scholarly community. Members of a network are mutually nominated when citations are the chosen variable, but membership could also be ascribed through an analysis of producer attributes (such as employment in the same laboratory), artifact attributes (such as article publication in a journal established by and for a particularly scholarly community), or concept clusters that are highly indicative of their research paradigm.

The second research question is actually a corollary of the first: How does the social network change over time? Any of the variables mentioned above can be measured longitudinally to provide data on this question.

The third research question concerns the evaluation of importance. "Importance" is usually defined in terms of quantities—of books or articles produced or of citations received. Sometimes the artifacts are ranked to give more weight, for example, to the high-prestige journals of a field. Other adjustments, such as weighting journals in an impact study to equate the number of citable articles that each publishes in a year, are debatable because the factor being held constant may actually be part of the dependent variable. For example, the definition of "journal importance" may include a high output of articles.

The final research question raised by Borgman concerns the diffusion of ideas. Both citations and concepts in text can be used to chart diffusion.

Up to the present time, almost all bibliometric studies can be classified within these four questions—social network structure, social network change, importance, or diffusion. We should ask, however: What are the new questions that researchers will be asking within bibliometrics' enlarged future charter?

Because of limited space in this chapter, only one additional set of questions will be proposed. Drawing upon the parallel with indicators research, we note a missing level of questions on the fundamental side of those raised by Borgman. These are "demographic" questions about the publication system and the social system behind it, such as (a) numbers of articles published in a wide range of scholarly subfields; (b) numbers of articles published on a wide range of important topics; (c) number of researchers actively publishing in each subfield according to the tabulations in (a) above; (d) number of researchers actively publishing on each topic according to the tabulations in (b) above; (e) national or geographic location and institutional affiliation of researchers identified in these analyses; (f) patterns of team research implied by the authorships per subfield or topic; or (g) characteristics of published articles per subfield or topic, including conceptual structures in the text, number of citations, average age of journal citations, and so on. In addition to the value of these demographic findings in themselves, they provide parameters for interpreting research on higher-level questions about social networks, importance, and diffusion.

## Statistical Contrasts

A larger matrix results when these questions are added to the set with which Borgman began this book. However, more unstated possibilities of research are found in individual cells of the matrix, where many different analyses can be performed on each category of data.

The lowest-level analysis in bibliometric research produces a number, such as the number of articles published on AIDS in 1989. The next level, producing a percentage, requires another number—a total number for the domain to which the first number belongs, such as the total number of articles in all journals that published at least one article on AIDS. Other numbers of the same order as the first (for example, on heart disease or lung cancer) enable rankings and difference percentages.

Any subdivision of these counts, for example, by country, enlarges the analysis to cross-tabulations or mean differences. We can then see the cross-tabulation of X disease articles, including AIDS, originating in Y countries. An alternative to these frequencies would be deviation scores from the mean number of articles per topic or country.

The introduction of other variables, such as the number of AIDS patients per country and national levels of funding for AIDS research, enables correlational analysis with country as the unit of analysis. With the inclusion of other variables specified by a predictive model, the simple correlations become a multivariate correlational analysis of the determinants of productivity in AIDS research.

Not mentioned yet is the significance of time in each of these possible analyses. Time is the only dimension that enters a study with its own statistical tools. Only the time dimension permits the analysis of "changes" rather than "differences."

All of these hypothetical analyses, as well as many others, can be performed in just one cell of the variables by questions matrix. Because of the abundance of bibliometric data yet to be used in any analysis, we expect to see many of these possibilities converted to valuable studies in the future.

## Conclusion

This chapter looks back over two generations of bibliometric research, focusing first on text-based and then on citation-based measures, and foresees a dramatic increase both in the overall number of bibliometric studies and in the number of studies that combine text-based measures, citation-based measures, and supplementary measures from nonbibliometric sources. One of the most difficult, or at least tedious, types of communication and information science research has become relatively easy and affordable, not only for researchers but also for students.

A sea of change in bibliometric research has occurred, but as yet it is fully understood by only a few hundred researchers worldwide. Each year in the 1990s will be marked by new waves of studies, larger, better designed, and better analyzed than those of the previous decades.

However, the enthusiasm for bibliometric research that is evident among the authors in this book may prove to be more transferable than their good judgment in data collection and analysis, which has been gained over years of experience in a more hands-on era. It is time for articles and textbooks to codify the procedures, models, and tests that have been largely intuitive until now.

Books like this, special issues of journals, and conferences help to define what bibliometric research is and what it can contribute to the understanding of both scholarly and public communication. Such self-definition is the prerequisite of significant progress in research. In a contemporary play, *Angels Fall* by Lanford Wilson, a young character recounts his journey toward self-understanding and his striving to become a successful athlete. He concludes by saying, "Once you know who you are, the rest is just work."

# References

Adler, M. J. (Ed.). (1952). *The great ideas: A syntopicon of great books of the western world* (Vol. 2). Chicago: Encyclopedia Britannica.

Ahlenius, H. (1932). *Georg Brandes i svensk litteratur t o m 1890*. Stockholm: Bonniers.

Allen, T. J. (1966). Performance of informational channels in the transfer of technology. *Industrial Management Review, 8*, 87-98.

Altman, D. (1986). *AIDS in the mind of America*. New York: Anchor/Doubleday.

Anonymous. (1983). Summarized proceedings of the workshop on population genetics, June 8, 1983 (National Institute of General Medical Sciences Administrative Document).

Arima, A., & Kanada, Y. (1984). Kenkyusha no katsudouryoku wo hakaru: Happyou ronbunsuu to ronbun inyousuu ni yoru jisseki hyouka no kokoromi [Measuring activities of researchers: An attempt of evaluation of researchers using numbers of publications and numbers of citations]. *Kagaku, 36*(6), 360-365.

Arvanitis, R., & Chatelin, Y. (1988). National strategies in tropical soil science. *Social Studies of Science, 18*, 113-146.

Asai, I. (1981a). A general formulation of Bradford's distribution: The graph-oriented approach. *Journal of the American Society for Information Science, 32*, 113-119.

Asai, I. (1981b). Adjusted age distribution and its application to impact factor and immediacy index. *Journal of the American Society for Information Science, 32*, 172-174.

Asai, I. (1987). The structure and usage of a "referation" database on microcomputers for personal document management. In K. D. Lehmann & H. Strohl-Goebel (Eds.), *The application of microcomputers in information documentation, and libraries* (pp. 510-517). Amsterdam: North-Holland.

Aspelin, K. (1975). *Textens dimensioner*. Stockholm: Norstedts.

Assman, A., & Assman, J. (Eds.). (1986-1987). *Kanon und Zensur, I-II*. Munich: Fink.

300

Bakker, P., & Righter, H. (1985). Editors of medical journals: Who and from where. *Scientometrics, 7*(1-2), 11-22.

Barnes, D. M. (1986). AIDS-related brain damage unexplained. *Science, 232,* 1091-1093.

Barnes, D. M. (1987). Brain damage by AIDS under active study. *Science, 235,* 1574-1577.

Barnouw, E. (Ed.). (1989). *International encyclopedia of communications* (Vols. 1-4). New York: Oxford University Press.

Barre-Sinoussi, F., Chermann, J. C., & Montagnier, L. (1987). Citation classic commentary on Science, 220, 868-71. *Current Contents / Life Sciences, 8,* 18.

Barre-Sinoussi, F., Chermann, J. C., Rey, F., Nugeyre, M. T., Chamaret, S., & Gruest, J. (1983). Isolation of a T-lymphotropic retrovirus from a patient at risk for Acquired Immune Deficiency Syndrome (AIDS). *Science, 220,* 868-871.

Bayer, A., Smart, J. C., & McLaughlin, G. W. (1984). *Mapping intellectual structures of a scientific subfield through author cocitation.* Paper presented at the annual meeting of the Society for Social Studies of Science, Ghent, Belgium.

Bazerman, C. (1983). Scientific writing as a social act: A review of the literature of the sociology of science. In P. V. Anderson (Ed.), *New essays in technical and scientific communication* (pp. 156-184). Farmingdale, NY: Baywood.

Bazerman, C. (1984). Modern evolution of the experimental report in physics: Spectroscopic articles in "Physical Review," 1893-1980. *Social Studies of Science, 14,* 163-196.

Bazerman, C. (1988). *Shaping written knowledge: The genre and activity of the experimental article in science.* Madison: University of Wisconsin Press.

Belkin, N. J., & Croft, W. B. (1987). Retrieval techniques. In M. E. Williams (Ed.), *Annual review of information science and technology* (Vol. 22, pp. 109-145). New York: Elsevier.

Beniger, J. R. (1986). *The control revolution: Technological and economic origins of the information society.* Cambridge, MA: Harvard University Press.

Beniger, J. R. (1988). Information and communication: The new convergence. *Communication Research, 15*(2), 198-218.

Bensman, S. J. (1982). Bibliometric laws and library usage as social phenomena. *Library Research, 4,* 279-312.

Berelson, B. R. (1952). *Content analysis in communication research.* New York: Free Press.

Berelson, B. R. (1959). The state of communication research. *Public Opinion Quarterly, 23,* 1-6.

Berger, C. R., & Chaffee, S. H. (Eds.). (1987). *Handbook of communication science*. Newbury Park, CA: Sage.

Bernal, J. D. (1948). Preliminary analysis of pilot questionnaire on the use of scientific literature. In *Royal Society Scientific Information Conference, reports and papers submitted*. (Paper no. 46, pp. 587-637). London: Royal Society.

Blashfield, R. K. (1984). The neo-Kraepelinian movement in American psychiatry. In R. K. Blashfield (Ed.), *The classification of psychopathology: Neo-Kraepelinian and quantitative approaches* (pp. 25-58). New York: Plenum.

Bolognesi, D. P. (1989). Progress in vaccines against AIDS. *Science, 246*, 1233-1234.

Bonnstetter, C. (1986). Magazine coverage of the mentally handicapped. *Journalism Quarterly, 63*(3), 623-627.

Borgman, C. L., & Rice, R. E. (in preparation). Convergence of fragmentation in communication and information science journal-to-journal citation networks, 1977-1987.

Borgman, C. L., & Schement, J. R. (1990). Information science and communication research: An essay on convergence. In A. E. Prentice (Ed.), *Information science as a discipline*. New York: Neal Schuman.

Bourdieu, P. (1975). The specificity of the scientific field and the social conditions of the progress of reason. *Social Science Information, 14*(6), 19-47.

Bourdieu, P. (1983). The field of cultural production, or: The economic world reversed. *Poetics, 12*, 311-356.

Bradford, S. E. (1934). Sources of information on specific subjects. *Engineering, 137*(3550), 85-86.

Braun, T., & Bujdoso, E. (1983). Gatekeeping patterns in the publication of analytical chemistry research. *Talanta, 30*(3), 161-167.

Brittain, J. M. (1979). Information services and the structure of knowledge in the social sciences. *International Social Science Journal, 31*, 711-728.

Broadus, R. M. (1987). Toward a definition of "bibliometrics." *Scientometrics, 12*(5-6), 373-379.

Brookes, B. C. (1971). Optimum P% library of scientific periodicals. *Nature, 232*, 458-461.

Brooks, T. A. (1986). Evidence of complex citer motivation. *Journal of the American Society for Information Science, 37*, 34-36.

Brooks, T. A. (in press-a). Clustering in comprehensive bibliographies and related literatures. *Journal of the American Society for Information Science*.

Brooks, T. A. (in press-b). Perfect Bradford multipliers: A definition and empirical investigation. *Information Processing and
Management*.

Burt, R. S. (1978). Stratification and prestige among elite experts in
methodological and mathematical sociology circa 1975. *Social
Networks, 1*, 105-158.

Burt, R. S. (1980). Models of network structure. *Annual Review of
Sociology*, pp. 79-141.

Burt, R. S. (1988). Some properties of structural equivalence measures derived from sociometric choice data. *Social Networks,
10*(1), 1-28.

Busch, L. (1980). Structure and negotiation in the agricultural
sciences. *Rural Sociology, 45*, 26-48.

Callon, M., Law, J., & Rip, A. (1986). *Mapping the dynamics of
science and technology*. London: Macmillan.

Cambrosio, A., & Keating, P. (1983). The disciplinary stake: The case
of chronobiology. *Social Studies of Science, 13*, 323-353.

Campbell, D. T., & Fiske, D. (1959). Convergent and discriminant
validation by the multitrait-multimethod matrix. *Psychological
Bulletin, 56*(1), 81-105.

Carpenter, M. P., & Narin, F. (1981). The adequacy of the Science
Citation Index (SCI) as an indicator of international scientific
activity. *Journal of the American Society for Information Science,
32*(6), 430-439.

Chapman, J., & Subramanyam, K. (1981). Cocitation search strategy. In *Proceedings of the National Online Meeting* (pp. 97-102).
Medford, NJ: Learned Information.

Chatterjee, S., & Price, B. (1977). *Regression analysis by example*.
New York: John Wiley.

Chubin, D. E. (1976). The conceptualization of scientific specialities.
*Scientometrics, 12*(5-6), 373-379.

Chubin, D. E. (1983). *Sociology of sciences: An annotated bibliography on invisible colleges, 1972-1981*. New York: Garland.

Chubin, D. E. (1985). Beyond invisible colleges: Inspirations and
aspirations of post-1972 social studies of science. *Scientometrics,
1*(3-6), 221-254.

Chubin, D. E. (1987). Research evaluation and the generation of big
science policy. *Knowledge: Creation, Diffusion, Utilization, 9*,
254-277.

Chubin, D. E., & Moitra, S. (1975). Content analysis of references:
Adjunct or alternative to citation counting. *Social Studies of
Science, 5*, 423-441.

Clark, P. (1982). Literature and sociology. In J. P. Barncelli & J. Gibaldi (Eds.), *Interrelations of literature*. New York: Modern Language Association.

Clark, T. N. (1973). *Prophets and patrons: The French university and the emergence of the social sciences*. Cambridge, MA: Harvard University Press.

Clegg, M. T., & Epperson, B. K. (1985). Recent developments in population genetics. *Advances in Genetics, 23*, 235-269.

Cohen, W. (1968). *Toward a social report*. Washington, DC: Department of Health, Education and Welfare.

Cole, J. (1970). Patterns of intellectual influence in scientific research. *Sociology of Education, 43*, 377-403.

Cole, J. R., & Cole, S. (1973). *Social stratification in science*. Chicago: University of Chicago Press.

Cole, S. (1975). The growth of scientific knowledge: Theories of deviance as a case study. In L. A. Coser (Ed.), *The idea of social structure: Papers in honor of Robert K. Merton* (pp. 175-220). New York: Harcourt Brace Jovanovich.

Cole, S. (1983). The hierarchy of the sciences? *American Journal of Sociology, 89*, 111-139.

Cole, S., Cole, J. R., & Dietrich, L. (1978). Measuring the cognitive state of scientific disciplines. In Y. Elkana, J. Lederberg, R. K. Merton, A. Thackray, & H. Zuckerman (Eds.), *Toward a metric of science: The advent of science indicators* (pp. 209-252). New York: Wiley-Interscience.

Cole, S., & Zuckerman, H. (1975). The emergence of a scientific specialty: The self-exemplifying case of the sociology of science. In L. A. Coser (Ed.), *The idea of social structure: Papers in honor of Robert K. Merton* (pp. 139-174). New York: Harcourt Brace Jovanovich.

Collins, H. M. (1975). The seven sexes: A study in the sociology of a phenomenon, or the replication of experiments in physics. *Sociology, 9*, 205-224.

Compton, B. (1973). Scientific communication. In I. Pool, W. Schramm, N. Maccoby, & E. B. Parker (Eds.), *Handbook of communication* (pp. 755-778). Chicago: Rand McNally.

Coser, L. A., Kadushin, C., & Powell, W. (1982). *Books: The culture and commerce of publishing*. New York: Basic Books.

Cottrill, C. A. (1987). *A co-citation study of the scientific literature of two innovation research traditions: Diffusion of innovations and technology transfer*. Unpublished doctoral dissertation, University for Experimenting Colleges and Universities, Cincinnati.

Cottrill, C. A., Rogers, E. M., & Mills, T. (1989). Co-citation analysis of the scientific literature of innovation research traditions. *Knowledge: Creation, Diffusion, Utilization, 11*(2), 181-208.

Cozzens, S. E. (1988). *Social control and multiple discovery in science: The opiate receptor case.* Albany: State University of New York Press.

Cozzens, S. E. (1989). What do citations count? The rhetoric-first model. *Scientometrics, 15*, 437-447.

Crane, D. (1967). The gatekeepers of science: Some factors affecting the selection of articles of scientific journals. *American Sociologist, 2*(4), 195-201.

Crane, D. (1969). Social structure in a group of scientists: A test of the "invisible college" hypothesis. *American Sociological Review, 34*(3), 335-352.

Crane, D. (1970). The nature of scientific communication and influence. *International Social Science Journal, 22*, 28-41.

Crane, D. (1971). Information needs and uses. In C. Cuadra & A. Luke (Eds.), *Annual review of information science and technology* (Vol. 6, pp. 1-39). Chicago: American Society for Information Science and Encyclopedia Britannica.

Crane, D. (1972). *Invisible colleges: Diffusion of knowledge in scientific communities.* Chicago: University of Chicago Press.

Crane, D. (1987). *The growth of the avant-garde in New York, 1940-1980.* New York: Free Press.

Crane, D. (1989). How scientists communicate. *Current Contents: Social & Behavioral Sciences, 21*(42), 18.

Crawford, J. W., & Crawford, S. (1980). Research in psychiatry-cocitation analysis. *American Journal of Psychiatry, 137*, 52-55.

Crawford, S. (1971). Informal communication among scientists in sleep research. *Journal of the American Society for Information Science, 22*, 301-310.

Cronin, B. (1981). The need for a theory of citing. *Journal of Documentation, 37*, 16-24.

Cronin, B. (1984). *The citation process: The role and significance of citations in scientific communication.* London: Taylor Graham.

Crow, J. F. (1986). *Basic concepts in population, quantitative, and evolutionary genetics.* New York: Freeman.

Culnan, M. J. (1986). The intellectual development of management information systems, 1972-1982: A cocitation analysis. *Management Science, 32*, 156-172.

Culnan, M. J. (1987). Mapping the intellectual structure of MIS, 1980-1985: A co-citation analysis. *MIS Quarterly, 22*, 341-353.

Cutlip, S. (1954). Content and flow of AP news: From trunk to TTS to reader. *Journalism Quarterly, 31*(3), 434-446.

Dahling, R. L. (1962). Shannon's information theory: The spread of an idea. In *Studies of innovation and of communication to the public* (pp. 118-139). Stanford, CA: Stanford University, Institute for Communication Research.

Davis, J. M. (1970). The transmission of information in psychiatry. *Proceedings of the annual meeting of the American Society for Information Science, 7,* 53-56.

Debons, A., King, D. W., Mansfield, U., & Shirey, D. L. (1981). *The information professional: Survey of an emerging field.* New York: Marcel Dekker.

Deese, J. (1965). *The structure of associations in language and thought.* Baltimore: Johns Hopkins University Press.

Delia, J. G. (1987). Communication research: A history. In C. R. Berger & S. H. Chaffee (Eds.), *Handbook of communication science* (pp. 20-98). Newbury Park, CA: Sage.

De Mey, M. (1982). *The cognitive paradigm: Cognitive science, a newly explored approach to the study of cognition applied in an analysis of science and scientific knowledge.* Dordrecht, the Netherlands: Reidel.

Dervin, B., & Voigt, M. (Eds.). *Progress in communication sciences* [Annual series]. Norwood, NJ: Ablex.

DiGiacomo, R., Kremer, J., & Shah, D. (1988). Clinical effects of fish-oil fatty acid ingestion in patients with Raynaud's phenomenon [Abstract]. *Arthritis and Rheumatism, 31*(4), (Suppl. 34).

Doreian, P. (1985). Structural equivalence in a psychology journal network. *Journal of the American Society for Information Science, 36*(6), 411-417.

Drake, D. C. (1989, January 29). The road to discovery. *Philadelphia Inquirer,* p. 1A.

Edge, D. O. (1977). Why I am not a co-citationist. *Society for Social Studies of Science Newsletter, 2,* 13-19.

Edge, D. O. (1979). Quantitative measures of communication in science: A critical review. *History of Science, 17,* 102-134.

Edge, D. O., & Mulkay, M. (1976). *Astronomy transformed: The emergence of radio astronomy in Britain.* New York: John Wiley.

Egghe, L. (1986). The dual of Bradford's law. *Journal of the American Society for Information Science, 37*(4), 246-255.

Escarpit, R. (1968). The sociology of literature. *International Encyclopedia of the Social Sciences, 9,* 417-425.

Essex, M., McLane, M. F., Lee, T. H., Falk, L., Howe, C. W. S., & Mullins, J. I. (1983). Antibodies to cell membrane antigens associated with human T-cell leukemia virus in patients with AIDS. *Science, 220*, 859-862.

Eto, H. (1984a). Model of R&D investment of firms and resulting new skew distribution. *International Journal of Systems Science, 15*(6), 673-684.

Eto, H. (1984b). Bradford law in R&D expending of firms and R&D concentration. *Scientometrics, 6*(3), 183-188.

Eto, H. (1988). Rising tail in Bradford distribution: Its interpretation and application. *Scientometrics, 13*(5-6), 271-287.

Eto, H., & Makino, K. (1983). Stochastic model for innovation and resulting skew distribution for technological concentration with verification in Japanese industry. *Scientometrics, 5*(4), 219-243.

Eveland, J. D. (1987). Diffusion, technology transfer, and implementation: Thinking and talking about change. *Knowledge: Creation, Diffusion, Utilization, 8*(2), 303-324.

Farber, P. L. (1982). *The emergence of ornithology as a scientific discipline: 1760-1850*. Boston: Reidel.

Faulstich, W. (1977). *Domînen der Rezeptionsanalyse*. Kronberg/TS: Athenaeum Verlag.

Ferment in the field. (1983). [Special issue]. *Journal of Communication, 33*(3).

Frame, J. D., & Carpenter, M. P. (1979). International research collaboration. *Social Studies of Science, 9*, 481-497.

Freeman, L. C. (1986). Boxicity and the social context of Swedish literary criticism, 1818-1883. *Journal of Social and Biological Structure, 9*, 141-149.

Freidheim, E. A. (1978). A quantitative procedure for classifying the content of theory/research works. *Sociological Quarterly, 19*, 234-252.

Fujiwara, S. (1984). Basic terms in science and technology as a communication tool for the promotion of better exchange of information. *International Forum on Information and Documentation, 9*(3), 22-26.

Fujiwara, S., Yokoyama, M., & Ueda, S. (1981). Analysis of keywords in chemistry. *Journal of Chemical Information and Computer Sciences, 21*(2), 66-70.

Fussler, H. H. (1949). Characteristics of the research literature used by chemists and physicists in the United States. *Library Quarterly, 19*, 19-35, 119-143.

Futuyma, D. J. (1986). *Evolutionary biology* (2nd ed.). Sunderland, MA: Sinauer Association.

Gaiser, G. (1983). Zur Empirisierung des Kanonbegriffs. *Spiel, 2*, 123-136.

Gallo, R. C. (1988). Citation classic commentary on Science 224, 500-3. *Current Contents: Life Sciences, 15*, 16-17.

Gallo, R. C., & Montagnier, L. (1987). The chronology of AIDS research. *Nature, 326*, 435-436.

Gallo, R. C., Sarin, P. S., Gelmann, E. P., Robert-Guroff, M., Richardson, E., & Kalyanaranman, V. S. (1983). Isolation of human T-cell leukemia virus in Acquired Immune Deficiency Syndrome (AIDS). *Science, 220*, 865-867.

Gardner, H. (1985). *The mind's new science: A history of the cognitive revolution.* New York: Basic Books.

Garfield, E. (1964). *The use of citation data in writing the history of science.* Philadelphia: Institute for Scientific Information.

Garfield, E. (1979a). Is citation analysis a legitimate evaluation tool? *Scientometrics, 1*, 359-375.

Garfield, E. (1979b). *Citation indexing: Its theory and application in science, technology and humanities.* New York: John Wiley.

Garfield, E. (1985). In tribute to Derek John deSolla Price: A citation analysis of *Little science, big science. Scientometrics, 7*, 487-503.

Garfield, E. (1986). In tribute to Derek John deSolla Price: A citation analysis of *Little science, big science.* In E. Garfield (Ed.), *Essays of an information scientist: Vol. 8. 1985: Ghostwriting and other essays* (pp. 232-240). Philadelphia: Institute for Scientific Information Press.

Garfield, E., Malin, M. W., & Small, H. (1978). Citation data as science indicators. In Y. Elkana, J. Lederberg, R. K. Merton, A. Thackray, & H. Zuckerman (Eds.), *Toward a metric of science: The advent of science indicators* (pp. 179-207). New York: John Wiley.

Garfield, E., Sher, I. H., & Torpie, R. J. (1964). *The use of citation data in writing the history of science.* Philadelphia: Institute for Scientific Information.

Garvey, W. D. (1979). *Communication: The essence of science.* New York: Pergamon.

Garvey, W. D., & Griffith, B. C. (1964). Scientific information exchange in psychology. *Science, 146*, 1655-1659.

Garvey, W. D., & Griffith, B. C. (1965). Scientific communication: Dissemination system in psychology and a theoretical framework for planning innovations. *American Psychologist, 20*(1), 157-164.

Garvey, W. D., & Griffith, B. C. (1971). Scientific communication: Its role in the conduct of research and creation of knowledge. *American Psychologist, 26*, 349-362.

Gerbner, G., & Gross, L. (1976). Living with television: The violence profile. *Journal of Communication, 26*(2), 173-179.

Gieryn, T. F. (1983). Boundary-work and the demarcation of science from non-science: Strains and interests in professional ideologies of scientists. *American Sociological Review, 48*, 781-795.

Gilbert, G. N. (1976). The transformation of research findings into scientific knowledge. *Social Studies of Science, 4*, 281-306.

Gilbert, G. N., & Mulkay, M. (1984). *Opening Pandora's box: A sociological analysis of scientists' discourse.* New York: Cambridge University Press.

Goffman, W., & Warren, K. S. (1969). Dispersion of papers among journals based on a mathematical analysis of two diverse medical literatures. *Nature, 221*(5187), 1205-1207.

Gottlieb, M. S., Schroff, R., Schanker, H. M., Weisman, J. D., Fan, P. T., & Wolf, R. A. (1981). Pneumocystis carinii pneumonia and mucosal candidiasis in previously healthy homosexual men. *New England Journal of Medicine, 305*, 1425-1431.

Graham, L., Lepenies, W., & Weingart, P. (Eds.). (1983). *Functions and uses of disciplinary histories.* Boston: Reidel.

Griffith, B. C. (1979). Science literature: How faulty a mirror of science? *Aslib Proceedings, 31*, 381-391.

Griffith, B. C. (Ed.). (1980). *Key papers in information science.* White Plains, NY: Knowledge Industry.

Griffith, B. C. (1987, October 21). *Studies of information and communication and the revolution in understanding science.* New Jersey chapter, American Society for Information Science Distinguished Lectureship School of Communication, Information and Library Studies, Rutgers University, New Brunswick, NJ.

Griffith, B. C., Drott, M. C., & Small, H. G. (1977). On the use of citations in studying scientific achievements and communication. *Society for Social Studies of Science Newsletter, 2*, 9-13.

Griffith, B. C., & Miller, A. J. (1970). Networks of informal communication among scientifically productive scientists. In D. E. Nelson & D. K. Pollock (Eds.), *Communication among scientists and engineers.* Lexington, MA: Heath Lexington.

Griffith, B. C., & Mullins, N. C. (1972). Highly coherent groups in scientific change. *Science, 177*(4053), 959-964.

Griffith, B. C., & Small, H. G. (1983). *The structure of the social and behavioral sciences literature.* Stockholm: Royal Institute of Technology Library. (Stockholm papers in library and information science, TRITA-LIB-6021)

Griffith, B. C., Small, H. G., Stonehill, J. A., & Dey, S. (1974). The structure of scientific literature, II: Toward a macro-structure for science. *Science Studies, 4*, 339-365.

Griswold, W. (1983). The devil's techniques: Cultural legitimation and social change. *American Sociological Review, 48*, 668-680.

Groeben, N. (1977). *Rezeptionsforschung als empirische Literaturwissenschaft: Paradigma—durch Methoden—diskussion an Untersuchungsbeispielen.* Kronberg/TS: Athenaeum Verlag.

Gustafson, A. (1961). *A history of Swedish literature.* Minneapolis: University of Minnesota Press.

Hagstrom, W. O. (1968). *The scientific community.* New York: Basic Books.

Hagstrom, W. O. (1973, July). Review of Crane's *Invisible colleges. Contemporary Sociology, 2*, 381-383.

Hagstrom, W. O. (1976). The production of culture in science. In R. A. Peterson (Ed.), *The production of culture* (pp. 91-106). Beverly Hills, CA: Sage.

Hammond, K. R., McClelland, G. H., & Mumpower, J. (1980). *Human judgment and decision making: Theories, methods, and procedures.* New York: Praeger.

Harada, M. (1974). Bibliometrics: Methods and applications. *Library and Information Science, 12*, 109-141.

Hargens, L. L., & Felmlee, D. H. (1984). Structural determinants of stratification in science. *American Sociological Review, 49*, 685-697.

Hargens, L. L., Mullins, N. C., & Hecht, P. K. (1980). Research areas and stratification processes in science. *Social Studies of Science, 10*, 55-74.

Harris, H. (1966). Enzyme polymorphisms in man. *Proceedings of the Royal Society of London* (Series B), *164*, 298-310.

Harris, H. (1969). Enzyme and protein polymorphism in human populations. *British Medical Bulletin, 25*, 5-13.

Hawkins, D. T. (1977). Unconventional uses of online information retrieval systems—online bibliometric studies. *Journal of the American Society for Information Science, 28*, 13-18.

Hayashi, Y., & Yamada, K. (Eds.). (1975). *Kagaku no raifu saikuru* [Life-cycles of sciences]. Tokyo: Chuo-Koron.

Hedrick, P. W. (1985). *Genetics of populations.* Boston: Jones & Bartlett.

Hilgard, E. R. (1963). Motivation in learning theory. In S. Koch (Ed.), *Psychology: A study of a science* (Vol. 5, pp. 253-283). New York: McGraw-Hill.

Hirsch, P. M. (1981). Institutional functions of elite and mass media. In E. Katz & T. Szecsk (Eds.), *Mass media and social change.* London: Sage.

Hopkins, F. L. (1984). New causal theory and ethnomethodology: Cocitation patterns across a decade. *Scientometrics, 3*, 33-53.

Hoshino, S. (Ed.). (1988). *Touyougaku kenkyuu shien dehta behsu no kenkyuu* [Studies on databases for supporting oriental studies]. Report of research supported by the Grant-in-Aid for Fundamental Scientific Research of the Education Ministry in fiscal 1987.

Hubby, J. L., & Lewontin, R. C. (1966). A molecular approach to the study of genic heterozygosity in natural populations. I: The number of alleles at different loci in Drosophila pseudoobscura. *Genetics, 54*, 577-594.

Hurt, C. D. (1983). A comparison of a bibliometric approach and an historical approach to the identification of important literature. *Information Processing & Management, 19*, 151-157.

Hutchins, R. M. (Ed.). (1952). *Great books of the western world* (54 vols.). Chicago: Encyclopedia Britannica.

Hymes, K. B., Cheung, T., Greene, J. B., Prose, N. S., Marcus, A., & Ballard, H. (1981). Kaposi's sarcoma in homosexual men: A report of eight cases. *Lancet, 2*, 598-600.

Ichikawa, Y., Kanada, Y., Oe, K., & Momota, H. (1979). Bunken jouhou kensaku ni motozuku kenkyuu doukou no keiryouteki bunseki [Quantitative analysis of research activities based on document information retrieval]. *Butsuri, 34*(12), 996-999.

Jablin, F., Putnam, L., Roberts, K., & Porter, L. (Eds.). (1987). *Handbook of organizational communication*. Newbury Park, CA: Sage.

Jauss, H. R. (1970). *Literaturgeschichte als Provokation*. Frankfurt: Suhrkamp.

Jensen, J. F. (1961). *Turgenjev i dansk åndsliv*. Copenhagen: Gyldendal.

Jensen, K. B., & Rosengren, K. E. (1990). Five traditions in search of the audience. *European Journal of Communication, 5*.

Jöreskog, K. G., & Sörbom, D. (1989). *LISREL 7: A guide to the program and applications* (2nd ed.). Chicago: SPSS.

Kadushin, C. (1966). The friends and supporters of psychotherapy: On social circles in urban life. *American Sociological Review, 31*, 786-802.

Kalyanaraman, V. S., Sarngadharan, M. G., Robert-Guroff, M., Miyoshi, I., Blayney, D., & Golde, D. (1982). A new subtype of human T-cell leukemia virus (HTLV-II) associated with a T-cell variant of hairy-cell leukemia. *Science, 218*, 571-573.

Kaneiwa, K., Adachi, J., Aoki, M., Matsuda, T., Midorikawa, N., Tanimura, A., & Yamazaki, S. (1988). A comparison between the journals Nature and Science. *Scientometrics, 13*(3-4), 125-133.

Kaneko, M., Itsumura, H., Saito, K., Ogawa, H., & Midorikawa, N. (1983). Characteristics of letter journals. *Annals of Japan Society of Library Science, 29*(1), 41-47.

Keen, P. G. W. (1987). MIS research: Current status, trends and needs. In R. A. Buckingham, R. A. Hirschheim, F. F. Land, & C. J. Tully (Eds.), *Information systems education: Recommendations and implementation* (pp. 1-13). Cambridge: Cambridge University Press.

Kepplinger, H. M. (1975). *Realkultur und Medienkultur: Literarische Karrieren in der Bundesrepublik.* Freiburg: Verlag Karl Alber.

Kerlinger, F. N. (1973). *Foundations of behavioral research* (2nd ed.). New York: Holt, Rinehart & Winston.

Kessler, M. M. (1963). Bibliographic coupling between scientific papers. *American Documentation, 14,* 10-25.

Kessler, M. M. (1965). Comparison of the results of bibliographic coupling and analytic subject indexing. *American Documentation, 16,* 223-233.

Kessler, M. M., & Heart, F. E. (1962). *Analysis of bibliographic sources in the "Physical review."* Cambridge: Massachusetts Institute of Technology.

Knapp, S. D. (1984). Cocitation searching: Some useful strategies. *Online, 8,* 43-48.

Knorr-Cetina, K. D. (1981). *The manufacture of knowledge: An essay on the constructivist and contextual nature of science.* New York: Pergamon.

Knorr-Cetina, K. D. (1988, December). *Thinking through talk: An ethnographic study of a molecular biology laboratory.* Paper presented at the 1988 Symposium on Science Communication, sponsored by the U.S. Environmental Protection Agency and the Annenberg School of Communications at the University of Southern California, Los Angeles.

Kochen, M. (1974). *Integrative mechanisms in literature growth.* Westport, CT: Greenwood.

Kochen, M. (1989). How well do we acknowledge intellectual debts? *Current Contents: Social & Behavioral Sciences, 21*(25), 7-14.

Kuhn, T. S. (1962). *The structure of scientific revolutions.* Chicago: University of Chicago Press.

Kuhn, T. S. (1970). *The structure of scientific revolutions* (2nd ed., enlarged). Chicago: University of Chicago Press.

Kuhn, T. S. (1977). Second thoughts on paradigms. In F. Suppe (Ed.), *The structure of scientific theories* (pp. 459-482). Urbana: University of Illinois Press.

Kulstad, R. (Ed.). (1986). *AIDS: Papers from Science, 1982-1985*. Washington, DC: American Association for the Advancement of Science.

Kurata, K. (1984). Scholarly productivity of political scientists in Japan. *Library and Information Science, 22*, 129-142.

Kurata, K. (1985). Determining factors of publication productivity of Japanese physical scientists. *Library and Information Science, 23*, 115-123.

Lachman, R., Lachman, J. L., & Butterfield, E. C. (1979). *Cognitive psychology and information processing: An introduction*. Hillsdale, NJ: Lawrence Erlbaum.

Latour, B. (1987). *Science in action: How to follow scientists and engineers through society*. Cambridge, MA: Harvard University Press.

Latour, B. (1988). *The pasteurization of France*. Cambridge, MA: Harvard University Press.

Latour, B., & Woolgar, S. (1979). *Laboratory life: The social construction of scientific facts*. Beverly Hills, CA: Sage.

Lenk, P. (1983). Mapping of fields based on nominations. *Journal of the American Society for Information Science, 34*, 115-122.

Lewison, G. (1989). *The evaluation of European community agricultural research*. Paper presented at the Conference of the Society for the Social Studies of Science, Irvine, CA.

Lewison, G., & Cunningham, P. (1989). The use of bibliometrics in the evaluation of community biotechnology research programmes. In A. F. J. van Raan, A. J. Nederhof, & H. F. Moed (Eds.), *Science and technology indicators, their use in science policy and their role in science studies*. Leiden, the Netherlands: University of Leiden, DSWO Press.

Lewontin, R. C. (1985a). Population genetics. *Annual Review of Genetics, 19*, 81-102.

Lewontin, R. C. (1985b). The week's citation classic. *Current Contents, 43*, 16.

Lewontin, R. C., & Hubby, J. L. (1966). A molecular approach to the study of genic heterozygosity in natural populations. II: Amount of variation and degree of heterozygosity in natural populations of Drosophila pseudoobscura. *Genetics, 54*, 595-609.

Leydesdorff, L. (1989). The relationship between qualitative theory and scientometric methods in science and technology studies. *Scientometrics, 15*, 333-347.

Lievrouw, L. A. (1988). Four programs of research in scientific communication. *Knowledge in Society, 1*(2), 6-22.

Lievrouw, L. A., Rogers, E. M., Lowe, C. U., & Nadel, E. (1987). Triangulation as a research strategy for identifying invisible colleges among biomedical sciences. *Social Networks*, *9*, 217-238.

Line, M. B. (1979). Influence of the type of sources used on the results of citation analysis. *Journal of Documentation*, *35*, 265-284.

Line, M. B., & Sandison, A. (1974). "Obsolescence" and changes in the use of literature with time. *Journal of Documentation*, *30*, 283-350.

Lingwood, D. A. (1969). *Interpersonal communication, research productivity, and invisible colleges*. Unpublished doctoral dissertation, Department of Communication, Stanford University, Stanford, CA.

Lippmann, W., & Merz, C. (1920). A test of the news. *New Republic* (Supplement to issue of August 4, 1920).

Lomnitz, L. A., Rees, M. W., & Cameo, L. (1987). Publication and referencing patterns in a Mexican research institute. *Social Studies of Science*, *17*, 115-133.

MacRoberts, M. H., & MacRoberts, B. (1986). Quantitative measures of communications in science: A study of the formal level. *Social Studies of Science*, *16*, 151-172.

MacRoberts, M. H., & MacRoberts, B. R. (1987a). Another test of the normative theory of citing. *Journal of the American Society for Information Science*, *38*, 305-306.

MacRoberts, M. H., & MacRoberts, B. R. (1987b). Testing the Ortega hypothesis: Facts and artifacts. *Scientometrics*, *12*, 293-295.

MacRoberts, M. H., & MacRoberts, B. R. (1988). Author motivation for not citing influences: A methodological note. *Journal of the American Society for Information Science*, *39*, 432-433.

MacRoberts, M. H., & MacRoberts, B. R. (1989). Problems of citation analysis: A critical review. *Journal of the American Society for Information Science*, *40*, 342-349.

Mann, P. H. (1983). The novel in British society. *Poetics*, *12*, 435-448.

Marshakova, I. V. (1981). Citation networks in information science. *Scientometrics*, *3*, 13-26.

Marton, J. (1983). Causes of low and high citation potentials in science: Citation analysis of biochemistry and plant physiology journals. *Journal of the American Society for Information Science*, *34*, 244-246.

Marx, J. L. (1982). New disease baffles medical community. *Science*, *217*, 618-621.

Marx, J. L. (1985). Indications of a new virus in MS patients. *Science*, *230*, 1028.

Masur, H., Michelis, M., Greene, J. B., Onorato, I., Zande-Stouwe, R. A., & Hozman, R. S. (1981). An outbreak of community-acquired pheumocystis carinii pneumonia: Initial manifestation of cellular immune dysfunction. *New England Journal of Medicine, 305,* 1431-1438.

Matsumoto, K., Miyamoto, S., & Nakayama, K. (1982). Computer application to the research of Chinese history: Indexing and statistical analysis of Chinese classics. In *Proceedings of the International Computer Symposium 1982* (pp. 121-129). Taiwan.

Matsumoto, K., Miyamoto, S., & Nakayama, K. (1984). Cluster analysis of Chinese texts: Section method and neighborhood method for generating similarities. In *Proceedings of the International Computer Symposium 1984* (pp. 218-225). Taiwan.

Mayr, E. (1963). *Animal species and evaluation.* Cambridge, MA: Harvard University Press.

Mayumi, I. (1984). Citation behavior in literary research: Citation content analysis in Shakespeare studies. *Library and Information Science, 22,* 119-128.

McCain, K. W. (1983). The author co-citation structure of macroeconomics. *Scientometrics, 5,* 277-289.

McCain, K. W. (1984). Longitudinal author co-citation mapping: The changing structure of macroeconomics. *Journal of the American Society for Information Science, 35,* 351-359.

McCain, K. W. (1985). *Longitudinal cocited author mapping and intellectual structure: A test of congruence in two scientific literatures.* Unpublished doctoral dissertation, Drexel University, Philadelphia.

McCain, K. W. (1986a). The paper trails of scholarship: Mapping the literature of genetics. *Library Quarterly, 56,* 258-271.

McCain, K. W. (1986b). Cocited author mapping as a valid representation of intellectual structure. *Journal of the American Society for Information Science, 37,* 111-122.

McCain, K. W. (1988). Evaluating cocited author search performance in a collaborative specialty. *Journal of the American Society for Information Science, 39,* 428-431.

McCain, K. W. (1989, June). *The production and exchange of research-related information in genetics.* Paper presented at the meeting of the International Society for the History, Philosophy, and Social Studies of Biology, London, Ontario, Canada.

McCain, K. W. (1990). *Mapping authors in intellectual space: A technical overview.* Manuscript submitted for publication.

McCain, K. W., & Turner, K. (1989). Citation context analysis and aging patterns of journal articles in molecular genetics. *Scientometrics, 17*, 127-163.

McCormack, T. (1982). Content analysis: The social history of a method. In T. McCormack (Ed.), *Studies in communications: A research annual: Culture, code, and content analysis* (pp. 157-183). Greenwich, CT: JAI.

McGhee, P. E., Skinner, P. R., Roberts, K., Ridenour, N. J., & Larson, S. M. (1987). Using online databases to study current research trends: An online bibliometric study. *Library and Information Science Research, 9*, 285-291.

Meadows, A. J. (1974). *Communication in science.* London: Butterworths.

Medawar, P. B. (1964, August 1). Is the scientific paper fraudulent? *Saturday Review*, pp. 42-43.

Meijer, R. F., Nederhof, A. J., & van Raan, A. F. J. (1990). *Aspects of knowledge transfer in agriculture in the Netherlands.* Leiden, the Netherlands: University of Leiden, Centre for Science and Technology Studies.

Melischek, G. (1984). Frames of reference of theater reviewers. In G. Melischek, K. E. Rosengren, & J. Stappers (Eds.), *Cultural indicators: An international symposium.* Vienna: Akademie der Wissenschaften.

Melischek, G., Rosengren, K. E., & Stappers, J. (Eds.). (1984). *Cultural indicators: An international symposium.* Vienna: Akademie der Wissenschaften.

Mendenhall, T. C. (1887). The characteristic curve of composition. *Science, 9*, 237-249.

Menzel, H. (1968). Informal communication in science: Advantages and analogues. In E. B. Montgomery (Ed.), *The foundations of access to knowledge: A symposium.* Syracuse, NY: Syracuse University, School of Library Sciences.

Merrill, D. J. (1981). *Ecological genetics.* Minneapolis: University of Minnesota Press.

Merton, R. K. (1942). Science and technology in a democratic order. *Journal of Legal and Political Sociology, 1*, 115-126.

Merton, R. K. (1957). Priorities in scientific discovery. *American Sociological Review, 22*(4), 635-659.

Merton, R. K. (1968). The Matthew effect in science. *Science, 159*, 56-63.

Merton, R. K. (1973). *The sociology of science.* Chicago: University of Chicago Press.

Merton, R. K. (1987). Three fragments from a sociologist's notebooks: Establishing the phenomenon, specified ignorance, and strategic research materials. *Annual Review of Sociology, 13,* 1-28.

Merton, R. K., Broom K., & Cottrell, L. S., Jr. (Eds.). (1959). *Sociology today: Problems and prospects.* New York: Basic Books.

Midorikawa, N. (1983). Citation analysis of physics journals: Comparison of subfields of physics. *Scientometrics, 5*(6), 361-374.

Midorikawa, N., Kurata, K., Mayumi, I., Oka, C., & Sugimoto, Y. (1986). *Investigative methods for library and information science.* Tokyo: Keiso-Shobo.

Midorikawa, N., Ogawa, H., Saito, K., Kaneko, M., & Itsumura, H. (1984). The relationships among the citation measures and the factors influence on them. *Information Services and Use, 4,* 417-424.

Miller, T., & Stebenne, D. (1988). The bibliometrics of politics. *Gannett Center Journal, 2*(4), 24-30.

Mitroff, I. I. (1974). *The subjective side of science.* New York: Elsevier.

Miwa, M., Ueda, S., & Nakayama, K. (1980). Characteristics of journal citations in the social sciences: Comparison of SSCI data of 1972 and 1977. *Library and Information Science, 18,* 141-155.

Miyamoto, S. (1989). Two approaches for fuzzy information retrieval through fuzzy associations. *IEEE Transactions on Systems, Man, and Cybernetics, 19,* 123-130.

Miyamoto, S., Miyake, T., & Nakayama, K. (1983a). Generation of a pseudothesaurus for information retrieval based on cooccurrences and fuzzy set operations. *IEEE Transactions on Systems, Man, and Cybernetics, 13*(1), 62-70.

Miyamoto, S., Miyake, T., & Nakayama, K. (1983b). Structure generation on bibliographic databases with citations based on a fuzzy set model. *Proceedings of IFAC Symposium on Fuzzy Information* (pp. 225-230). Marseille.

Miyamoto, S., & Nakayama, K. (1980). A hierarchical representation of citation relationships. *IEEE Transactions on Systems, Man, and Cybernetics, 10*(12), 899-903.

Miyamoto, S., & Nakayama, K. (1981). Determination of the conservation time of periodicals and optimal shelf maintenance of a library. *Journal of the American Society for Information Science, 32,* 268-274.

Miyamoto, S., & Nakayama, K. (1983). A technique of two-stage clustering applied to environmental and civil engineering and related methods of citation analysis. *Journal of the American Society for Information Science, 34*(3), 192-201.

Miyamoto, S., & Nakayama, K. (1984). A directed graph representation based on a statistical hypothesis testing and application to citation and association structures. *IEEE Transactions on Systems, Man, and Cybernetics*, *14*(2), 203-221.

Moed, H. F., de Bruin, R. E., & Straathof, A. (1989). *A bibliometric study of agricultural research within the European community* (Research report to the Commission of the European Communities, Report CWTS 89-03). Leiden, the Netherlands: University of Leiden, Centre for Science and Technology Studies.

Moed, H. F., & Vriens, M. (1989). Possible inaccuracies occurring in citation analysis. *Journal of Information Science*, *15*, 95-107.

Moravcsik, M. J., & Murugesan, P. (1975). Some results on the function and quality of citations. *Social Studies of Science*, *5*, 86-92.

Moravcsik, M. J., & Murugesan, P. (1979). Citation patterns in scientific revolutions. *Scientometrics*, *1*, 161-169.

Mosteller, F., & Wallace, D. L. (1963). Inference in an authorship problem. *Journal of the American Statistical Association*, *58*(3), 275-309.

Mulkay, M. (1974). Methodology in the sociology of science: Some reflections on the study of radio astronomy. *Social Science Information*, *13*, 109-119.

Muller, C. (1976). Statistique lexicale et théorie du lexique. *Cahiers de Lexicologie*, *24*, 91-101.

Mullins, N. C. (1966). *Social networks among biological scientists*. Unpublished doctoral dissertation, Harvard University.

Mullins, N. C. (1968). The distribution of social and cultural properties in informal communication networks among biological scientists. *American Sociological Review*, *33*, 786-797.

Mullins, N. C. (1973). *Theory and theory groups in contemporary American sociology*. New York: Harper & Row.

Mullins, N. C. (1975). New causal theory: An elite specialty in social science. *History of Political Economy*, *7*, 499-529.

Mullins, N. C., Hargens, L. L., Hecht, P. K., & Kick, E. L. (1977). The group structure of co-citation clusters: A comparative study. *American Sociological Review*, *42*, 552-562.

Munch-Petersen, E. (1931). Bibliometrics and fiction. *Libri*, *31*, 1-21.

Murray, S. O. (1982). The dissolution of "classical ethnoscience". *Journal of the History of the Behavioral Sciences*, *18*, 163-175.

Nadel, E. (1981). Citation and co-citation indicators of a phased impact of the BCS theory in the physics of superconductivity. *Scientometrics*, *3*, 203-221.

Nadel, E. (1983). Commitment and co-citation: An indicator of in-commensurability in patterns of formal communication. *Social Studies of Science, 13*, 255-283.

Nakayama, K., Ueda, S., & Miyamoto, S. (1979). Hierarchical structure of scientific disciplines using Social Sciences Citation Index. *Proceedings of the 20th Conference of the Information Processing Society of Japan, 5J-1*, 749-750.

Narin, F. (1976). *Evaluative bibliometrics: The use of publication and citation analysis in the evaluation of scientific activity* (Report No. 704 R). Washington, DC: Computer Horizons.

Narin, F., & Moll, J. K. (1977). Bibliometrics. In M. E. Williams (Ed.), *Annual review of information science and technology* (Vol. 12, pp. 35-58). White Plains, NY: Knowledge Industry.

Nei, M. (1987). *Molecular evolutionary genetics*. New York: Columbia University Press.

Newell, A. (1973). Artificial intelligence and the concept of mind. In R. C. Schank & K. M. Colby (Eds.), *Computer models of thought and language* (pp. 1-60). San Francisco: Freeman.

Noma, E. (1986). *Subject classification and influence weights for 3,000 journals*. Cherry Hill, NJ: Computer Horizons.

Nomoto, K., Wakayama, S., Kirimoto, T., & Kondo, M. (1987). *A fuzzy retrieval system based on citations* (Preprints of Second IFSA Congress, pp. 723-726). Tokyo.

Norman, C. (1985). Patent dispute divides AIDS researchers. *Science, 230*, 640-642.

Oberschall, A. (1972). *The establishment of empirical sociology: Studies in continuity, discontinuity, and institutionalization.* New York: Harper & Row.

O'Connor, D. O., & Voos, H. (1981). Empirical laws, theory construction, and bibliometrics. *Library Trends, 30*, 9-20.

Ogawa, H., Midorikawa, N., Yoshikawa, C., Saito, K., Itsumura, H., Kaneko, M., & Niki, E. (1989). How much of cited conference materials can be found using bibliographic tools? *Journal of the American Society for Information Science, 40*(5), 350-355.

Oi, K., Miyamoto, S., Abe, O., Katsuya, A., & Nakayama, K. (1986). Analysis of cognitive structures of environment of local residents through word association methods. *Ecological Modelling, 32*, 29-41.

Oleson, A., & Voss, J. (Eds.). (1979). *The organization of knowledge in modern America, 1860-1920*. Baltimore: Johns Hopkins University Press.

Onodera, N. (1988). A frequency distribution function derived from a stochastic model considering human behaviors and its comparison with an empirical bibliometric distribution. *Scientometrics*, *14*(1-2), 143-159.

Oppenheim, C. (1985). Use of online databases in bibliometric studies. In *Proceedings of the 9th International Online Information Meeting* (pp. 355-364). Oxford: Learned Information.

Oromaner, M. (1981). Cognitive consensus in recent mainstream American sociology: An empirical analysis. *Scientometrics*, *3*, 73-84.

O'Sullivan, M., Fave, A., Galante, E., Henning Petersen, P., Henrichsmeyer, W., Sanchez Monge, E., & Wilson, G. (1989). *Evaluation of the agricultural programmes (1976-1978, 1979-1983, and 1984-1988)* (Research evaluation Report no. 39). (Available from the Office for Official Publications of the European Communities, EUR 12147)

Paisley, W. J., (1964). Identifying the unknown communicator in painting, literature and music: The significance of minor encoding habits. *Journal of Communication*, *14*(4), 219-237.

Paisley, W. J. (1965). *The flow of (behavioral) science information: A review of the research literature*. Stanford, CA: Stanford University, Institute for Communication Research.

Paisley, W. J. (1966). The effects of authorship, topic, structure, and time of composition on letter redundancy in English texts. *Journal of Verbal Learning and Verbal Behavior*, *5*(1), 28-34.

Paisley, W. J. (1968). Information needs and uses. In C. Cuadra & A. Luke (Eds.), *Annual review of information science and technology* (Vol. 3, pp. 1-30). Chicago: American Society for Information Science and Encyclopedia Britiannica.

Paisley, W. J. (1972, April). The role of invisible colleges in scientific information transfer. *Educational Researcher*, *1*(4), 5-19.

Paisley, W. J. (1984). Communication in the communication sciences. In B. Dervin & M. Voigt (Eds.), *Progress in the communication sciences* (Vol. 5, pp. 1-43). Norwood, NJ: Ablex.

Paisley, W. J. (1986). The convergence of communication and information science. In H. Edelman (Ed.), *Libraries and information science in the electronic age* (pp. 122-153). Philadelphia: ISI.

Paisley, W. J. (1989a). Bibliometrics, scholarly communication and communication research. *Communication Research*, *16*(5), 701-717.

Paisley, W. J. (1989b). Public communication campaigns: The American experience. In R. Rice & C. Atkin (Eds.), *Public communication campaigns* (2nd ed., pp. 15-38). Newbury Park, CA: Sage.

Paisley, W. J. (in press). An oasis where many trails cross: The improbable co-citation networks of a multidiscipline. *Journal of the American Society for Information Science.*

Parker, E., & Paisley, W. J. (1966). Research for psychologists at the interface of the scientist and his information system. *American Psychologist, 21*(11). 1061-1072.

Parker, E. B., Paisley, W., & Garrett, R. (1967). *Bibliographic citations as unobtrusive measures of scientific communication.* Stanford, CA; Stanford University, Institute for Communication Research.

Patterson, A. M. (1945). Literature references in "Industrial and engineering chemistry" for 1939. *Journal of Chemical Education, 22,* 514-515.

Patterson, O. (1984). Analysis of television coverage of the Vietnam War. *Journal of Broadcasting, 28*(4), 397-404.

Pelz, D. C., & Andrews, F. M. (1966). *Scientists in organizations.* New York: John Wiley.

Penan, H. (1989). *Pour une Gestion Bibliometrique de l'Information Scientifique et Technique des Entreprises: Application en Théorie Microéconomique et Financiere.* Unpublished doctoral dissertation, Universite de Toulouse I, Toulouse, France.

Persson, O. (1986). Online bibliometrics: A research tool for everyman. *Scientometrics, 10,* 69-75.

Pickering, A., & Nadel, E. (1987). Charm revisited: A quantitative analysis of the HEOP literature. *Social Studies of Science, 17,* 87-113.

Polanyi, M. (1958). *Personal knowledge: Towards a post critical philosophy.* Chicago: University of Chicago Press.

Popper, K. R. (1972). *Objective knowledge: An evolutionary approach.* Oxford: Clarendon.

Popper, K. R., & Eccles, J. C. (1977). *The self and its brain.* London: Springer.

Porter, A. L., Chubin, D. E., & Jin, X. (1988). *Scientometrics, 13*(3-4), 103-124.

Pratt, A. D. (1977). A measure of class concentration in bibliometrics. *Journal of the American Society for Information Science, 28*(5), 285-292.

Prentice, A. E. (Ed.). (1990). *Information science as a discipline.* New York: Neal Schuman.

Price, D. J. (1961). *Science since Babylon.* New Haven, CT: Yale University Press.

Price, D. J. (1963). *Little science, big science.* New York: Columbia University Press.

Price, D. J. (1965). Networks of scientific papers. *Science, 149,* 510-515.

Price, D. J. (1975). *Science since Babylon* (enlarged ed.). New Haven, CT: Yale University Press.

Price, D. J. (1979). The revolution in mapping of science. *Proceedings of the American Society for Information Science Annual Meeting, 16,* 249-253.

Price, D. J., & Beaver, D. (1966). Collaboration in an invisible college. *American Psychologist, 21,* 1011-1018.

Pritchard, A. (1968). *Computers, statistical bibliography and abstracting services.* Unpublished manuscript.

Pritchard, A. (1969). Statistical bibliography or bibliometrics? *Journal of Documentation, 25,* 348-349.

Pritchard, A. (1980). Citation analysis vs. use data [Letter to the editor]. *Journal of Documentation, 36,* 268-269.

Pritchard, A., & Wittig, G. (1981). *Bibliometrics: A bibliography and index (1874-1959)* (Vol. 1). Watford, England: ALLM.

Raisig, L. M. (1962). Statistical bibliography in the health sciences. *Bulletin of the Medical Library Association, 50,* 450-461.

Ramadan, N. M., Halvorson, H., Vande-Linde, A., Levine, S. R., Helpern, J. A., & Welch, K. M. A. (1989). Low brain magnesium in migraine. *Headache, 29.*

Ravetz, J. R. (1971). *Scientific knowledge and its social problems.* Oxford: Clarendon.

Reardon, K. K., & Rogers, E. M. (1988). Interpersonal versus mass media communication: A false dichotomy. *Human Communication Research, 15,* 284-303.

Rees, C. J. van (1983a). Introduction: Advances in the empirical sociology of literature and the arts: The institutional approach. *Poetics, 12,* 285-310.

Rees, C. J. van (1983b). How a literary work becomes a masterpiece: On the threefold selection practiced by literary criticism. *Poetics, 12,* 397-418.

Rees, C. J. van (1985). Editorial: Empirical sociology of cultural productions. *Poetics, 14,* 5-11.

Reeves, B., & Borgman, C. L. (1983). A bibliometric evaluation of core journals in communication research. *Human Communication Research, 10*(1), 119-136.

Reitz, K. (1988). Social groups in a monastery. *Social Networks, 10*(4), 343-357.

Restivo, S. (1983). *Supporting laboratory life: Funds and funding sources as contingencies in the social production of science* (Report to the National Science Foundation, Division of Policy Research and Analysis). Troy, NY: Rensselaer Polytechnic Institute, Department of Science and Technology Studies.

Rice, R. E., Borgman, C. L., Bednarski, D., & Hart, P. J. (1989). Journal-to-journal citation data: Issues of validity and reliability. *Scientometrics*, *15*(3-4), 257-282.

Rice, R. E., Borgman, C. L., & Reeves, B. (1988). Citation networks of communication journals, 1977-1985: Cliques and positions, citations made and citations received. *Human Communication Research*, *15*, 256-283.

Rice, R. E., & Richards, W., Jr. (1985). An overview of network analysis methods. In B. Dervin & M. Voigt (Eds.), *Progress in communication sciences* (Vol. 6, pp. 105-165). Norwood, NJ: Ablex.

Rice, R. E. et al. (1984). *The new media: Communication, research, and technology*. Beverly Hills, CA: Sage.

Rigter, H. (1986). Evaluation of performance of health research in the Netherlands. *Research Policy*, *15*, 33-48.

Rogers, E. M. (1983). *Diffusion of innovations*. New York: Free Press.

Rosengren, K. E. (1961). *Turgenev i Sverige*. Unpublished licentiate thesis in literature, University of Lund, Sweden.

Rosengren, K. E. (1966). *The literary system*. Unpublished licentiate thesis in sociology, University of Lund, Sweden.

Rosengren, K. E. (1968). *Sociological aspects of the literary system*. Stockholm: Natur och Kultur.

Rosengren, K. E. (1981). Cultural indicators: Sweden, 1945-1975. *Mass Communication Review Yearbook*, *2*, 717-737.

Rosengren, K. E. (1983). *The climate of literature: Sweden's literary frame of reference, 1953-1976*. Lund: Studentlitteratur.

Rosengren, K. E. (1984). Cultural indicators for the comparative study of culture. In G. Melischek, K. E. Rosengren, & J. Stappers (Eds.), *Cultural indicators: An international symposium*. Vienna: Akademie der Wissenschaften.

Rosengren, K. E. (1985a). Media linkages between culture and other societal systems. *Communication Yearbook*, *9*, 19-56.

Rosengren, K. E. (1985b). Time and literary fame. *Poetics*, *14*, 157-172.

Rosengren, K. E. (1986). *Sociological aspects of the literary system*. Stockholm: Natur och Kultur.

Rosengren, K. E. (1987). Literary criticism: Future invented. *Poetics*, *16*, 295-325.

Rosengren, K. E. (1988). *The study of media culture: Ideas, actions, and artifacts*: Vol. 10. *Lund Research Papers in the Sociology of Communication*. Lund, Sweden: University of Lund, Department of Sociology.

Rosengren, K. E., & Arbelius, B. (1971). Frames of reference as systems: Size and other variables. *General Systems, 16*, 205-210.

Rosengren, K. E., & Windahl, S. (1989). *Media matter: Television in the lives of children and adolescents.* Norwood, NJ: Ablex.

Rossel, S. H. (1982). *A history of Scandinavian literature.* Minneapolis: University of Minnesota Press.

Rossi, R. J., & Gilmartin, K. J. (1980). *The handbook of social indicators: Sources, characteristics, and analysis.* New York: Garland STPM.

Rossum, W. (1989). Operationalizing developments in a problem field: The case of MBD. *Scientometrics, 15*(5-6), 509-526.

Rousseau, R. (1987). The nuclear zone of a Leimkuhler curve. *Journal of Documentation, 43*(4), 322-333.

Roy, R., Roy, N. R., & Johnson, G. G., Jr. (1983). Approximating total citation counts from first author counts. *Scientometrics, 4*, 411-416.

Ruben, B. (Ed.). *Information and behavior* (Annual series). New Brunswick, NJ: Transaction.

Russett, B. M. (1970). Methological and theoretical schools in international relations. In N. D. Palmer (Ed.), *A design for international relations research: Scope, theory, methods, and relevance* (Monograph 10, pp. 87-105). Philadelphia: American Academy of Political and Social Science.

Saito, Y. (1984). Identification of the specialties in library and information science using cocitation analysis. *Library and Information Science, 22*, 61-74.

Sammons, J. (1977). *Literary sociology and practical criticism: An inquiry.* Bloomington: Indiana University Press.

Saris, W., & Stronkhorst, H. (1984). *Causal modelling in nonexperimental research.* Amsterdam: Sociometric Research Foundation.

Sarngadharan, M. G., Popovic, M., Bruch, L., Schupbach, J., & Gallo, R. C. (1984). Antibodies reactive with human T-lymphotropic retroviruses (HTLV-III) in the serum of patients with AIDS. *Science, 224*, 506-508.

Schiffman, S. S., Reynolds, M. L., & Young, F. W. (1981). *Introduction to multidimensional scaling: Theory, methods and applications.* Orlando, FL: Academic Press.

Schmidt, S. J. (1988). Empirical studies in literature and the media today. *Siegneer Periodicum zur Internationalen Empirischen Literaturwissenschaft, 7*, v-xi.

Schmuck, L. (1981). Literaturkritik und literarische Wertung. *Zeitschrift für Literaturwissenschaft und Linguistik, 12*, 96-115.

Schott, T. (1988). International influence in science: Beyond center and periphery. *Social Science Research*, *17*, 219-238.

Schramm, W. (1983). The unique perspective of communication: A retrospective view. *Journal of Communication*, *33*(3), 6-17.

Schramm, W. (1985). The beginnings of communication study in the United States. In E. M. Rogers & F. Balle (Eds.), *The media revolution in America and in Western Europe*. Norwood, NJ: Ablex.

Segers, R. T. (1978). *The evaluation of literary text*. Leiden: de Ridder.

Segers, R. T. (1989). Understanding contemporary literature: Some characteristic reviewing procedures in Dutch newspapers and weeklies. *Siegener Periodicum zur Internationalen Empirischen*, *8*, 131-156.

Self, P. C., Filardo, T. W., & Lancaster, F. W. (1989). Acquired Immunodeficiency Syndrome (AIDS) and the epidemic growth of its literature. *Scientometrics*, *17*, 49-60.

Shils, E. (1981). *Tradition*. London: Faber and Faber.

Siegal, F. P., Lopez, C., Hammer, G. S., Brown, A. E., Kornfeld, S. J., & Gold, J. (1981). Severe acquired immunodeficiency in male homosexuals, manifested by chronic perianal ulcerative herpes simplex lesions. *New England Journal of Medicine*, *304*, 1439-1444.

Simon, H. A. (1955). On a class of skew distribution functions. *Biometrika*, *42*, 425-440.

Small, H. G. (1973). Cocitation in the scientific literature: A new measure of the relationship between two documents. *Journal of the American Society for Information Science*, *24*, 265-269.

Small, H. G. (1974). Multiple citation patterns in scientific literature: The circle and hill models. *Information Storage and Retrieval*, *10*, 393-402.

Small, H. G. (1976). Structural dynamics of scientific literature. *International Classification*, *3*, 67-74.

Small, H. G. (1977). A cocitation model of a scientific specialty: A longitudinal study of collagen research. *Social Studies of Science*, *7*(5), 139-166.

Small, H. G. (1978). Cited documents as concept symbols. *Social Studies of Science*, *8*, 327-340.

Small, H. G. (1979). Co-citation context analysis: The relationship between bibliometric structure and knowledge. *Proceedings of the American Society for Information Science* (Vol. 16, pp. 270-275). White Plains, NY: Knowledge Industry.

Small, H. G. (1980). Cocitation context analysis and the structure of paradigms. *Journal of Documentation, 36,* 183-196.

Small, H. G. (1981). The relationship of information science to the social sciences: A cocitation analysis. *Information Processing and Management, 17,* 39-50.

Small, H. G. (1982). Citation context analysis. In B. J. Dervin & M. J. Voigt (Eds.), *Progress in communication sciences* (Vol. 3, pp. 287-310). Norwood, NJ: Ablex.

Small, H. G. (1984). The lives of a scientific paper. In K. Warren (Ed.), *Selectivity in information systems* (pp. 83-97). New York: Praeger.

Small, H. G. (1986). The synthesis of specialty narratives from co-citation clusters. *Journal of the American Society for Information Science, 37,* 97-110.

Small, H. G. (1987). The significance of bibliographic references. *Scientometrics, 12,* 339-341.

Small, H. G. (1988). Contributions of citation analysis to understanding scientific communication. In E. M. Rogers (Ed.), *1988 Symposium on Science Communication: Environmental and Health Research, December 15-17, 1988, Los Angeles, CA.* Los Angeles: University of Southern California, Annenberg School of Communications.

Small, H. G., & Crane, D. (1979). Specialties and disciplines in science and social science: Examination of their structure using citation indexes. *Scientometrics, 1,* 445-461.

Small, H. G., & Garfield, E. (1985). The geography of science: Disciplinary and national mappings. *Journal of Information Science, 11,* 147-159.

Small, H. G., & Garfield, E. (1989). Verification of results that logically related noninteractive literatures are potential sources of new knowledge [Letter to the editor]. *Journal of the American Society for Information Science, 40,* 152.

Small, H. G., & Greenlee, E. (1980). Citation context analysis of a co-citation cluster: Recombinant DNA. *Scientometrics, 2,* 277-301.

Small, H. G., & Greenlee, E. (1986). Collagen research in the 1970s. *Scientometrics, 10,* 95-117.

Small, H. G., & Greenlee, E. (1989). A co-citation study of AIDS research. *Communication Research, 16,* 642-666.

Small, H. G., & Griffith, B. C. (1974). The structure of scientific literature I: Identifying and graphing specialties. *Science Studies, 4,* 17-40.

Small, H. G., & Sweeney, E. (1985). Clustering the Science Citation Index using co-citations. 1: A comparison of methods. *Scientometrics, 7*, 391-409.

Small, H. G., Sweeney, E., & Greenlee, E. (1985). Clustering the Science Citation Index using co-citations (Vol. 2). Mapping science. *Scientometrics, 8*, 321-340.

Smeenk, J., & Hagendijk, R. (1989). The analysis of national subfields: A case study of a Dutch fresh-water ecology. *Scientometrics, 15*(5-6). 485-508.

Smith, L. E. (1981). Citation analysis. *Library Trends, 30*, 83-106.

Snelson, P. (1989). *Scientific communication and bibliometrics: A literature review.* New Brunswick, NJ: School of Communication, Information, and Library Studies, Rutgers University.

So, C. (1988). Citation patterns of core communication journals: An assessment of the developmental status of communication. *Human Communication Research, 15*, 236-255.

Sparkes, V. (1978). Flow of news between Canada and the United States. *Journalism Quarterly, 55*(2), 260-268.

Splichal, S. (1989). Indigenization versus ideologization: Communication science on the periphery. *European Journal of Communication, 4*, 329-359.

*SPSSX: Statistical Package for the Social Sciences User's Guide* (1986). (2nd ed.). New York: McGraw-Hill.

Storer, N. W., & Parsons, T. (1968). The discipline as a differentiating force. In E. B. Montgomery (Ed.), *The foundation of access to knowledge* (pp. 101-121). Syracuse, NY: Syracuse University.

Subramanyam, K. (1981). *Scientific and technical information resources.* New York: Marcel Dekker.

Sullivan, D., Koester, D., White, D. H., & Kern, R. (1980). Understanding rapid theoretical change in particle physics: A month-by-month co-citation analysis. *Scientometrics, 2*, 309-319.

Sullivan, D., White, D. H., & Barboni, E. J. (1977). Co-citation analyses of science: Evaluation. *Social Studies of Science, 7*, 223-240.

Svensson, C. (1985). *The construction of poetic meaning: Linking studies in arts and science* (Vol. 2). Malm: Liber.

Swanson, D. R. (1986a). Fish oil, Raynaud's syndrome, and undiscovered public knowledge. *Perspectives in Biology and Medicine, 30*, 7-18.

Swanson, D. R. (1986b). Undiscovered public knowledge. *Library Quarterly, 56*, 103-118.

Swanson, D. R. (1987). Two medical literatures that are logically but not bibliographically connected. *Journal of the American Society for Information Science, 38*, 228-233.

Swanson, D. R. (1988). Migraine and magnesium: Eleven neglected connections. *Perspectives in Biology and Medicine, 31*, 526-557.

Swanson, D. R. (1989a). Online search for logically-related non-interactive medical literatures: A systematic trial-and-error strategy. *Journal of the American Society for Information Science, 40*(6), 356-358.

Swanson, D. R. (1989b). A second example of mutually-isolated medical literatures related by implicit, unnoticed connections. *Journal of the American Society for Information Science, 40*(6), 432-435.

Swanson, D. R. (1990a). Integrative mechanisms in the growth of knowledge: A legacy of Manfred Koche. *Information Processing and Management.*

Swanson, D. R. (1990b). Medical literature as a potential source of new knowledge. *Bulletin of the Medical Library Association.*

Swanson, D. R. (1990c). Somatomedin C and Arginine: Implicit connections between mutually-isolated literatures. *Perspectives in Biology and Medicine.*

Symposium on mass and interpersonal communication. (1988). [Special issue]. *Human Communication Research, 15*(2).

Tamiya, H. (1931). Eine mathematische Betrachtung über die Zahlenverhaltnisse der in der "Bibliographie von Aspergillus" zusammengestellen Publikationen. *Botanical Magazine, 45*, 530, 62-71.

Tamura, S., Midorikawa, N., & Inoue, N. (1985). A comparison of the "production and use" patterns of literature by Japanese and Russian chemists. *Library and Information Science, 23*, 104-114.

Thackray, A. (1978). Measurement in the historiography of science. In Y. Elkana et al. (Eds.), *Toward a metric of science: The advent of science indicators* (pp. 11-30). New York: John Wiley.

Tijssen, R. J. W., & Moed, H. F. (1989). Literature-based statistical analyses of international scientific cooperation: An exploratory case study of the Netherlands. In A. F. J. van Raan, A. J. Nederhof, & H. F. Moed (Eds.), *Science and technology indicators, their use in science policy and their role in science studies*. Leiden, the Netherlands: University of Leiden, DSWO Press.

Todorov, R., & Glanzel, W. (1988). Journal citation measures: A concise review. *Journal of Information Science, 14*, 47-56.

Tuchman, G., & Fortin, N. E. (1984). Fame and misfortune: Edging women out of the great literary tradition. *American Journal of Sociology, 90,* 72-96.

Ueda, S., Midorikawa, N., Yoshikawa, C., Itsumura, H., Kaneko, M., & Harada, T. (1987). *Scientific and technical literature: Characteristics and use.* Tokyo: Keiso-Shobo.

Van Maanen, J. (1983). Reclaiming qualitative methods for organizational research: A preface. In J. VanMaanen (Ed.), *Qualitative methodology,* (pp. 9-18). Beverly Hills, CA: Sage.

Verdaasdonk, H. (1983). Social and economic factors in the attribution of literary quality. *Poetics, 12,* 383-396.

Vickery, B. C., & Vickery, A. (1987). *Information science in theory and practice.* London: Butterworths.

Viehoff, R. (1976). Über ein Versuch den Erwartungshorizont zeitgenssischer Literaturkritik empirisch zu objektivieren. *Zeitschrift für Literaturwissenschaft und Linguistik, 6,* 96-124.

Viehoff, R. (1988). Literarisches Verstehen. *Internationales Archiv für Sozialgeschichte der deutschen Literatur, 13,* 1-39.

Wallace, B. (1981). *Basic population genetics.* New York: Columbia University Press.

Weaver, K. (1989). [Letter to the editor]. *Perspectives in Biology and Medicine, 33,* 151-152.

Webb, E. J., Campbell, D. T., Schwartz, R. D., & Sechrest, L. (1966). *Unobtrusive measures: Nonreactive research in the social sciences.* Chicago: Rand McNally.

Webb, E. J., Campbell, D. T., Schwartz, R. D., Sechrest, L., & Grove, J. B. (1981). *Nonreactive measures in the social sciences* (2nd ed.). Boston: Houghton Mifflin.

Weimann, R. (1977). *Structure and society in literary history.* London: Lawrence and Wishart.

White, H. D. (1950). The "gatekeeper": A case study in the selection of news. *Journalism Quarterly, 27*(2), 383-390.

White, H. D. (1981a). Cocited author retrieval online: An experiment with the social indicators literature. *Journal of the American Society for Information Science, 32,* 16-22.

White, H. D. (1981b). Bradfordizing search output: How it would help online users. *Online Review, 5,* 47-54.

White, H. D. (1983). A cocitation map of the social indicator movement. *Journal of the American Society for Information Science, 34,* 307-312.

White, H. D. (1986). Cocited author retrieval. *Information Technology & Libraries, 5,* 93-99.

White, H. D. (1989). Toward automated search strategies. In *Proceedings of the 13th International Online Information Meeting* (pp. 33-47). Oxford: Learned Information.

White, H. D., & Griffith, B. C. (1981a). Author cocitation: A literature measure on intellectual structure. *Journal of the American Society for Information Science, 32*, 163-172.

White, H. D., & Griffith, B. C. (1981b). A cocitation map of authors in judgment and decision research. In B. F. Anderson, D. H. Deane, K. R. Hammond, G. H. McClelland, & J. C. Shanteau (Eds.), *Concepts in judgement and decision research: Definitions, sources, interrelationships, and comments* (Frontispiece, pp. 261-271). New York: Praeger.

White, H. D., & Griffith, B. C. (1982). Authors as markers of intellectual space: Cocitation in studies of science, technology and society. *Journal of Documentation, 38*, 255-272.

White, H. D., & McCain, K. W. (1989). Bibliometrics. In M. E. Williams (Ed.), *Annual review of information science and technology* (Vol. 24, pp. 119-186). Amsterdam: Elsevier.

Whitley, R. D. (1969). Communication nets in science: Status and citation patterns in animal physiology. *Sociological Review, 17*, 219-233.

Whitley, R. D. (1982). The establishment and structure of the sciences as reputational organizations. In N. Elias et al. (Eds.), *Scientific establishments and hierarchies* (pp. 313-357). Boston: Reidel.

Whitley, R. D. (1984). *The intellectual and social organization of the sciences*. Oxford: Clarendon.

Wiemann, J. M., Hawkins, R. P., & Pingree, S. (1988). Fragmentation in the field and the movement toward integration in communication science. *Human Communication Research, 15*, 236-255.

Williams, M. (Ed.). *Annual review of information science and technology* (Annual series). Amsterdam: Elsevier.

Wilson, P., & Farid, M. (1979). On the use of records of research. *Library Quarterly, 49*, 127-145.

Winstanley, M. (1976). Assimilation into the literature of a critical advance in molecular biology. *Social Studies of Science, 6*, 545-549.

Witt, W. (1972). Multivariate analysis of new flow in a conservation issue. *Journalism Quarterly, 49*(1), 91-97.

Yule, G. U. (1944). *The statistical study of literary vocabulary*. Cambridge, UK: Cambridge University Press.

Zima, P. V. (1977). Le texte comme objet: Une critique de la sociologie empiriqu e de la littrature. *Homme et Societ, 43*, 151-170.

Ziman, J. M. (1968). *Public knowledge: An essay concerning the social dimension of science*. Cambridge: Cambridge University Press.

Zipf, G. K. (1935). *Psycho-biology of language*. Boston: Houghton Mifflin.

Zsindely, S., Schubert, A., & Braun, T. (1982a). Citation patterns of editorial gatekeepers in international chemistry journals. *Scientometrics*, *4*(1), 69-76.

Zsindely, S., Schubert, A., & Braun, T. (1982b). Editorial gatekeeping patterns in international science journals: A new science indicator. *Scientometrics*, *4*(1), 57-68.

Zuckerman, H. (1977). *Scientific elite: Studies of Nobel laureates in the United States*. Chicago: University of Chicago Press.

Zuckerman, H. (1987). Citation analysis and the complex problem of intellectual influence. *Scientometrics*, *12*, 329-338.

# Author and Work Index

## SCOPE OF INDEX

This index is much more comprehensive than a traditional author index, in recognition of its value as a bibliometric device. It gives the page locations for all mentions of all the cited works in the reference section (e.g., Price [1961]), as well as individuals mentioned (Price, D. J.). Other works mentioned in the text, whether in print form (*Scientific American*) or electronic form (ERIC) are included as well. Electronic systems (DIALOG) and software packages (LISREL) are listed in the Subject Index.

*Dee Andy Michel, Indexer*

# Subject Index

## SCOPE OF INDEX

This Subject Index includes traditional topics (External validity), as well as places (Ireland), names of institutions (Duke University), and eponyms (Price's Index). Electronic systems (DIALOG) and software packages (LISREL) also will be found in the Subject Index. Note that three entries in the Subject Index having to do with research methology contain an especially large number of references: Evaluation of research, Research methods, and Statistics.

*Dee Andy Michel, Indexer*

# About the Authors

**James R. Beniger** is Associate Professor at the Annenberg School of Communications, University of Southern California. His research interests include information technology, communication theory, and societal change, with particular attention to the implications for social control, popular culture, and the arts. His second book, *The Control Revolution: Technological and Economic Origins of the Information Society* (1986), won the 11th Annual Association of American Publishers award for "the most outstanding book in social and behavioral sciences." He has a Bachelor of Arts degree (magna cum laude) in history from Harvard as well as a Master of Science degree in statistics, and a Master of Arts and a doctorate in sociology, all from the University of California, Berkeley.

**Christine L. Borgman** (M.L.S., University of Pittsburgh, Ph.D., Stanford University) is Associate Professor at the University of California, Los Angeles, in the Graduate School of Library and Information Science and in the Communication Studies program. She is on the editorial boards of *Communication Research*, the *Journal of the American Society for Information Science*, the *Annual Review of Information Science and Technology*, and *Interacting with Computers*. Her research interests focus both on human-computer interaction and on scholarly communication; her articles have appeared in a variety of information science and communication research journals. She is a Fellow of the American Association for the Advancement of Science.

**Terrence A. Brooks** (M.L.S., McGill University, M.B.A, York University, Ph.D., University of Texas at Austin) is Assistant Professor at the Graduate School of Library and Information Science at the University of Washington. He has contributed a number of articles to *Library and Information Science Research* and the *Journal of the American Society for Information Science* on the topics of forecasting, citer motivations, relational database design, and bibliometrics. He is the designer of the *Bibliometrics Toolbox*.

**Charlotte A. Cottrill** (Ph.D., Union Institute) is a social scientist in the U.S. Environmental Protection Agency's Health Effects Research Laboratory in Cincinnati. Her academic interests center on knowledge utilization and the social studies of science.

**Renger E. de Bruin** received his doctorate in history from the University of Utrecht, where he worked in the International Relations Section of the Department of History. Since 1987 he has been a researcher at CWTS at the University of Leiden. His publications include studies of political structures, the impact of revolutions, the use of bibliometric indicators and knowledge transfer in the social sciences and humanities, and international scientific cooperation.

**Edwin Greenlee** (B.A., SUNY Buffalo, M.A., Ph.D. [Cand.] Temple University) is the Manager of Research Programming at the Institute for Scientific Information and a graduate student in the anthropology department of Temple University. In addition to scientometrics, his research interests center on medical anthropology and the use of critical theory in anthropology. His dissertation research applies Foucault's model of discourse analysis to a cultural and historical examination of hypertension research in the United States.

**Belver C. Griffith** (Ph.D., University of Connecticut) has been Professor at the College of Information Studies at Drexel University since 1969. Earlier he had worked in experimental psychology and was coauthor of the three volumes of *The Reports of the American Psychological Association's Project on Scientific Information Exchange in Psychology* (1963-1969). He edited *Key Papers in Information Science* (1980). His recent articles include "Exact Fits to Large Ranked, Bibliometric Distributions" (*JASIS*) and "Derek Price's Puzzles: Numerical Metaphors for the Operation of Science" (*Science, Technology, & Human Values*). He has held visiting and honorary posts in several European institutions, most recently at the Royal Institute of Technology, Stockholm. He is interested in a variety of topics regarding systems and scientific communication and information.

**Leah A. Lievrouw** (M.A., University of Texas Southwestern Medical Center at Dallas, Ph.D., University of Southern California) is Assistant Professor in the Department of Communication at Rutgers University. She is coeditor of *Mediation, Information and Communication: Information and Behavior*, (Vol. 3, Transaction, 1988). She has contributed articles to a number of journals, including *Social Networks, Knowledge in Society, Critical Studies in Mass Communication*, and *Telecommunications Policy*. Her recent research focuses on scientific and scholarly communication and on the social impacts of telecommunication technologies.

**Katherine W. McCain** (M.S., Western Washington University, Ph.D., Drexel University) is Associate Professor at Drexel University in the College of Information Studies. She is on the editorial board of *Library Quarterly*. Her recent published work includes articles in the *Journal of the American Society for Information Science, Information Processing and Management*, and *Scientometrics*; she is also coauthor (with Howard D. White) of a recent review of bibliometrics literature from 1977 to 1988 (*Annual Review of Information Science and Technology*, 1989). Among her current research interests are studies of the intellectual structure of scholarly literatures, the diffusion of research innovations in biomedicine, and the evaluation of information retrieval systems.

**Nobuyuki Midorikawa** (M.A., Keio University) is Associate Professor at the University of Library and Information

Science. He has contributed a recent article to *Scientometrics*. His research interests center on communication in science, bibliometrics, and the communication media.

**Sadaaki Miyamoto** (Ph.D., Kyoto University) is Associate Professor at the University of Tsukuba in the Institute of Information Sciences and Electronics. He has contributed a recent article to *IEEE Transactions on Systems, Man, and Cybernetics*. His research interests include information retrieval and cluster analysis based on fuzzy sets as well as analysis of bibliographic information using digraph representations.

**Henk F. Moed** studied mathematics and physics at the University of Amsterdam and received his doctorate in quantitative studies of science from the University of Leiden. Since 1981 he has been a senior researcher at the University of Leiden. He is a permanent staff member of CWTS, supervising various projects in the field of science studies. His publications include studies of the use of bibliometric indicators for the assessment of research performance, the use of online literature databases, (co-)citation analysis, and international scientific cooperation.

**Kazuhiko Nakayama** (M.S., International Christian University, Japan) is Professor at the University of Tsukuba in the Institute of Information Sciences and Electronics. He has contributed a recent article to *IEEE Transactions on Systems, Man, and Cybernetics*. His research interests include the development of scientific information systems and computer-assisted instruction.

**William Paisley** (Ph.D., Stanford University) is Executive Vice President and cofounder of Knowledge Access International, an electronic publishing company in Mountain View, California. He taught at Stanford from 1965 to 1985 and held visiting appointments at Syracuse University and the University of California, Berkeley. While at Stanford, he served as director of the ERIC Clearinghouse on Information Resources and administered the information science doctoral program. He has published widely in the fields of communication and information science. His research and writing focus on communication in science and the professions as well as the uses of technology to improve the flow of information.

**Sydney J. Pierce** (M.L.S., State University of New York at Albany, Ph.D. in English, University of Rochester, Ph.D. in sociology, Indiana University) is Assistant Professor of Library and Information Studies and Sociology at the University of Oklahoma. She previously taught library and information studies at the University of California, Los Angeles (where this chapter was written), at Emory University, at Indiana University, and as a Fulbright Lecturer at the Federal University of Minas Gerais in Brazil. Her current research deals with the development of standards for the presentation of research in American disciplinary literatures.

**Ronald E. Rice** (Ph.D., Stanford University, 1982) is Associate Professor, School of Communication, Information and Library Studies, Rutgers University, New Brunswick, New Jersey. He is coeditor or coauthor on *Public Communication Campaigns* (1981, 1989, Sage), *The New Media: Communication, Research and Technology* (1984, Sage), *Managing Organizational Innovation* (1987, Columbia University Press), and *Research Methods and New Media* (1988, Free Press). He has published widely in the areas of diffusion of innovations, network analysis, and organizational computer-mediated communication systems.

**Everett M. Rogers** (Ph.D., Iowa State University) is Walter H. Annenberg Professor, Annenberg School of Communication, University of Southern California. His main scholarly interest over the past several decades has been the diffusion of innovations.

**Karl Erik Rosengren** is Professor of Sociology at the University of Lund, Sweden. His publications include books and articles on the sociology of literature, communication, and culture. His most recent book (with Sven Windahl and others, 1989) is *Media Matter: Television in the Lives of Children and Adolescents*.

**András Schubert** (Ph.D., Technical University, Budapest, Hungary) is the Head of the Department of Scientometrics at the Library of the Hungarian Academy of Sciences. His main concern is the theory and application of scientometric indicators in the analysis and assessment of scientific research. He is a member of the editorial board of *Scientometrics*, in which much of his research has been published. He is coauthor of several books, including *Scientometric Indicators: A 32-Country Comparative Evaluation of Publishing Performance and Citation Impact* (World Scientific, 1985), with T. Braun and W. Glanzel, and *Literature of Analytical Chemistry: A Scientometric Evaluation* (CRC Press, 1987), with T. Braun and E. Bujdosó.

**Henry Small** (Ph.D., University of Wisconsin) is Director of Corporate Research at the Institute for Scientific Information in Philadelphia, Pennsylvania. He has recently completed a bibliometric analysis of the research literature on aging for the Institute of Medicine and an analysis of federal support of leading-edge research for the Office of Technology Assessment. His interests are the application of clustering and scaling methods to bibliometric data for mapping scientific fields and studying their development.

**Don R. Swanson**, whose degrees are in physics (B.S. with honor, California Institute of Technology; M.A., Rice University; Ph.D., University of California, Berkeley), is Professor at the University of Chicago (Center for Information and Language Studies and the Graduate Library School). He has also served as Dean of the Graduate Library School and as a research scientist for TRW. His current research interests include online search strategies, knowledge representation, bibliometrics, and the structure of scientific literature. Recent publications appear in *Perspectives in Biology and Medicine, Journal of the American Society for Information Science, Information Processing and Management,*

*Bulletin of the Medical Library Association*, and the *Library Quarterly*.

**Howard D. White** (M.L.S., Ph.D., University of California, Berkeley) is Professor, College of Information Studies, Drexel University, Philadelphia, Pennsylvania, which he joined in 1974. He has published articles on co-citation analysis, evaluation of library collections and reference service, innovative online searching, social science data archives, library publicity, and American attitudes toward library censorship. With Katherine McCain, he is the coauthor of the chapter "Bibliometrics" in the 1989 *Annual Review of Information Science and Technology*.

**Sándor Zsindely** (M.A., Ph.D., Roland Eotvos University, Budapest, Hungary) is Senior Research Fellow in the Department of Scientometrics at the Library of the Hungarian Academy of Sciences. His main research interest is quantitative studies of the gatekeeping system of science and certain scientific subcommunities, such as university professors, journal editors, or participants in scientific meetings.

# NOTES

# NOTES

# NOTES

# NOTES

# NOTES